THE POLITICS OF C
SERVICES REF

Re-examining Two Decades of
Policy Change

Carl Purcell

Foreword by Sir Paul Ennals

First published in Great Britain in 2020 by

Policy Press
University of Bristol
1-9 Old Park Hill
Bristol
BS2 8BB
UK
t: +44 (0)117 954 5940
pp-info@bristol.ac.uk
www.policypress.co.uk

North America office:
Policy Press
c/o The University of Chicago Press
1427 East 60th Street
Chicago, IL 60637, USA
t: +1 773 702 7700
f: +1 773-702-9756
sales@press.uchicago.edu
www.press.uchicago.edu

British Library Cataloguing in Publication Data
A catalogue record for this book is available from the British Library

Library of Congress Cataloging-in-Publication Data
A catalog record for this book has been requested

ISBN 978-1-4473-4877-1 (paperback)
ISBN 978-1-4473-4876-4 (hardcover)
ISBN 978-1-4473-4879-5 (ePub)
ISBN 978-1-4473-4878-8 (ePdf)

Cover design by Qube Design Associates, Bristol.
Front cover image: Shutterstock: big-ben-label-450w-87221995
Printed and bound in Great Britain by CMP, Poole
Policy Press uses environmentally responsible print partners.

For Ruwani, Nimali and Nelum

Contents

List of abbreviations

ADCS	Association of Directors of Children's Services
ADSS	Association of Directors of Social Services
AILC	Association of Independent LSCB Chairs
APPG	All Party Parliamentary Group
APSW	Association of Professors of Social Work
ASBO	Anti-Social Behaviour Order
BASW	British Association of Social Workers
CAF	Common Assessment Framework
CIAG	Children's Inter-Agency Group
CSJ	Centre for Social Justice
CWDC	Children's Workforce Development Council
CYP Directorate	Children and Young People's Directorate
CYPU	Children and Young People's Unit
DCMS	Department for Culture, Media and Sport
DCS	Director of Children's Services
DCSF	Department for Children, Schools and Families
DfE	Department for Education
DH	Department of Health
DWP	Department for Work and Pensions
ECM	Every Child Matters
ECPC	End Child Poverty Coalition
EIF	Early Intervention Foundation
EIG	Early Intervention Grant
GSCC	General Social Care Council
HCPC	Health and Care Professionals Council
JUCSWEC	Joint University Council Social Work Education Committee
KSS	Knowledge and Skills Statement
LEA	Local education authority
LGA	Local Government Association
LMCS	Lead Member for Children's Services
LSCB	Local Safeguarding Children Board
NAO	National Audit Office
NCB	National Children's Bureau
NEET	Not in education, employment or training
NEF	New Economics Foundation
NGOs	Non-governmental organisations
NSPCC	National Society for the Prevention of Cruelty to Children

PAT 12	Policy Action Team 12
PCF	Professional Capabilities Framework
PFI	Private Finance Initiative
PMDU	Prime Minister's Delivery Unit
SEU	Social Exclusion Unit
SWAN	Social Work Action Network
SWRB	Social Work Reform Board
SWTF	Social Work Task Force

Acknowledgements

First, I owe a huge debt to everyone who agreed to be interviewed as part of the research for this book, most of whom remain anonymous. At the beginning of the project, I doubted how many people would be willing to talk to me about their involvement in this area of policymaking. Thankfully, my scepticism was entirely misplaced, and throughout the project, I have been impressed by the willingness of interviewees to share their insights, as well as put me in touch with former colleagues.

The book started off as an Economic and Social Research Council (ESRC)-funded PhD research project at Durham University, beginning in 2012. I would like to thank friends and colleagues in Durham, but particularly Dr Danny Chow for encouraging me to apply for the studentship in the first place and for his support thereafter. I would also like to thank Professor Ray Jones for his help when I was writing up the PhD and for encouraging me to submit a book proposal to Policy Press. Colleagues at King's College London, particularly Professor Jill Manthorpe, have also helped immeasurably with the task of turning the PhD thesis into something more readable. I am also very grateful to Sir Paul Ennals for his kind and thought-provoking foreword to the book. Finally, I owe my biggest debt of gratitude to Professor Martin Laffin for supporting me all the way through what turned out to be an eight-year project.

Foreword

Sir Paul Ennals

Writing in late 2019, it can feel as if government policies are largely driven by dogma. The checks and balances that normally contribute to good policy formation seem far away. The role of evidence, the input of professional civil servants, the balancing views of key elements of civil society – none of these seem visible. However, it is important to remember that it was not always like this – and, indeed, that, even today, much policy is still being filtered through the proper processes before bursting into government implementation.

Back in 1989, the Children Act provided a textbook example of how effective policy can be developed. A group of civil servants with profound understanding of their topic were willing to engage openly and directly with those key agencies who were working with the issues that children faced. Local authorities were deeply involved, and so too were a plethora of voluntary organisations. Debates were open and honest; research evidence was commissioned and studied; children and families were consulted. The result was an Act that has stood the test of time and still provides the backbone to our systems for keeping children safe, delivered by a Conservative government under Secretary of State Ken Clarke.

Carl Purcell has illuminated the processes that have been followed over the last two decades as children's policies have developed. He has dug under the surface to challenge what can become lazy assumptions as to why a particular policy emerged. His key conclusion that the big changes in policy were not directly due to the more famous child abuse scandals of the age (Victoria Climbié and Baby Peter) is, I think, correct. So too is his conclusion that current policy has swerved away from the 'child welfare' approach that was promoted by Labour, towards a more restrictive 'child protection' approach.

For those of us engaged in children's services, the period from 2000 to 2010 was a fruitful time. The favourable financial climate played a huge part – it is so much easier to be innovative and bold when there is increased funding every year (until 2008 at least). There were several examples of policymaking at its best. Sure Start was conceived by a great civil servant, Norman Glass, in response to a clear policy direction set out by Gordon Brown and his colleagues. Norman gathered the best evidence together, convened a series of seminars outside government (the first was in my office at the National Children's Bureau), consulted with front-line practitioners and helped inexperienced ministers think through the options available to government. The programme was rolled out in waves, with rigorous monitoring and evaluation, and engaging widely across the sector. Experts from the field (such as Naomi Eisenstadt) were brought in to run the programme. Mistakes were made, plenty of them, and later phases of the programme changed in the light of them, but there was an openness and willingness to learn that seem a world away from today's policy environment.

Perhaps it was easier because the government as a whole seemed almost impregnable: Blair's government did not seem under threat until the financial crisis, so they were more willing to ask for the views of people who might challenge them. From the voluntary sector, we felt under no pressure to be polite to them beyond common decency; rather, we felt able to probe, suggest, question, disagree and propose. Perhaps there were some cultural commonalities that helped: the politicians felt comfortable among public sector leaders and voluntary sector operatives – we spoke each other's language.

One other factor was important, I think. Normal civil service practice is to circulate senior civil servants across briefs – as with the politicians, it is not thought to be a good idea for civil servants to become too expert in their fields. The image of the entirely objective civil servant, who can apply their skills to any topic, has endured for centuries. However, in my experience, on the occasions where civil servants are allowed to stay in their brief for long enough to gain a real reputation, the quality of policy and delivery improves. We had some genuinely great civil servants during those ten years, who remained in post, motivated and enthused to see improvements in children's lives. I do not believe that they ever became subject to the 'provider capture' that some in the civil service feared, where their loyalty might move away from implementing the policy of politicians, to becoming the true creators of policy themselves. However, it is always a matter of balance. Any successful policy has many who claim parenthood – it is failure that is an orphan. Indeed, in moments of hubris, I have sometimes claimed partial parenthood of Every Child Matters myself. However, if driven to name one parent of that overarching policy framework that was so influential on a generation of children, I would suggest the civil servant Tom Jeffery.

The real truth, though, is that good policy never has just one parent. The children's sector was ready and able to work together, compromise views, find common principles and negotiate with the government as equals. Local government, health, police, the voluntary sector, civil servants, researchers – all worked together. That is why a 'child welfare' approach emerged, emphasising the need for early intervention and progressive universalism. After the crash, when budgets were being cut, it is not so surprising (though disappointing) that public policy has reverted so quickly to a narrow focus on child protection. In a world of cuts, it is harder for politicians and civil servants to engage openly and warmly with the sector too, so the use of independent evidence declines, as does the willingness to consult openly with real people. It will take a mature government, perhaps imbued with more money than has been evident over this last decade, to return to the days of effective child-centred policymaking. When those days come, Carl's book will help to point the way ahead.

Sir Paul Ennals was Chief Executive of the National Children's Bureau from 1998 to 2011, and Chair of the Children's Workforce Development Council from 2008 to its closure in 2012. He is now independent chair of several children's safeguarding partnerships.

Introduction

Protecting children from harm is one of the most important and undisputed responsibilities of the modern state. However, the nature of state involvement and the way in which it is organised and resourced differs between countries. Comparative research has identified two broad types of child welfare system. In *child protection* systems, the principal remit of welfare agencies is to identify and respond to actual or potential incidences of child abuse or maltreatment. These systems are characterised by highly legalistic interventions to protect children from deviant parents. In contrast, *family service* systems are characterised by a stronger spirit of partnership between the state and families facing difficulties, and an emphasis on working to prevent the escalation of needs and the necessity for coercive state intervention. It is suggested that child welfare systems reflect the broader cultural and socio-economic context of different countries. Child protection systems are found in neoliberal political economies with 'safety-net' welfare systems. Family service systems are generally located in social-democratic countries offering more generous welfare support (Gilbert et al, 2009: 174; Parton, 2014: ch 1).

There is a strong case for identifying the English child welfare system as a child protection system. National policy places a strong emphasis on the child protection responsibilities of welfare agencies, but particularly those of social work professionals. Under the Coalition and Conservative governments (2010–19), policy initiatives prioritised the reform of social work and the restructuring of local welfare services, including the privatisation of child protection services (Jones, 2019). On the other hand, elements of the family service approach can also be found in the English system. Under the Labour government's (1997–2010) Every Child Matters (ECM) programme (HM Government, 2003) there was a much stronger focus on the provision of preventative services. Local authority children's services departments, set up under ECM, retain responsibility for the commissioning and delivery of a diverse range of welfare services, including preventative services. They also continue to employ, directly or indirectly, a diverse workforce drawn from multiple professions and occupational groups in addition to social workers. Furthermore, the moral and economic case for the provision of preventative services, made by campaigning organisations in the children's sector over several decades, continues to command widespread support. Even after withdrawing central funding (Action for Children et al, 2019) the Conservative government continued to emphasise the importance of local 'early help' services (HM Government, 2018a). The example of English children's services reveals changes and tensions in welfare policy that cannot be explained with reference to fixed cultural and socio-economic conditions alone.

Policy changes in the English system are often depicted as responses to child abuse inquiries and scandals. Under the spotlight of the media, politicians promise that lessons will be learned and that steps will be taken to address the failings of the agencies and, typically, social workers involved. Thus, different waves of reform have become closely associated with the apparent failings of local services and professionals highlighted in successive inquiries. Labour's ECM reforms were presented as a response to the Victoria Climbié inquiry (Lord Laming, 2003). Similarly, the case of 'Baby P' (later identified as Peter Connelly) has been tied to subsequent child protection reforms, including the reform of social work (Biehal, 2019). The outsourcing of child protection services to the private and voluntary sector was increasingly promoted following child sexual exploitation inquiries in Rotherham (Jay, 2014) and Oxfordshire (Oxfordshire Safeguarding Board, 2015), but also in response to a rise in local authority children's social care services judged as 'inadequate' or 'requires improvement' by Office for Standards in Education (Ofsted) inspectors (Jones, 2019).

This book challenges this narrative by turning the spotlight on the process of policymaking at the national level to highlight the underlying political drivers of policy change. It provides a unique insight into the reform process by drawing on 45 interviews with prominent policymakers, including ministers, political advisers, civil servants, local authority directors, representatives of non-governmental organisations (NGOs) and social work researchers. Although the book includes extensive discussion of child protection and social work policies, a broad understanding of *children's services*, incorporating preventative services, is retained throughout. The findings presented add to existing research on English child welfare policy but the book is also intended as a contribution to wider debates about the drivers of welfare reform in the UK and beyond. The book also draws on public policy theory and offers a modest contribution to research in this field. It is also hoped that the book can inform wider public understanding of children's services reform in England and provide a useful analysis for individuals and organisations involved in this important area of public policy.

The book builds on an Economic and Social Research Council (ESRC)-funded PhD thesis undertaken at Durham University between 2012 and 2016. My interest in studying children's services reform was prompted by 11 years of working in English local government. As a 'back office' policy and performance manager, my role, supported by my colleagues, was to monitor compliance with central government reform initiatives and reporting requirements. The intense scrutiny from central government and Ofsted inspectors meant that this was a prominent role that involved close working with senior management. The art was to make sure that the demands placed on practitioners were not too onerous, but also to ensure that the data and information collated could be used to inform practice, as well as meeting central government requirements. Unclear or contradictory policy objectives, unrealistic reporting requirements, and the sheer volume of new or changing central government initiatives made this very difficult to achieve. However, this experience provided me with a good knowledge of children's services policy that I was able to build on during the research, as well as a few useful contacts to get me started!

The first chapter considers the question: 'What drives children's services reform?' Two distinct narratives are identified in existing research on children's services and child and family social work. The case for further research drawing on competing theories of the policymaking process is made. The chapter also provides an overview of the approach taken to the research, including details of the interviewees. Chapters 2 to 6 examine the Labour years (1997–2010). Chapter 2 considers the early development of Labour's children's policy. This chapter highlights the tensions between the priorities of Blair and Brown that would shape the development of policy over the coming years. It also examines how the Treasury, under Brown's leadership, sought to establish greater control over key areas of social policy, including children's services. Chapters 3 provides a comprehensive examination of how proposals for the structural reform of local authorities took shape both before and after the Victoria Climbié inquiry. Chapter 4 then interrogates the official claim that it was the recommendations of this inquiry that informed the ECM reforms. Chapters 5 and 6 discuss the challenge of implementing the ECM reforms during Blair's final years and under Brown's premiership. Chapter 6 includes a discussion of the political context of the 'Baby P' case and the government's response. Chapters 7 to 9 examine the development of children's services policy under the Coalition and Conservative governments (2010–19). This begins in Chapter 7 with a discussion of the social policy priorities of the Coalition and Conservatives leaders. Chapters 8 and 9 examine different aspects of children's services policy. Chapter 8 focuses on schools reform and early intervention policy. Chapter 9 focuses on the development of policy on child and family social work since 2010. The concluding chapter reflects on the research findings and the implications for those who seek to engage in the policymaking process.

1

What drives children's services reform?

Introduction

This chapter reflects on the existing literature on children's services reform and makes the case for further research following a different approach. Two overarching narratives on children's services reform can be identified in the existing literature. Both of these narratives emphasise the importance of contextual factors: the first highlights the role of the media and the significance of child abuse inquiries and scandals; and the second points towards the importance of the broader socio-economic context of the English welfare system. It is argued that neither of these perspectives takes full account of tensions and contradictions in children's policy or the range of interests involved in policymaking. The chapter also draws on competing theoretical perspectives on contemporary British policymaking to provide a guide for this research. An overview of the research design and process is provided in the final section.

Child abuse inquiries and scandals

Inquiries into the apparent failings of local welfare agencies are now commonplace (Stanley and Manthorpe, 2004). In recent decades, welfare reform has often followed scandals generated by media coverage of inquiry findings and the ensuing public outrage generated. Butler and Drakeford (2005: 5) comment that 'Scandals are the policy equivalent of the earthquake; they are a powerful signal that change is occurring, or that the pressure for change has reached unsustainable levels.' Children's services reform in England has been closely associated with scandals that have followed the publication of inquiries into serious cases of child abuse. Thus, Stafford et al (2012: 31) argue that 'the media has been and remains one of the main drivers of system change'. In Warner's (2015: 2, emphasis in original) view, 'emotions can be seen as *the* driving force behind policy and practice'. From this perspective, policymakers and professionals working in children's services are compelled to respond to the public anger and grief generated by media coverage of inquiries.

The Maria Colwell inquiry in 1974 (Secretary of State for Social Services, 1974) has been consistently identified as having marked a turning point for social services and the social work profession (Parton, 1985; Butler and Drakeford, 2012). Maria was murdered in 1973 after having suffered an extended period of abuse at the hands of her mother's partner, William Kepple. The inquiry highlighted the failure of multiple agencies and professionals to share information and work together to better protect Maria. However, media coverage focused predominantly on the failings of the social services department and the social workers involved in the case. The political response challenged the broad welfare focus of social service departments, established following the Seebohm Report (Seebohm Committee, 1968), as well as the trust placed in social work professionals. The reforms that followed 'changed the face of social work practice irrevocably in so far as social work was to be an extraordinarily closely "managed" profession from this point on' (Butler and Drakeford, 2012: 174). Moreover, it was from this point that *child and family* social work started to emerge as a distinct specialism supporting a strong child protection focus in England (Parton, 1985, 2014; Butler and Drakeford, 2012).

Over the last 20 years, two high-profile cases stand out for the volume and ferocity of media coverage, as well as the political reforms that they have come to be associated with. The first of these was the case of Victoria Climbié. Victoria died in the London borough of Haringey in 2000 after suffering months of horrific abuse. She had been known to multiple statutory and charitable agencies across London. The Victoria Climbié inquiry (Lord Laming, 2003) uncovered familiar failings in inter-agency working. Media coverage again focused upon the failings of the social workers involved in Victoria's case. Butler and Drakeford (2005: ch 11) comment that the Victoria Climbié inquiry also provoked serious debate about child welfare services nationally. The inquiry itself included a series of seminars with representatives of the children's services sector, who were invited to provide feedback on proposals for reform. Labour's ECM Green Paper (HM Government, 2003) and the subsequent Children Act 2004 were presented as the government's direct response to Lord Laming's report. Simon and Ward (2010: xi) argue that ECM was 'one of the biggest social policy initiatives of the post-war years, affecting all aspects of the lives of children and their families: education, social services and health'. ECM applied a broad understanding of child welfare that extended well beyond child protection, leading to major structural changes in the organisation of local services. Biehal (2019) argues that 'the official inquiry into the killing of Victoria Climbié led to a major overhaul of child welfare policy'.

However, the broader approach introduced under ECM was challenged following media reporting of the Baby P case. Baby P (later identified as Peter Connelly) was killed in 2007 while in the care of his mother and her partner. Like Victoria, he was known to various agencies in Haringey, including the new children's services department. The case was first reported publicly following the conviction of Baby P's mother and her partner in November 2008. Again, media reporting focused on the failings of the social workers involved, as well as the Director of Children's Services (DCS) Sharon Shoesmith. However, the volume and tone of media coverage surpassed that of previous cases. The Baby P case generated an unprecedented level of public anger and clamour for reform (Jones, 2014; Parton, 2014: ch 5; Warner, 2015; Shoesmith, 2016). Responding to significant political and public pressure, Secretary of State for Children, Schools and Families Ed Balls announced a new review by Lord Laming and the establishment of a Social Work Task Force (SWTF). These steps were notable because they marked a departure from the broader approach of ECM. Lord Laming's (2009) review focused specifically on child protection services. The establishment of the SWTF offered an implicit acknowledgement that the reform of social work had not been sufficiently prioritised by the government. Stafford et al (2010: 79) argue that the Baby P case pushed the 'system to safeguard children in England back in the direction where it came from towards a more narrow focus on child protection'.

In Warner's (2015: 3) view, the Baby P case marked 'a step–change in the intensity of the cycle of crisis and reform'. She introduces the concept of *emotional politics* to explain the ferocity of media coverage and the political response that this was seen to generate. Warner (2015: 12) explains that 'Emotional engagement by politicians can be understood as indicative of a deeper malaise in politics and the democratic process.... Matters of principle have diminished in their importance in terms of the struggle for parties to differentiate themselves and gain political advantage.' The concept highlights the way in which contemporary politicians respond to, and mobilise, public displays of anger and grief in order to seek public approval. Warner (2015: ch 4) analyses a speech made in 2013 by Michael Gove, then Secretary of State for Education, to illustrate how emotional politics has shaped recent shifts in children's services policy. In this speech, Gove promotes the swifter removal of children from abusive parents and carers, challenging policies that emphasise the importance of working *with* families. Gove cites a series of high-profile child abuse cases, including Baby P, to make his point. For Warner (2015: 76), the 'emotional politics at work' is exemplified by Gove's binary discourse on child protection in which a more interventionist approach is presented as morally superior. The speech also 'reflects the political necessity of always being, or appearing to be, in control in the face of a consistent stream of failures, scandals and disasters' (Warner, 2015: 79).

Children's services and neoliberalism

A second narrative on children's services reform emphasises the importance of the socio-economic context of children's policy. The development of the English child protection system following the Maria Colwell inquiry coincided with the onset of a fiscal crisis and the fracturing of the post–war social-democratic consensus in the mid-1970s. Criticism of the broad remit of social services departments, and the levels of trust placed in social work professionals, formed part of a wider critique of spending on welfare services and the power of public sector professionals. This culminated in the election of the Thatcher-led Conservative government in 1979 and the emergence of a neoliberal approach to economic and social policy. Policy developments since Maria Colwell, including responses to subsequent high-profile inquiries, are seen to have been influenced (or constrained) by neoliberal ideology. Rogowski (2011: 922) pinpoints 'the ideological changes of the last thirty years being at the root of social work's current crisis'. Lee (2014: 2136) argues that 'There should be no underestimation of the extent to which the neo-liberal orthodoxy has penetrated the daily experience of social work.'

The imprint of neoliberal ideology is detected in concerted attempts to limit professional autonomy. The introduction of private sector management techniques, including performance targets, financial planning and competency frameworks, is cited as evidence of a new 'managerialism' in the UK public sector (Clarke and Newman, 1997). The dominance of managerialism, and thus the de-professionalisation of practice, has been a recurring theme in children's social work research (Harris, 1998; Jones, 2001; Munro, 2004; White et al, 2008; Ferguson and Woodward, 2009; Broadhurst et al, 2010a, 2010b; Dominelli, 2010; Wastell et al, 2010; Rogowski, 2016). For Munro (2004), the purpose of introducing new processes and management controls was to try to make social work 'auditable'. Butler and Drakeford (2012: 198) suggest that the culmination of this has been the development of the

Ofsted inspection regime. On the other hand, Rogowski (2016: 109) argues that neoliberal-inspired reforms have also been designed to 'imitate market relationships' and thereby ensure that social workers are 'engrossed in the bracing competitive stimulus of market forces'. Jones (2015, 2019) argues that the 'end game' has turned out to be the privatisation of child protection and social work.

Neoliberalism is also associated with a shift from universal/collective welfare provision towards targeted services and more punitive state interventions in family life. Levitas (2005) argues that neoliberal approaches to social policy are informed by a 'moral underclass' perspective on poverty and life chances. This emphasises the behavioural deviances of individuals and families while denying the relevance of social and economic inequalities. Thus, in recent decades, social policy has focused on the development of surveillance technologies and interventions designed to create 'responsible' (Featherstone et al, 2014: 24–26; Liebenberg et al, 2015) and 'resilient' (Garrett, 2016) citizens. A 'new punitiveness' (Garrett, 2009a: 19) in social policy is reflected in policies that prioritise protecting the community from 'problem' families. In this context, Featherstone et al (2014: 22) argue that social work has taken on 'a role in risk regulation and as expert mediator for problematic populations and vulnerable people'. Rogowski (2011: 928) argues more forcefully that 'what remains of social work is increasingly tied to a system primarily concerned with the management of risk by controlling the behaviour of young people who represent a threat to the wider community'. Parton (2014: 139) connects children's services reform with 'a clear agenda to establish … an authoritarian neo-liberal state'.

Furthermore, analysis of the socio-economic context of children's services policy has tended to downplay the relevance of ideological differences between Labour and Conservative-led governments. Tony Blair's claim that the Labour government was committed to pursuing a 'Third Way' in British politics is widely dismissed as a rhetorical device used to mask an underlying commitment to economic and social policies first introduced by the Conservatives (Ferguson and Woodward, 2009: 41–2; Garrett, 2009a: 14; Rogowski, 2011: 922). Ferguson and Woodward (2009: 35) comment that 'the UK has borne the brunt of efforts by both Conservative and New Labour politicians to marginalise the role of the state in dealing with social problems and to introduce a business agenda to welfare services'. Rogowski (2011: 924) goes further, arguing that 'New Labour out Toried the Tories by consolidating the Conservatives' reforms so that social work was drawn deeper into managerial, market-oriented ways of thinking and practising'. Garrett (2009a) does acknowledge that Labour's reforms to children's services included some progressive elements, marking a departure from Conservative policies. However, he is ultimately dismissive of the broader child welfare focus provided by ECM, arguing that this was outweighed by more punitive interventions into family life. Moreover, he claims that Labour policy documents on children's services reform were shallow and largely promotional, being part of a 'branding of particular programmes of governance ... to mask the deeply ideological content of much of the "transformational reform agenda"' (Garrett, 2009a: 3). In his view, they merely contributed to 'doing neo-liberalism the New Labour way' (Garrett, 2009a: 21–2).

More recent policies introduced under the Coalition and Conservative governments are seen to have marked the intensification of four decades of largely uninterrupted reform inspired by neoliberal ideology. Jones (2019: 2) argues that 'The journey leading to the current position ... is a long one, going back forty years to the mid-1970s'. In his analysis, the drive to privatise child protection and social work marks the culmination of successive waves of managerial reform that have sought to constrain professional autonomy and subject social work to the discipline of market forces. Featherstone et al (2018: 27) describe a consistent focus on the narrow child protection responsibilities of welfare agencies and social workers, as well as a pull away from preventative family support services. In their view: 'With the exception of a few decades of the 20th century, history shows a strong tendency towards individual social engineering to produce model citizens, with parenting practices the primary focus of state attention' (Featherstone et al, 2018: 27).

The case for re-examining children's services reform

In my view, the reform of children's services over the last two decades needed to be re-examined for three reasons. First, neither of the narratives outlined earlier chime completely with my experience of working in local government between 2000 and 2011. Local authorities had to respond to a constant stream of new or revised national policy initiatives. ECM was a major landmark. However, the programme was comprised of multiple separate initiatives. Many of these were already in train before the publication of the report of the Victoria Climbié inquiry (Lord Laming, 2003). Furthermore, central government policymakers were continuously involved in the redesign of local service delivery arrangements, both before and after media reporting of the Victoria Climbié and Baby P cases. This does not fit the narrative of sporadic reforms driven by serious case inquiries and scandals. Ministers and civil servants were far more proactive. Furthermore, there were often ideological contradictions and tensions between different policy initiatives. The narrow child protection focus described by social work researchers is recognisable. However, this ran alongside more progressive initiatives, such as Sure Start, which expanded the provision of preventative services. We must be able to better account for regular shifts and contradictions in policy.

Second, the claim that the Labour government pursued broadly similar social policies to those inherited from the Conservatives has been contested by British political researchers. Driver and Martell (2006) identify three competing perspectives in the literature on 'New' Labour. Advocates of the 'accommodation view' argue that Labour did not depart significantly from the priorities of the Conservatives. The neoliberal narrative of children's services reform is consistent with this view. However, advocates of the 'revisionist view' argue that the Labour government pursued a broadly social–democratic policy agenda. Driver and Martell (2006), on the other hand, promote an alternative 'composite view'. They argue that Labour's economic and social policies were largely shaped by electoral pressures and characterised by shifting and sometimes conflicting priorities, reflecting both neoliberal and social–democratic ideas. Moreover, after ten years of public sector austerity under the Coalition and Conservative governments, it may now be a good time to reappraise Labour's children's services reforms.

Third, case studies of policymaking suggest that we must take account of the roles played by competing interest groups. This requires us to move beyond the 'critical and sceptical reading of texts' (Garrett, 2009a: 2), which has provided the basis for much of the existing research on children's services reform. Case studies of policymaking commonly draw upon interviews with policymakers to get a sense of what happened behind the scenes. Hall's (1976) *Reforming the Welfare* drew on interviews with members of the Seebohm Committee, government ministers, civil servants and external pressure groups. The study demonstrated that the establishment of local authority social services departments followed concerted pressure from social work activists. Nelson (1984) also analysed the roles played by different interest groups in her study of the emergence of child abuse as a national priority in the US. No similar investigation of the children's services reform process over recent years has been carried out in England or elsewhere.

Understanding the policymaking process

Public policy theory challenges us to look beyond formal policy statements and to examine the informal behind-the-scenes aspects of policymaking and the range of interests involved. The *process* of policymaking incorporates the pre-legislative phase of policy *formulation* and the post-legislative phase of policy *implementation* (Hill, 2009: 143; Cairney, 2012: 43); it does not begin and end with official policy statements. Moreover, public policy theories challenge the assumption that policy is structurally determined. As Cairney (2012: 131) explains:

> Most modern theories try to conceptualize this dynamic process in which structures influence agents and agents mediate or reconstitute the structural constraints within which they operate. They identify not only how socio-economic factors constrain behaviour, but also how policy-makers mediate these factors by interpreting or weighting their significance in different ways.

However, the question of which agents influence policy, and the extent to which they are constrained (or empowered) by contextual factors, is the subject of much debate among public policy theorists. It is not possible to provide a comprehensive overview of all the different theories here; what follows is only a brief discussion of the application of public policy theory in the British context. The three different perspectives introduced are based on competing interpretations of the contemporary political and socio-economic context of British policymaking, and the dominant interests driving (or resisting) reform. These perspectives provide an essential guide to answering the question: *what drives children's services reform?*

Groups and networks

One of the key discussion points among public policy theorists is the role played by non-governmental pressure groups (Hill, 2009; Cairney, 2012; John, 2012). The origins of this debate can be traced back to the 1950s and the development of pluralist theory by US political scientists. Pluralist theory challenged research that focused mainly on the formal policymaking arena. Advocates of the pluralist perspective argued that the importance of behind-the-scenes engagement between governmental policymakers and non-governmental pressure groups was not sufficiently recognised. Richardson and Jordan's

(1979: 41) *Governing under Pressure* highlighted the importance of the 'government–civil service–pressure group network' in British policymaking. They argued that it is 'the practices of co-option and the consensual style, that perhaps better account for policy outcomes than do examinations of party stances, manifestoes or of parliamentary influence' (Richardson and Jordan, 1979: 74). Marsh and Rhodes (1992) built upon this earlier research in their study of *Policy Networks in British Government*. In their view, the influence of non-state groups within discrete policy networks is dependent upon the resources they control. In certain policy areas, central government dependence on the organisational and informational resources controlled by groups such as professional or industry bodies is reflected in their greater influence over policy.

In his subsequent work, Rhodes (1997, 2007, 2017) has argued that private and voluntary organisations now play a pivotal role in British policymaking in general. This is because changes in the political and socio-economic context of policymaking are deemed to have 'hollowed out' the capacity of central government. In Rhodes's 'differentiated polity', central government has been hollowed out externally by globalisation and the development of European political institutions. Internally, central government has been hollowed out by New Public Management reforms that have created a fragmented public sector and increased central government dependence upon private and voluntary sector agencies. From this perspective, policymaking has become a more decentred process increasingly dominated by 'self-steering inter-organisational networks' (Rhodes, 1997: 5). In Rhodes's differentiated polity, Britain's 'tradition of strong executive leadership founders on the bargaining games within and between networks' (Rhodes, 1997: 22).

Rhodes's writing on policy networks is introduced here because it has strongly influenced research into British policymaking (Marinetto, 2003; Marsh, 2011; Laffin, 2013; Richardson, 2018). Furthermore, the involvement of a diverse range of NGOs and independent advisers has been a consistent feature of children's services policymaking in recent decades. Under Labour, representatives of NGOs in the children sector enjoyed unprecedented levels of access to ministers and senior civil servants. The involvement of non-partisan experts, including Lord Laming and Professor Munro, author of *The Munro Review of Child Protection* (Munro, 2011), has also been a defining feature of children's services policymaking. Close working between central government policymakers and sector representatives was also evident following the publication of the report of the Victoria Climbié inquiry and after the publication of the Baby P serious case review (SCR).

Whitehall

The emphasis placed on the influence of groups or policy networks has been challenged by institutional theorists, who have sought to bring the state back into public policy analysis (Hill, 2009: 68). Marsh and others (Marsh et al, 2001, 2003; Richards and Smith, 2002, 2004; Marsh, 2008, 2011; Richards, 2008) argue that Rhodes's perspective on British policymaking overstates the extent to which central government has been hollowed out and policymaking resources have been more widely dispersed. In their view, the centralisation of British policymaking reflects broader socio-economic inequalities and the continued dominance of a governing elite. They acknowledge that non-state groups can influence policy but argue that British policymaking 'is not an even playing field ... enduring slopes and gullies favour some interests over others' (Marsh et al, 2003: 310). Several studies of policy implementation under the Labour government (1997–2010) also lead us to question the claim that groups or networks drive policymaking. Rather, there is strong evidence to suggest that central government continued to dominate policymaking in the Labour period, and even developed new mechanisms to extend central control over local agencies (Davies, 2002; Bache, 2003; Wilson, 2003; Goodwin and Grix, 2011; Laffin, 2013).

More specifically, Marsh et al claim that it is Whitehall departments that largely drive British policymaking, not groups or policy networks. In their view, 'Departments are a concentration of political and bureaucratic resources. They are the source of most policy and they hold overall responsibility for delivering policies' (Marsh et al, 2001: 1). An important implication of this is that ministers rarely seek to challenge established policy objectives or patterns of working. Richards and Smith (2004: 778) argue that, 'generally, the relationship between ministers and civil servants is harmonious'. Moreover, Marsh et al argue that ministers and civil servants pursue a shared interest in preserving the dominance of departments. Both sides promote the idea of a 'British political tradition' that emphasises a representative understanding of democracy and the need for strong leadership and decisive action (Marsh et al, 2001, 2003; Marsh and Hall, 2007, 2016) – in other words, a view that 'government knows best' (Marsh et al, 2003: 312).

This perspective suggests that departmental ministers and officials work together to retain control over policy and resist reform. Marsh and Hall (2016: 138) argue that 'Change tends to threaten the position, and indeed the interests of politicians and bureaucrats and the socio-economic elites, who resist fundamental change; Thus change, such that it is, is likely to be minimised, unless it facilitates their interests.' Research inspired by Marsh et al's framework has highlighted the difficulties that Blair faced as Prime Minister when he sought to reform the civil service and challenge the dominance of departments within Whitehall (Marsh and Hall, 2007; Marsh, 2008; Richards, 2008; Diamond, 2014: 104). The influence of Blair is deemed to have been checked by the concentration of resources within departments. This perspective on British policymaking suggests that ministers and officials can resist or reshape reform proposals under pressure from other interests, both inside and outside of government.

Politicised policymaking

A third perspective suggests that policymaking has become a more politically driven process over recent decades. This perspective emphasises the influence of the leaders of the ruling party and senior ministers. It therefore challenges not only the view that policymaking is predominantly shaped by discrete policy networks with significant autonomy from central government, but also the alternative view that emphasises the autonomy of departmental ministers and civil servants. Both the policy network and Whitehall perspectives question the capacity of the ruling party leadership to implement 'meta-policy' or get ministers to sing from the same 'hymn sheet' (Richardson, 2018: 219). However, Richardson (2018: 220–3) argues that since the beginning of the fiscal crisis of the mid-1970s, party leaders and the Treasury have consistently imposed fiscal discipline on Whitehall. Thus, one of the main challenges for ministers has been to resist demands for increased expenditure from within their departments and from NGOs. This pressure has intensified in recent years under the programme of severe public austerity initiated by the Coalition government's 2010 Spending Review (Richardson, 2018: 223; Diamond, 2019).

Furthermore, party leaders have not restricted themselves to setting the financial parameters of departmental policymaking. Following the collapse of the post-war welfare consensus, various attempts have been made to implement public services reforms affecting both the civil service and public sector professionals. This has involved taking on diverse groups, including miners, doctors, lawyers and higher education institutions (Richardson, 2018: 223–5). Party leaders have also sought to implement personal priorities and manifesto commitments by throwing their weight behind specific policy projects, or even establishing new policy units to take closer personal control. Blair's involvement in education policy provides a good example of this (Shaw, 2007: ch 3).

The centre of government now also plays a more prominent role in relation to media management and responding to events (Davis and Rentoul, 2019: ch 3; Gregory, 2019). The intervention of party leaders has been a defining feature of government responses to the child abuse scandals discussed earlier, particularly the Baby P case (Jones, 2014; Parton, 2014). This does not mean that the centre now dominates Whitehall. However, King and Crewe (2014) suggest that these trends may have added to the complexity of policymaking. In their study, *The Blunders of our Governments*, they conclude that 'Almost all of the blunders we studied in detail exhibited some combination of, on the one hand, fragmented departmentalism ... on the other, a Number 10 whose interventions were almost invariably sporadic and occasionally completely ineffectual' (King and Crewe, 2014: 307).

A further layer of complexity in policymaking can arise from ideological divisions within government. Dorey and Garnett (2016) analyse disagreements on policy within the Conservative–Liberal Coalition government and show how the working relationship between the two parties deteriorated over time. However, *intra-party* disagreements can also affect policymaking. In his study of *The Problem of Party Government*, Richard Rose (1976) highlighted the existence of competing *policy parties* within government. In his view, 'every British government is a coalition government, because of the existence of differing groups within an electoral party' (Rose, 1976: 323). Davis and Rentoul's (2019) more recent study of the Labour government also underlines the importance of understanding the impact of intra-party tensions on the development of policy. They argue that there was greater mistrust between the two sides of the 'Blair–Brown Coalition' than there was between the Conservatives and the Liberal Democrats (Davis and Rentoul, 2019: 17). From their perspective, any analysis of policymaking between 1997 and 2007 (when Blair stepped down) must start by recognising 'a division between institutionally and ideologically distinct "parties": the Blairites and the Brownites' (Davis and Rentoul, 2019: 16).

The pressure on ministers to respond to the priorities of party leaders, and the underlying dynamics of inter- and intra–party competition, may also be reflected in changes to the policymaking process at the departmental level. It is important to remember that even though 'the centre cannot hold', the Prime Minister has the power to reshuffle ministers and create or abolish departments (King and Crewe, 2014: 306). The appointment of partisan ministerial special advisers, and even the process for appointing civil servants, is cited as evidence of the politicisation of departmental policymaking (Richards and Smith,

2016; Richardson, 2018; Diamond, 2019: chs 3–4). Richards and Smith (2016) argue that the relationship between ministers and civil servants is now better characterised as a hierarchical principal–agent relationship rather than a partnership of equals. Thus, civil servants are expected to simply implement policy and not offer any critique (Diamond, 2019: ch 5). Richardson (2018: 225) suggests that civil servants are now expected to be 'the "carriers" of ministerial ideas, willing to try to implement policies even when lacking broad policy community support'.

Another feature of politicised policymaking is the activism of ministers. King and Crewe (2014: 323) argue that the ever-present threat of the reshuffle means that in ministers' minds, 'making an immediate impact is almost certain to trump promoting lines of policy that have a good chance of becoming permanently bedded down'. Moran (2007: 190) argues that contemporary British policymaking is characterised by 'hyper-innovation':

> Hyper-innovation is the product of democratic politics dominated by adversarial competition, where politicians are forced to intervene to shape policy around the short term imperatives of the adversarial battle, and the management of their own careers. The effect has been to produce a shift to micro-management of projects by senior ministers.

The activism of ministers is evident in concerted efforts to take on perceived vested interests in the civil service and the public services professions, as denoted by the 'ubiquity of institutional reorganisation' (Moran, 2007: 131). Diamond (2019: 6) warns that 'Politicians are busy pursuing their agenda of reform and transformation, but neglect what is required to ensure a reliable supply of well-informed public policy advice. Worst of all, ministers undermine the space for reflection about long-term policy-making in government.' In this context, consultation takes placed within 'restricted parameters' as ministerial reforms are 'enforced against the resistance of at least some organised groups' (Richardson, 2018: 216). Thus, King and Crewe (2014: ch 27) suggest that the British policymaking process is now characterised by 'a deficit of deliberation'.

The research design and process

Studying how public policies are formulated and implemented requires a researcher to develop a detailed understanding of the interactions between multiple actors across multiple arenas. Sabatier (1991: 148) argues that a researcher needs to acquire substantive policy knowledge in a particular policy area in order to understand the technical nature of discussions between policy actors. Furthermore, he suggests that the ideal time frame for such research is a minimum of a decade (Sabatier, 1991: 149). In Sabatier's view, policy studies following a shorter time frame are problematic for two main reasons: (1) they often judge the impact of policy reform too prematurely; and (2) policy change often occurs gradually and can therefore go unnoticed. This research examined the development of children's services between 1997 and 2019. This allowed for an examination of:

- the emergence of new children's services priorities during the first Labour term;
- the development of the ECM Green Paper and the Children Act 2004;
- the post-legislative period of ECM delivery;
- the development of children's services policy under the Coalition government, including its response to the policy framework that it inherited from Labour; and
- the development of children's services policy under the Conservatives before and after the European Union (EU) referendum in June 2016.

Understanding the drivers of children's services reforms required a detailed investigation into the interactions between a range of elite policy actors, as well as an appreciation of the political and organisational context of policymaking. Both the formal legislative and the informal behind-closed-doors arenas of policymaking needed to be considered. Elite interviews are an inevitable component of in-depth policy research (Davies, 2001: 74–5). Richards (1996: 199) defines an elite as 'a group of individuals, who hold or have held, a privileged position in society and as such ... are likely to have had more influence on political outcomes than general members of the public'. Elite individuals are likely to hold a more in-depth knowledge and understanding of the public policy process than that which can be ascertained from formal records alone. Elite interviews enable us to develop an understanding of the political and organisational context of policymaking and appreciate the importance of the ideologies, beliefs and motivations of policy actors (Aberbach and Rockman, 2002; Lilleker, 2003).

However, there are a number of challenges and potential pitfalls to research relying on data generated through elite interviews. The first challenge is to gain access to elite actors and ensure that the programme of interviews is sufficiently representative of the various interests engaged in policymaking. In other words, it is important to hear all sides of the story (Goldstein, 2002; Aberbach and Rockman, 2002). Second, in conducting the interviews, the researcher must be sufficiently prepared in order to maximise the utility of the interview, but without prejudicing the interview conversation. Richards (1996) suggests that researchers should compile a dossier on interviewees, as well as an interview schedule to be used as an aide-memoire. Third, analysing interview data also presents significant challenges. Richards (1996: 200) argues that interviews must not be conducted with a view to establishing 'the truth'. It must be recognised that different interviewees will hold different recollections of events or promote their own interpretation of the policymaking process. Data from different interviews need to be triangulated against other sources of evidence, such as official and media reports, in order to try to arrive at a consensus view. Where this is not possible, the researcher must present disagreements or ambiguities explicitly in the reported findings (Davies, 2001).

The challenge of gaining access to elite policymakers was successfully overcome through a strategy of 'snowballing' and 'polite persistence' (Aberbach and Rockman, 2002: 673). Interviewees were selected for the prominent role that they played in relation to one or more aspect of children's services policymaking, as well as to ensure a good representation of politicians, government officials, interest group representatives and independent experts. The total of 45 participants included seven ministers, three political advisers, 12 civil servants, eight charity sector leaders, six local authority directors and nine academics/ independent expert advisers. Several participants moved between the civil service, the charity sector and local government during the time frame of this research. However, to minimise the risk of identification, these interviewees have been categorised according to the sector that they primarily represented in the policymaking process.

The following participants agree to be named:

- Paul Boateng (Labour Chief Secretary to the Treasury, 2002–05)
- Charles Clarke (Labour Secretary of State for Education, 2002–04)
- Margaret Hodge (Labour Children's Minister, 2003–04)
- Beverley Hughes (Labour Children's Minister, 2005–09)
- Ed Balls (Labour Secretary of State for Children, Schools and Families, 2007–10)

- Tim Loughton (Shadow Children's Minister, 2001–10; Conservative Children's Minister, 2010–12)
- Edward Timpson (Conservative Children's Minister, 2012–17) (written responses only)
- Professor Dame Eileen Munro (who led *The Munro Review of Child Protection*, 2010–11)
- Dame Moira Gibb (Chair of the Social Work Taskforce/Reform Board, 2009–12)
- Sir Martin Narey (Chief Executive of Barnardo's, 2005–11, and independent adviser to the Coalition/Conservative governments)

Forty of the interviews were carried out between 2012 and 2015, as part of the original PhD research project. An additional five interviews were carried out in 2018 and 2019. Unless indicated otherwise, interview quotes included in the book are taken from the original interviews carried out between 2012 and 2016. Interviews were semi-structured and several interviewees requested an interview schedule in advance. Questions were tailored towards the specific involvement that interviewees had had in the children's services policymaking process. Interviews were recorded and transcribed in full, except for one participant who provided written responses to interview questions and did not participate in a recorded interview. The collected data were coded in accordance with the three perspectives on British policymaking outlined earlier. Inevitably, interviewees sometimes had different recollections of events and attributed varying degrees of influence to the actors involved in policymaking. Therefore, applying the principle of triangulation, interview data were cross-referenced against approximately 500 official policy publications, select committee minutes and media reports. A chronology of selected key reports is included in the Appendix. It is recognised that this approach can never provide a definitive account of 'the truth'. To provide transparency and to invite counter-argument, the chapters that follow present the findings of this research in detail.

PART I

Children's services reform under the Labour government (1997–2010)

2

The Labour leadership and children's policy

Introduction

> Ask me my three main priorities for government and I tell you: education, education and education. (Blair, 1996)

> We will be tough on crime and tough on the causes of crime, and halve the time it takes persistent juvenile offenders to come to court. (Labour Party, 1997)

> Tackling child poverty and disadvantage is not about providing either more money or better public services; it is of necessity about both. (Brown, in HM Treasury, 2001: foreword)

The election of a Labour government in 1997, with a substantial majority in Parliament, was an exciting prospect for the children's sector. After decades of campaigning and debate around children's policy, there was a strong sense of hope that action would now follow. This chapter asks what changed in the early years of the new government, assessing the extent to which this hope was well founded or misplaced. First, competing assessments of Labour's overarching approach to economic and social policy are briefly discussed. Many commentators on children's services reform have pointed towards the acceptance of policy priorities inherited from the Conservatives, as the discussion in Chapter 1 revealed, but alternative assessments must also be considered. This provides the platform for a discussion of three key areas of children's policy of interest to Blair and Brown in the second section: education, 'problem' young people and child poverty. The third section then focuses on the Treasury's engagement with Whitehall in the early Labour years. This includes a discussion of the role played by NGOs representing the children's charity sector, and the emergence of the flagship Sure Start programme. The chapter begins to examine the main drivers of children's policy while providing an essential platform for further discussions of the Labour period in subsequent chapters.

Labour economic and social policy

Following a fourth successive election defeat in 1992, Labour embarked upon a major review of its approach to economic and social policy. The report of the Commission on Social Justice (1994) was critical of the neoliberal approach pursued by the Conservative government since 1979, highlighting significant increases in social inequality and the degradation of public services. However, the commission's report also urged Labour to acknowledge the importance of private enterprise and accept that social justice could not be achieved through greater state control over the economy and public services alone. As the report stated:

> The values of social justice are for us essential. They are: the equal worth of all citizens, their equal right to be able to meet their basic needs, the need to spread opportunities and life chances as widely as possible, and finally the requirement that we reduce and where possible eliminate unjustified inequalities. Social justice stands against fanatics of the free market economy; but it also demands and promotes economic success. The two go together. (Commission on Social Justice, 1994: 1)

Blair's statements on economic and social policy in the run-up to the 1997 election and in office were consistent with this analysis. He consistently sought to distance 'New' Labour from the Conservatives, as well as from past Labour administrations deemed to have followed an overly interventionist approach to economic and social policy. Blair drew upon the concept of a 'Third Way' to chart a new approach. As he explained:

> The Third Way is not an attempt to split the difference between right and left. It is about traditional values in a changed world. And it draws vitality from uniting the two great streams of left-of-centre thought – democratic socialism and liberalism – whose divorce this century did so much to weaken progressive politics across the West. Liberals asserted the primacy of individual liberty in the market economy; social democrats promoted social justice

with the state as its main agent. There is no necessary conflict between the two, accepting as we now do that state power is one means to achieve our goals, but not the only one and emphatically not an end in itself. (Blair, 1998)

However, the extent to which the Labour government turned out to be markedly different from previous Conservative and Labour administrations has been the subject of considerable debate. Driver and Martell (2006) identify three competing views, which now need to be briefly considered.

The accommodation view

The neoliberal narrative of children's services reform, discussed in Chapter 1, highlights continuities between the policies of the Conservative and Labour governments. This perspective is consistent with what Driver and Martell (2006) identify as the *accommodation view*. Advocates of this view argue that the Labour leadership largely abandoned the party's social-democratic traditions and accepted the neoliberal economic and social policy framework inherited from the Conservatives. They highlight Labour's commitment to monetary policy, fiscal prudence, the deregulation of financial markets and commitment to flexible labour markets as evidence of policy continuity. The decision to stick to Conservative spending plans for the first two years is also widely cited as evidence of the Labour leadership's abandonment of the party's social-democratic ideals. Critics of the Labour government argue that the leadership was more concerned with securing the continued support of business leaders and the middle classes than it was with serving the interests of working-class supporters (Hay, 1999; Heffernan, 2000; Hall, 2003; Watson and Hay, 2003; Lee, 2008, 2009).

Labour's focus on reducing welfare dependency and commitment to a tough approach to tackling crime and anti-social behaviour are also cited as evidence of policy continuity (Peck, 1999; Hall, 2003; Levitas, 2005; Faucher-King and Le Galès, 2010). Levitas (2005) argues that these policies reflected a 'moral underclass' perspective on poverty. In her view, this was particularly evident in the work of the Social Exclusion Unit (SEU) set up in 1997. The SEU highlighted the importance of behavioural traits (labelled 'risk factors') in explaining 'social exclusion'. This shifted the focus of social policy towards interventions targeted at specific groups, downplaying the economic determinants of poverty and the importance of redistributive social policies. Labour's approach to public services reform also led critics to question the leadership's commitment to state-directed welfare services. Advocates of the accommodation view have also argued that the extension of the Private Finance Initiative (PFI), the contracting out of public services and Blair's emphasis on choice and competition demonstrated a commitment to a market-based welfare system. For critics of this approach, centrally prescribed performance targets and league tables are viewed as key components of this market-based system (Clarke et al, 2000; Cutler and Waine, 2000; Leys, 2001; Newman, 2001; Hall, 2003; Faucher-King and Le Galès, 2010).

The revisionist view

The *revisionist view* of the Labour government is more sympathetic towards the Labour leadership. Advocates of this view emphasise the economic constraints that the party faced in government and point towards an ongoing commitment to progressive social policies. This was a view that Blair (2002) himself promoted during the second term. Anthony Giddens, author of *The Third Way: The Renewal of Social Democracy* (Giddens, 1998), has also promoted this assessment of Labour's record. Giddens (2002, 2007) argues that critics of the Labour government have tended to downplay the significance of globalisation and the constraints that this placed on economic and social policy. Advocates of the revisionist view highlight Labour's development of a 'social investment' approach to social policy. This emphasised the importance of positive state intervention to create a highly skilled workforce equipped to compete in the new knowledge-intensive global economy (Giddens, 1998; Lister, 2003; Buckler and Dolowitz, 2004; Dolowitz, 2004; Dobrowolsky and Lister, 2008). The concept of social investment was used to justify significant increases in public spending after the first two years of sticking to Conservative spending plans. Education spending rose from 4.5 per cent of national income in 1996/97 to 5.4 per cent by 2006/07. Health spending rose over the same period from 5.4 per cent to 7.5 per cent of national income (Beech, 2008). The introduction of the national minimum wage, childcare places and enhanced maternity and paternity rights are also highlighted as evidence of Labour's social-democratic credentials. Income transfers through benefits and tax reform also ensured that poor families were better off (Driver, 2008: 56). Furthermore, from the revisionist perspective, public services reforms were aimed at ensuring that new money was spent effectively, and that welfare services were equipped to tackle the more complex needs of a diverse population. From this perspective, Labour's public services reforms were more about the renewal of the welfare state than privatisation (Blair, 2002; Prabhakar, 2003).

The composite view

However, Driver and Martell (2006) argue that both the accommodation and revisionist views of the Labour government overstate its ideological coherence. The alternative *composite view* suggests that the overriding priority of the Labour leadership was to keep winning elections. Advocates of this perspective suggest that the party leadership drew upon competing ideological traditions to develop policies that appealed to different groups in society. Smith (2003: 224) highlights the importance of presentation to the Labour leadership and suggests that the same policies were often spun in different ways. Advocates of this interpretation point towards the pragmatic approach taken to economic policy, arguing that although the leadership worked hard to maintain an image of neoliberal orthodoxy, the government's approach to economic policy was, in fact, an eclectic blend of macroeconomic pragmatism, monetarist ideas and New Keynesian ideas (Annesley and Gamble, 2003; Smith, 2014). Annesley and Gamble (2003: 157) suggest that this was part of a deliberate strategy of 'credit avoidance' for the moderate redistribution of economic resources that benefitted working-class families. Labour's position on workers' rights also contained ideological tensions. On the one hand, the Labour leadership refused to repeal Conservative trade union legislation and expressed commitment to the principle of flexible labour markets. Yet, on the other, Labour introduced the national minimum wage and improved maternity and paternity rights. It is acknowledged that Blair wanted to demonstrate that Labour could be as tough as the Conservatives when it came to tackling welfare dependency, crime and anti-social behaviour. However, it is also pointed out that Labour prioritised reducing child poverty and invested in the expansion of universal public services, including youth services (Diver and Martell, 2006: 107–11).

Contradictions and shifts in Labour's approach to public services reform have also been highlighted (Smith, 2003; Driver and Martell, 2006; Shaw, 2007). These reflected disagreements between Blair and Brown over Labour's approach to public services reform. On the one hand, Blair (2002) promoted the expansion of competition and choice as the key to improving public services. On the other, Brown spoke about the importance of equity and emphasised the limitations of a more market-based welfare system (Shaw, 2007; Davis and Rentoul, 2019: 226–9). Underlying these disagreements was an ongoing struggle between No 10 and the Treasury to control social policy. Following the 'Granita deal', named after a restaurant in Islington, Brown claimed that in exchange for backing Blair to be party leader, he was promised a much broader domestic policy role for the Treasury (Davis and Rentoul, 2019: 19–20). The remainder of the chapter examines the early development of children's services policy, paying careful attention to policymaking arrangements in the 'Blair–Brown coalition' (Davis and Rentoul, 2019) government.

The children's policy priorities of the Labour leaders

Blair and education reform

At the 1996 Labour Party conference, Blair (1996) famously declared that the three main priorities of a future Labour government would be 'education, education, education'. His prioritisation of education reform was also reflected in the 1997 election manifesto (Labour Party, 1997). Education reform was important to Blair because it attracted middle-class voters to the party and reassured working-class supporters that Labour remained committed to improving public services. Under the social investment narrative, increased spending on education was justified because it would reduce wasteful future spending on unemployment benefits. Furthermore, Blair framed a commitment to improving 'equality of opportunity' as a modernised version of Labour's historic commitment to the levelling of economic inequality (Shaw, 2007: ch 3). The following quotation taken from the government's first education White Paper, *Excellence in Schools*, captures these arguments:

> To overcome economic and social disadvantage and to make equality of opportunity a reality, we must strive to eliminate, and never excuse, under-achievement in the most deprived parts of our country.... We are talking about investing in human capital in the age of knowledge. To compete in the global economy, to live in a civilised society and to develop the talents of each and every one of us, we will have to unlock the potential of every young person. (DfEE, 1997: 3)

However, critics on the Left argue that Labour's approach to education reform did not signal a break with Conservative 'local management of schools' policies. A central aim of Conservative reforms had been to limit the control of local education authorities (LEAs) over schools.

Thus, schools were granted greater control of their own budgets and encouraged to opt out of LEA control altogether. Conservative ministers argued that this would create greater diversity and competition in the school system, and that parental choice over schools would drive innovation and raise standards. New city technology colleges and grant-maintained schools were also created outside of LEA control. These reforms were opposed at the time by Labour as they were interpreted as an attack on the principle of comprehensive education, a central pillar of the state-directed welfare state (Shaw, 2007: ch 3). However, the Labour government's focus on 'standards not structures' (DfEE, 1997: 66) meant that the thorny issues of how schools were governed was sidestepped. To Labour's critics, this signalled an unwillingness to reverse the direction of education policy set by the Conservatives. What was presented by the government as a non-partisan focus on standards was interpreted as facilitating an extension of market principles in the governance of education. Targets, league tables and inspections were viewed as essential to establishing competition between schools (Muschamp et al, 1999; Naidoo and Muschamp, 2002).

However, this interpretation fails to acknowledge the substantial centralisation of education policymaking that occurred during Labour's first term. Furthermore, the government's stated aim was to even out disparities in the education system nationally. First, there was a commitment to improving access to, and the quality of, early-years (pre-school) education. The headline pledge was a free nursery education place for all four years olds whose parents wanted it. Second, in relation to primary schools, there was a target of class sizes of no more than 30 for five to seven year olds. Third, new national and school-level performance targets were introduced for primary and secondary schools. These were backed up by an enhanced inspection regime and the publication of more detailed performance tables. At the primary level, mandatory literacy and numeracy hours were added to the national curriculum in order to drive the achievement of English and maths performance targets.

Furthermore, Blair also sought to strengthen No 10's influence over education policymaking in Whitehall. The key institutional change introduced was the creation of the education Standards and Effectiveness Unit. Importantly, the focus on education standards also required the government to reinvigorate the capacity of LEAs to intervene in failing schools (DfEE, 1997: ch 3). Although there would be no reversal of financial controls devolved to schools under the Conservatives, the White Paper stressed that LEAs had 'to challenge schools to raise standards continuously and apply pressure where they do not' (DfEE, 1997: 27). LEAs were required to submit detailed education development plans outlining their commitment to driving up school standards in line with national targets as a condition of increased funding for school improvement work. They were effectively set up as local agents of the DfEE.

Blair and 'problem' young people

The manifesto commitment to be 'tough on crime and tough on the causes of crime, and halve the time it takes persistent juvenile offenders to come to court' (Labour Party, 1997), provided an example of Blair's more authoritarian populist (Hall and Jacques, 1983) perspective on young people. The origins of this strand of Labour children's policy can be traced back to Blair's time as Shadow Home Secretary, when he competed with the then Conservative Home Secretary Michael Howard to sound tough on law and order. Blair placed a strong emphasis on youth justice in the inter-party-political battles of this period, most notably, following the murder of two-year-old Jamie Bulger in February 1993 by two ten-year-old boys (Frost and Parton, 2009: 86).

Charman and Savage (2008: 105) argue that Blair remained mindful of the electoral imperatives of law-and-order policy, including youth justice, when in office. Thus, as with education policy, Blair sought to establish a greater degree of central control over policymaking. Under the Crime and Disorder Act 1998, a new national Youth Justice Board was created. In each local authority area, new Youth Offending Teams (YOTs) were also set up. YOTs sat outside of social services departments, reporting directly to local authority chief executives. One of the priorities for these new institutions was to increase the number of offences brought to justice. By 2007, this resulted in a 26 per cent increase in the number of young people subjected to criminal prosecution. Lower-level anti-social behaviour was addressed through the issuing of Anti-Social Behaviour Orders (ASBOs). Also introduced under the 1998 Act, the initial uptake of ASBOs was slow. However, this increased dramatically following the intervention of Blair. In January 2003, he set up the Anti-Social Behaviour Unit in the Home Office and pushed the subsequent Anti-Social Behaviour Act 2003. By 2005, approximately 600 orders were issued per quarter, with juveniles accounting for 50 per cent of the total (Frost and Parton, 2009: 86–91).

Additional policy initiatives were also developed to tackle a broader range of perceived problem behaviours among young people and to pressure Whitehall departments to reallocate policymaking resources. Responsibility for the development of a cross-departmental children and family's strategy was initially handed to the Home Secretary, Jack Straw. Straw's report, *Supporting Families* (Home Office, 1998), reflected the conservative tone of Blair's 'rights-and-responsibilities discourse', placing a strong emphasis on the importance of the traditional family unit rather than the state. Moreover, a more targeted approach to tackling the problem behaviours of a small number of families and adolescents was advocated (Home Office, 1998; ch 5). This more targeted approach to social policy was influenced by the work of the SEU, discussed earlier. The SEU's focus on the 'risk factors' linked to social exclusion meant that particular groups of young people became the focus of specific policy initiatives. The key risk factors faced by young people that were identified included: poor early development; poor school attendance; being in care; contact with the police; drug misuse; teenage parenthood; and not participating in education, employment or training (NEET) between the ages of 16 and 18 (SEU, 1999, cited in DSS, 1999: 43–4).

Brown and child poverty

Although it was Blair (1999a) who announced Labour's target to end child poverty in a generation, it was Brown who spoke more frequently about tackling economic disadvantage and it was the Treasury that drove policy in this area. Brown identified tax and benefits reform as the most effective lever available to the Treasury to reduce child poverty. However, Brown needed to tread carefully so as not to break pre-election promises on income tax and to maintain a distance from 'tax-and-spend' Labour chancellors of the past. The term 'progressive universalism' came to describe the Treasury approach to reform. In his biography of Gordon Brown, Peston (2005: 277) explained that 'Progressive universalism is brunch for welfare theoreticians: it's not classic means testing; and it's not a universal payment. It is financial help for the vast majority of people that tapers down to nil for those whose earnings are well above the average.' However, over time, both fiscal and social policies were tied to the Treasury's progressive universalism approach to reducing child poverty. Naomi Eisenstadt (2011: 65), the former head of Labour's Sure Start Unit, identifies the pre-Budget report *Tackling Child Poverty: Giving Every Child the Best Possible Start in Life* (HM Treasury, 2001) as a clear statement of this dual approach. In his foreword to the report, Brown states:

> As Beveridge knew, tackling child poverty and disadvantage is not about providing either more money or better public services; it is of necessity about both. It will require more resources to be devoted to raising the incomes of poor families (to tackle the need and unemployment Beveridge identified) and also to deliver the services on which we all depend (to provide high-quality healthcare, world-class education system and decent housing for all). It will also require us to ensure that public services take more account of the level of need in a locality. (HM Treasury, 2001: iii)

By tying social policy to the government's strategy to tackle child poverty, the Treasury significantly extended the potential cohort of children and young people requiring enhanced support. Moreover, the Treasury called upon *universal services* to develop more focused programmes to support economically disadvantaged families and 'respond effectively to early signs of difficulties, rather than waiting until there is a crisis' (HM Treasury, 2001: 3). This challenged more targeted policy initiatives informed by the SEU's analysis of 'risk factors' and Blair's prioritisation of action to tackle relatively small groups of problem young people. The emphasis placed on the role of universal services also highlighted the important role that schools needed to play. From the progressive universalism perspective, the narrow focus on standards of achievement (measured through statutory tests) in education policy overlooked the broader range of challenges faced by children growing up in poverty. Policy on schools would later emerge as a key point of tension in Labour children's policy, as subsequent chapters will demonstrate.

The Treasury and Whitehall

One of the first steps taken by Brown as Chancellor was to hand over responsibility for the setting of interest rates to the Bank of England. An important implication of this was that the Treasury now had greater capacity to oversee public spending. Furthermore, following the deal struck with Blair, Brown envisaged an extended role for the Treasury in shaping social policy. In his memoirs, Brown states:

The Treasury may have lost control of one empire – the control of monetary policy – but it had assumed an even bigger task in long-term fiscal management and overseeing public sector reform. The success or failure of public services was now measured not by the Treasury's traditional focus on inputs – what was spent – but on what really matters: outputs and outcomes. What counted now was not simply the level of spending but whether programmes achieved their stated purposes and what difference they had on people's lives. (2017: 134–5)

Blair set up the Standards and Effectiveness Unit to give No 10 greater control over education policy, as highlighted earlier. Michael Barber was appointed to head up the unit. He subsequently headed up the Prime Minister's Delivery Unit (PMDU), which was responsible for monitoring the implementation of a broader range of Blair's domestic policy priorities during the second Labour term. In his memoirs, Barber (2007: ch 9) reflects upon the challenges that he faced in trying to influence the work of departmental policymakers, pointing out that even after the establishment of new policy units, No 10 still commanded limited policymaking resources. In contrast, the Labour Treasury was better placed to influence departmental policymaking. Barber comments that:

There is no doubt that by agreeing to concede so much power to his Chancellor, Blair constrained his own influence. Brown was the master of the Budget and management of the economy. Spending reviews were a matter of a hard-fought card game, in which the Treasury held the trump cards on timing and information. (2007: 305–6)

This is not to say that the input of No 10 was unimportant. Rather, Barber alerts us to tensions in Labour policy created by competition between No 10 and the Treasury. He describes the implications for departmental policymakers as follows:

Reading signals not just from their own ministers but from interaction with No 10 advisers and Treasury officials, they [sought] to pick their way across a minefield ... the system of dual power at the top and, more particularly the way it was played out in practice, caused real problems. (Barber, 2007: 306–7)

The departmental Spending Review process

Control over the departmental Spending Review process provided the key mechanism for the Treasury to shape departmental policymaking. It was clear from the outset that the Treasury would use the Spending Review process to promote Brown's public services reform priorities (HM Treasury, 1998). Moreover, the Treasury consistently used the Spending Review process to promote policies aimed at reducing and alleviating the impact of child poverty. Negotiations between the Treasury and departments were shaped by clear policy objectives, not just arguments about resources. As one Treasury official closely involved in the Spending Review process explained:

> 'The Chancellor had put into its [The Treasury's] objectives not only some of the obvious things you'd expect as a finance and economics department, but things like child poverty. So, to have a Treasury that actually took child poverty, reduction of, as part of its objectives, I would guess, was relatively unique. It potentially changes the whole way the organisation is supposed to think.' (Interview with Treasury official)

Under the Spending Review process, beginning with the 1998 Spending Review, the Treasury negotiated Public Service Agreements (PSAs) with every government department. PSAs set out the Treasury's three-year allocation of resources to departments alongside an agreed list of performance targets. The inclusion of performance targets tied future spending allocations to compliance with policy priorities approved by the Treasury. However, in addition to these bilateral agreements, the Treasury also sought to establish closer control over policymaking in key areas. As part of the Spending Review process, the Treasury set up 'cross-cutting' reviews in areas of policy that were deemed to cross departmental boundaries. Furthermore, these reviews provided an opportunity for Treasury ministers and officials to engage with a wide range of NGOs and independent experts, and thereby avoid being over-reliant on the advice of perceived vested interests in Whitehall. Significantly, services for children were subject to a cross-cutting review in every spending round under the Labour government. The case of the Sure Start review is discussed later.

This determination to shape the content of departmental policy as well as financial planning required the input of social policy experts. Consequently, Brown and his close advisers Ed Balls and Ed Miliband "were interested in spending time with, and in and around, people that knew something about policy and policy implementation" (interview with Treasury official). Experienced outsiders were recruited to bolster the capacity of the Treasury and limit dependence on the advice of departmental officials. In 2000, Lucy de Groot, Chief Executive of Bristol City Council, was recruited to the post of Public Services Director and played a lead role in Treasury–department negotiations. De Groot was replaced in 2003 by Ray Shostak. Shostak had previously served as a director at Hertfordshire Council, where he created the first integrated education and children's social services department in England, well ahead of the statutory requirement introduced under the Children Act 2004. Shostak acted as a key adviser to the Chief Secretary to the Treasury Paul Boateng when he led the development of the ECM Green Paper (discussed in Chapter 4). However, the Treasury also looked towards representatives of the children's charity sector for advice on social policy.

The relationship with the children's charities

Close ties with representatives of the children's charity sector had been formed during Labour's long period of opposition. The charities provided the party with evidence of the negative impact of Conservative policies, as well as ideas to inform a more progressive approach to social policy. Thus, the contribution of the charitable sector was eulogised in early Labour social policy statements. For example, Brown stated that 'A partnership between Government and the voluntary, community and faith sectors is the best way to tackle poverty and support families, as demonstrated by the fact that some of the most innovative projects of recent years have partnership with community organisations at their heart' (HM Treasury, 2001: iii). In the early Labour years, representatives of the children's charity sector gained unprecedented levels of access to ministers, political advisers and officials, including those based in the Treasury. Before her appointment to head up the Sure Start Unit, Eisenstadt was Chief Executive of the Family Services Unit charity. In her book, she recalls hosting visits from Treasury officials:

> For those of us outside government, hosting visits from Treasury officials was a completely new experience. We had spent years trying to convince the DoH [Department of Health] and the DfEE [Department for Education and Employment] that investment in early years was critical to child outcomes. We were now meeting a wholly different

kind of bureaucrat, one who knew virtually nothing about
services for poor children, was extremely keen to learn and
had huge influence in deciding how public money should
be spent. (Eisenstadt, 2011: 24)

However, although it was often the small community-based local
charities that were eulogised in official discourse, it was the more
established voices in the children's charity sector that enjoyed the best
access to senior officials and ministers. This reflected the superior
lobbying and policymaking resources available to the largest charities,
including the National Society for the Prevention of Cruelty to
Children (NSPCC), Barnardo's, the NCH (later called Action for
Children) and the Children's Society. The National Children's Bureau
(NCB) can also be added to this list. The NCB was formed in 1963
to represent a diverse range of organisations working across the
charitable and statutory sectors. As such, it could claim to represent
a wide range of interests. Furthermore, the NCB was primarily a
policy development organisation. As one interviewee put it, "it was
full of policy wonks". Together, these charities performed a "think-
tank function", helping ministers to turn vague reform priorities into
concrete proposals that "would feel right to the sector" (interview
with Treasury official). The work of the NCB was particularly
important. Throughout the Labour period, NCB Chief Executive
Paul Ennals enjoyed direct access to senior officials, ministers and
Gordon Brown. A senior Department for Education and Skills
(DfES) official described Ennals as an "adroit operator" who became
a familiar face in Whitehall.

Importantly, close working between Labour policymakers and
representatives of the children's charity sector was also founded upon a
shared ideological commitment to address child poverty. This provided
the basis for the relationship formed during the Conservative years
and that lasted after Labour came to power. Ministers felt that they
could trust the charities because they shared the same basic goals.
Furthermore, there were close personal connections between the
charities and Labour. As one interviewee explained:

'There was a great commonality of interests and ambition,
even though we might have fallen out with government
sometimes about whether we thought they were a bit too
interfering, micromanaging, too structural. There were
different strands of thought and policy within government
on children which changed throughout the Labour years,

but, basically, it was a very close and comradely kind of relationship, and the truth is lots of people working in the children's sector at that time were Labour Party members, Labour Party activists and were just very at home. It was very easy to work together, very much shared values.' (Interview with charity leader seconded into the DfEE)

The reference to the different strands of Labour policy in the preceding quote is important. The sector welcomed the Treasury's progressive universalism approach but was generally critical of some of Blair's more authoritarian initiatives. Thus, it supported Brown in his intra-party battle to progress the Treasury's child poverty strategy. The example of the End Child Poverty Coalition (ECPC) illustrated how the Treasury sought to nurture external critique of Labour social policy in order to progress the Treasury's policy priorities. The ECPC was formed in 2003 and brought together a wide range of NGOs that shared the objective of eliminating child poverty. Sir Martin Narey chaired the ECPC when he was the Chief Executive at Barnardo's. He recalled that "Ed [Balls] was very encouraging of me making a noise about poverty. He was very much a minister who believed that one of the roles of the charities was to make some political space into which politicians could enter. He welcomed the pressure to spend more on child poverty" (interview with Sir Martin Narey, 2019). However, the influence of the children's charities was not limited to their role as external pressure groups. The Sure Start initiative provides an example of how representatives of the sector came to play a more prominent role in shaping the detail of policy alongside ministers and civil servants during the early Labour years.

Sure Start

The Sure Start programme was widely regarded as the flagship Treasury social policy. When it was launched in 1998, the programme established 250 local schemes in the most economically disadvantaged parts of the country. In tune with the principle of progressive universalism, each local scheme was tasked with developing the early intervention and preventative role of mainstream health and pre-school services for children under the age of five and their parents. A substantial investment of £450 million over three years was allocated to these first local schemes. By 2004, £500 million per year was committed to fund the establishment of 3,500 Sure Start children's centres nationwide (HM Treasury, 2004; Eisenstadt, 2011).

Officially, the programme was presented as an outcome of the Sure Start review, one of the cross-cutting reviews in the 1998 Spending Review. The review process considered evidence from a wide range of external sources. Furthermore, the programme was presented as being modelled on the Head Start programme in the US. This programme, also targeted at pre-school children, had first been established in the 1960s as a Great Society programme and strong evidence had been gathered demonstrating its effectiveness. Furthermore, this evidence supported the economic argument that early intervention saved public money in the long run by preventing the development of acute problems later in childhood. The establishment of Sure Start was spearheaded by the Treasury civil servant Norman Glass but with the strong support of Labour ministers, including Tessa Jowell, who chaired the programme's ministerial group (Eisenstadt, 2011: 22).

However, high-level political backing for the programme was evident from the outset. A Treasury official involved in the review explained that:

> 'They [Labour] were really interested in how to do better for poor families and poor children; that was very much a feature of their government. That created a space within which officials like Norman [Glass] could be quite radical and say "Right, we will go out and talk to the voluntary sector and listen to what they are saying", which felt quite radical at the time, and the political emphasis on the importance of child poverty definitely helped make the space for that…. We were told by the top of the office that we ought to think big on this. By which they meant – don't just come up with a proposal for ten pilots that cost 10k each.' (Interview with Treasury official)

Beverley Hughes, Children's Minister between 2004 and 2009, agreed that there was a prior commitment to establish the programme:

> 'Certainly, we recognised the economic argument, and that is very much evident in the findings from the States – they reckon there is a one-in-seven return on investment in children and young people. But the reason this was a policy priority was to do with our commitment to reducing inequality in society.' (Interview with Beverley Hughes)

The review team also recognised that it could not simply transfer a policy initiative embedded in the US welfare system. The review also looked for examples of effective schemes at home. However, there was a predisposition towards the evidence presented by representatives of the children's charity sector, who were more trusted than the perceived vested interests in central and local government. One of the charity leaders who gave evidence to the review recalled how uncritically evidence from the charity sector was received:

> 'They called for evidence from all these outside groups like the charity I was working for, and it was quite funny because we all wrote in stuff that we believed, that the Treasury thought was evidence. There was no scientific basis; it was what we believed. But for some reason, they took more credence against what we wrote in than from what the departments were telling them.... Was any of this tested against really rigorous evaluation? No.' (Interview with charity leader)

Having led the review, the Treasury went on to lead the process of setting up the Sure Start Unit in government. The appointment of Naomi Eisenstadt, Chief Executive of the Family Services Unit children's charity, to lead the unit, has already been highlighted. Although Eisenstadt was officially appointed as a civil servant, the recruitment process and the management arrangements for the new unit were designed to protect ministerial authority and minimise the potential for the capture of the unit by departmental officials. Although based in the DfEE, the Sure Start Unit was established as an inter-departmental unit with a ring-fenced budget, and with reporting lines into ministers in both the DfEE and Department of Health (DH). A DfEE official interviewed for this research commented that officials such as Eisenstadt were more trusted than career officials because they were considered to have a greater knowledge of service delivery and, above all, a commitment to reform:

> 'They had a degree of independence from the department. The leaders of these units had a status which was more prominent than us civil servants.... There was quite a hands-on delivery operation as well as developing some of the policy, and it was very much in the spirit of New Labour, experimentation with different ways of doing things in government.' (Interview with DfEE official)

The elevated position of officials such as Eisenstadt in Whitehall was matched by the central role given to charities at the local level. Key ministers saw statutory service providers, but particularly local government, as potential obstacles to innovation. Ministers saw the charities as a source of innovation and dynamism in the heart of local communities. As Secretary of State with responsibility for Sure Start, David Blunkett was a strong advocate of community- and voluntary sector-led local delivery partnerships (Eisenstadt, 2011: 33). It was hoped that charity sector leadership of multi-agency partnerships, which included statutory public agencies from local government and health, would drive innovation and prevent the capture of new resources by the statutory agencies. Of course, the charities welcomed the promise of new resources and the chance to influence how they were allocated.

Discussion

So was the optimism of campaigners and stakeholders from the children's sector at the beginning of the Labour period well founded? For many, the fiscal prudence of the early Labour years was a major disappointment. After 18 years of Conservative rule, many wanted to see Labour prioritise reducing economic inequality and reinvesting in public services. Early policy announcements on welfare dependency, crime and anti-social behaviour also suggested, to some, that Labour would continue to follow social policy priorities inherited from the Conservatives. On the other hand, more sympathetic commentators point out that in the context of globalisation, Labour could not significantly increase taxes and public spending. Moreover, increased spending on education and health was prioritised after 2000. Supporters of the government also highlight progressive reforms, including the national minimum wage, enhanced maternity and paternity rights, childcare places, and tax and benefit changes.

However, more nuanced assessments suggest that the Labour government cannot easily be characterised as having pursued either a neoliberal or social-democratic agenda. Rather, it is suggested that the Labour government sometimes pursued contradictory policies as it sought to appeal to both business leaders and middle-class supporters alongside more traditional working-class voters. Competition between Blair and Brown added a further layer of complexity to Labour social policy, and the early development of children's policy must be viewed in this context. On education policy, Blair did not commit to reversing market-imitating reforms introduced by the Conservatives. However, he did drive the centralisation of education policy in the early Labour years, seeking to even out disparities in access to education and levels of achievement. On the other hand, Blair largely stuck to the more authoritarian agenda of the Conservative era when it came to policy on youth crime and anti-social behaviour. Yet, Blair's and Brown's commitment to reducing child poverty placed the government on more traditional Labour territory. Under Brown's leadership, the Treasury redistributed significant resources to raise the incomes of poorer families. Furthermore, the Treasury's commitment to addressing inequality was evident in the substantial investment in the Sure Start programme. Thus, on balance, the election of the Labour government did lead to important shifts in social policy, especially policy relating to children and families.

This chapter has also highlighted important developments in relation to the policymaking process during the early Labour years. Both Blair and Brown sought to establish closer control over policymaking resources in Whitehall as they pursued their separate interests in relation to children's policy. Blair established new policy units to try to steer policy on education, youth justice and social exclusion. However, the Treasury's control of public spending provided it with a more effective lever to shape both social policy spending and departmental priorities. The establishment of the Sure Start programme provided an example of how the Treasury sought to direct significant investment in early years services in support of its child poverty strategy. Significantly, efforts to direct policymaking in Whitehall also saw the Treasury look to representatives of the children's charity sector for support. At the national level, the charities provided Treasury policymakers with an alternative source of expertise to perceived vested interests in Whitehall departments. Ministers also envisaged the charity sector playing a lead role in relation to the design and implementation of Sure Start at the local level, where local statutory agencies were viewed as potential obstacles to the effective investment of new resources. Chapter 3 explains how this pattern of policymaking developed as the Labour leaders and senior ministers grew increasingly impatient at the perceived slow pace of policy delivery and came to contemplate the structural reform of statutory children's services.

3

Structural reform and the Victoria Climbié inquiry

Introduction

> We had come to power in 1997 saying it was 'standards not
> structures' that mattered. This was fine as a piece of rhetoric
> ... it was bunkum as a piece of policy. Structures beget
> standards. How a service is configured affects outcomes.
> (Blair, 2010: 265, cited in Timmins, 2017: 588)

> We cannot undo the wrongs done to Victoria Climbié.
> We can, though, seek to put right for others what so
> fundamentally failed for her. That is what Lord Laming's
> report demands, and that is what the Government is
> determined to do. (Milburn, 2003)

Public service reform was one of the dominant themes of Labour's
second term. The Party leadership and senior ministers expressed
concern about the perceived slow implementation of new policy
initiatives even before the election victory in 2001. Moreover, reform
was deemed necessary to ensure that significant increases in public
spending in key areas such as health and education, announced in
the 2000 Spending Review, were not wasted (Driver and Martell,
2006: ch 5). Following the Children Act 2004, all local authorities in
England were required to merge education and children's social care
services in order to create new children's services departments led by
a single DCS. In the government's official narrative, this structural
change provided a direct response to the Victoria Climbié inquiry
(Lord Laming, 2003). This chapter begins to question this claim by
examining the earlier development of structural reform proposals in
the context of wider debates within the government regarding public
services reform.

To begin with, it is necessary to consider the dual role played by
local authority social services departments to protect children and to
support families. Under Labour's *Modernising Social Services* programme

(DH, 1998a), new performance objectives and targets were introduced but structural reform appeared to have been ruled out. However, following the SEU's (2000) review of policy on services for 13 to 19 year olds, chaired by the then Home Office minister Paul Boateng, this position was challenged. The second section of the chapter discusses this shift. The background to Lord Laming's (2003) inquiry and his recommendations for structural reform are then examined in the third section. As Secretary of State for Health, Alan Milburn held responsibility for social services and had agreed to establish Lord Laming's inquiry. The final section of the chapter therefore considers Milburn's response to the inquiry on behalf of the DH and the government. By questioning the origins of Labour's plans for structural reform, the chapter addresses the key theme of inquiries and scandals in children's services policymaking. In doing so, it also begins to assess the extent to which organisational structures in children's services have been shaped by ministers seeking to implement political priorities.

The role of local authority social services departments

The report of the Seebohm Committee

The *Report of the Committee on Local Authority and Allied Personal Social Services*, more commonly referred to as the Seebohm Committee (1968), considered evidence provided by a diverse range of experts and agencies involved in the delivery of welfare services. The committee's report initially received a mixed reception and was not immediately acted upon (Hall, 1976). However, after a period of successful campaigning by 'a newly emergent, diverse and politically inexperienced lobby – the social workers' (Hall, 1976: xiii), Labour Secretary of State for Social Services Richard Crossman eventually agreed to implement the committee's key recommendation. Thus, local authority social services departments were established under the Local Authority and Social Services Act 1970.

The broad remit envisaged for the new social services departments reflected the optimism of the post-war period of welfare state expansion. The committee's report stated:

> We recommend a new local authority department, providing a community based and family oriented service, which will be available to all. This new department will, we believe, reach far beyond the discovery and rescue of social casualties; it will enable the greatest possible number of

individuals to act reciprocally, giving and receiving service for the well-being of the whole community. (Seebohm Committee, 1968: para 2)

The committee also emphasised the importance of preventative work and the need to coordinate the work of different agencies across the voluntary and statutory sectors:

Much more ought to be done in the fields of prevention, community involvement, the guidance of voluntary workers and in making fuller use of voluntary organisations. We believe that the best way of achieving these ends is by setting up a unified social service department which will include the present children's and welfare services together with some of the social services functions of health, education and housing departments. (Seebohm Committee, 1968: para 139)

Frost and Parton (2009: 10) comment that the new departments were regarded as the 'fifth social service ... the personalized, humanistic dimension of the welfare state'. Furthermore, they point out that the 'primary tool' available to social services departments was 'the professional worker's personality and understanding of human relationships' (Frost and Parton, 2009: 10). Thus, in Frost and Parton's (2009: 10) view, 'the early 1970s marked the high point of optimism and confidence in social work'.

Section 17 of the Children Act 1989

However, this optimism and confidence was short-lived because social services departments were created at a moment when the post-war welfare consensus was starting to fracture. In the mid-1970s, fiscal crisis and declining public and political confidence in public service professionals led to significant restructuring across the welfare system in the decades that followed. This also provided the context to the Maria Colwell inquiry (Secretary of State for Social Services, 1974) discussed in Chapter 1. This inquiry marked a turning point for social services and the social work profession, after which a much stronger focus on identifying and responding to serious cases of child abuse emerged (Parton, 1985, 2014; Butler and Drakeford, 2012). Following a series of subsequent inquiries over the years that followed, the duty of social workers to protect children from 'significant harm' was more clearly codified under Section 47 of the Children Act 1989. However, following the Cleveland inquiry (Secretary of State for Social Services, 1988), this legislation also responded to concerns that social workers can sometimes move too quickly to remove children from their families. Thus, Section 17 of the Children Act 1989 reaffirms the broader responsibility of social services departments and social workers to provide support to the families of 'children in need'. Section 17 specifies:

> It shall be the general duty of every local authority: (a) to safeguard and promote the welfare of children within their area who are in need; and (b) so far as is consistent with that duty, to promote the upbringing of such children by their families, by providing a range and level of services appropriate to those children's needs.

It also specifies that 'Every local authority – shall facilitate the provision by others (including in particular voluntary organisations) of services which it is a function of the authority to provide by virtue of this section.' Thus, Section 17 reaffirms the broader child and family welfare remit envisaged by the Seebohm Committee (1968). However, the balance reached for in the Children Act 1989 was not achieved in practice. The DH-commissioned report *Child Protection: Messages from Research* (DH, 1995) revealed that in most social services departments, resources were primarily focused on meeting responsibilities specified under Section 47. Only limited resources were directed towards the implementation of Section 17 of the Act. In other words, social services departments continued to concentrate on identifying and responding to children judged to be at significant risk of harm. The broader remit in relation to child and family welfare continued to be neglected. In the run-up to the 1997 general election, campaigners called for a 'refocusing' of resources to address this imbalance (Frost and Parton, 2009: 16–17).

Labour's Modernising Social Services *White Paper*

When Labour came to power in 1997, responsibility for policy on social services (covering children and adults) remained with the DH. The White Paper *Modernising Social Services* (DH, 1998a) set out the department's plans for reform. Labour's new Secretary of State for Health, Frank Dobson, stated in the foreword that 'One big trouble social services have suffered from is that up to now no Government has spelled out exactly what people can expect or what the staff are expected to do. This Government is to change all that' (DH, 1998a: foreword). However, notwithstanding the modernisation rhetoric, the White Paper did not signal any significant change in government policy on social services departments' responsibilities towards vulnerable children and families. The three 'priority aims' set out in the White Paper were broadly consistent with existing legislation:

- to ensure that children are protected from sexual, physical and emotional abuse, and from neglect;
- to raise the quality of care of children in care so that it is as close as possible to the care provided by loving and responsible parents; and
- to improve the life chances of children in care, and of others ('children in need') who need social services' support, in particular through improving their health and education and support after they leave care.

The first aim reflected social services departments' responsibilities to protect children from significant harm, as specified under Section 47 of the Children Act 1989. The second was consistent with duties towards children in care, covered principally by Section 22 of the Act. The third aim is more vaguely specified but alludes to social services departments' responsibilities under Section 17.

One of the key policy developments that did follow the White Paper was the creation of a new framework of objectives and performance indicators (DH, 1998b, 1999). The introduction of centrally prescribed objectives and performance indicators placed significant new demands on social services departments. However, DH policymakers worked closely with sector representatives on the development and implementation of this new framework. Under the Quality Protects programme (DH, 1998b), a network of regional advisers recruited from social services departments was set up to provide support for the development of new performance planning and data-collection systems at the local level. Furthermore, the DH allocated funding to social services departments to contribute towards meeting the cost of this work. Thus, the new performance framework was cautiously welcomed by social services leaders.

The DH (2000a) also introduced the *Framework for the Assessment of Children in Need and their Families*. This provided a clearer specification of the specific needs of vulnerable children that social services departments needed to identify and respond to. However, this development did not directly address concerns relating to the resourcing of social services departments' Section 17 responsibilities. The government was investing significant new resources in child and family welfare services at this time, notably, through the Sure Start initiative. However, these resources were not explicitly allocated to supporting the fulfilment of Section 17 responsibilities. As the *Modernising Social Services* White Paper stated:

> Social services for children cannot be seen in isolation from the wider range of children's services delivered by local authorities and other agencies. The Government is committed to taking action through a broad range of initiatives to strengthen family life, to reduce social exclusion and anti-social behaviour among children, and to give every child the opportunity of a healthy, happy, successful life.... Children's social services must be seen within this wider context. However, this must not mean that social services lose their focus on the most vulnerable children. (DH, 1998a: paras 3.4–3.5)

Social services departments were not positioned as the central coordinating agencies as they are under Section 17. At best, they were viewed as one of a range of agencies with a role to play in the delivery of Labour's child and family welfare policies. Moreover, government policymakers signalled that social services departments ought to continue to prioritise working with a relatively small number of vulnerable children and families. This reflected the emphasis placed on the contribution of universal public services and the voluntary sector in delivery arrangements for programmes such as Sure Start.

Boateng's case for reform

Although social services departments were not positioned as the key coordinating agencies in relation to child and family welfare services, the DH did appear to rule out the possibility of structural reform. As the *Modernising Social Services* White Paper stated:

> Although there are often difficulties in bringing together different agencies' responsibilities, major reorganisation of services boundaries – always a tempting solution – does not provide the answer. This would create new boundaries and lead to instability and diversion of management effort. Instead, the Government is fostering a new spirit of flexible partnership working which moves away from sterile

conflicts over boundaries to an approach where this wasted time and effort is directed positively towards working across them. (DH, 1998a: para 6.3)

However, this position came to be questioned towards the end of the first term as ministers re-examined arrangements for the delivery of key policy initiatives. A policy review commissioned by the SEU provoked a debate regarding structural arrangements for the delivery of child and family welfare services, and a re-examination of the role of social services departments. The SEU had been set up by Blair in 1997 to lead on key areas of social policy that crossed departmental boundaries, as discussed earlier. The SEU established a series of 'policy action teams' to review existing departmental policies and to recommend ways in which policymaking could be better 'joined up' across government and at the local level. Policy Action Team 12 (PAT 12) was chaired by the then Home Office minister Paul Boateng.

Although PAT 12 had been asked to focus on policies affecting young people aged 13–19, its report emphasised the need to invest in services targeted at children and young people aged between five and 13 (SEU, 2000). The rationale provided was that the best way to address the problem behaviours and poor outcomes experienced by some 13–19 year olds was to invest in preventative services targeted at the younger cohort. Furthermore, the report argued that this investment should be weighted in favour of those growing up in the most economically disadvantaged communities, commenting that 'Emerging evidence suggests that on average the state spends 14 per cent less money on young people in the most deprived areas than on the average young person' (SEU, 2000: 49). This emphasis on economic disadvantage challenged Blair's more authoritarian perspective on problem young people, as well as earlier SEU reports that called for more targeted initiatives to address specific 'risk factors' associated with social exclusion (SEU, 1999). On the other hand, the emphasis on economic disadvantage was consistent with the Treasury's principle of progressive universalism. Moreover, the case made for investment in preventative services for 5–13 year olds echoed earlier arguments made during the Sure Start review of services for the under fives.

Following the 2000 Spending Review, the Treasury made £450 million available over three years to fund the expansion of preventative services under the Children's Fund programme (HM Treasury, 2000). Delivery arrangements for the Children's Fund programme replicated those for Sure Start at both the national and local levels. A new inter-departmental Children and Young People's

Unit (CYPU), reporting to Boateng in the Home Office, was created to oversee the roll-out of the programme. As with the Sure Start unit, key staff were recruited from outside of government. Althea Efunshile was recruited from the London Borough of Lewisham to head up the CYPU. Her deputy, Barbara Hearn, was seconded from the NCB. All local authority areas were required to set up partnership boards to bring together key agencies across the statutory and charitable sectors, and to collectively agree how resources should be distributed. As with Sure Start, ministers envisaged local charities playing a pivotal role. The Children's Fund also emphasised the role that universal services (schools and health) needed to play in the early identification of problems faced by children and their families. Underpinning this was the claim that joined-up working across different agencies and professional groups was key to preventing the escalation of problems and the need for expensive specialist interventions later.

Significantly, the report also reflected wider concerns about the effectiveness of policy delivery arrangements and the ability of vested interests in Whitehall and in the wider public sector to resist reform. Blair (1999b) had by now made a speech in which he complained about the uphill challenge of public service reform, famously referring to 'the scars on my back'. At the national level, Whitehall interests were seen to be resistant to efforts to join up policymaking across departmental boundaries. At the local level, ministers recognised that, in most areas, statutory agencies remained dominant, despite efforts to elevate the position of the charity sector. In most Sure Start local partnerships, the local authority was the only agency that had the capacity to act as the financially accountable body. The PAT 12 report expressed the view that reform was therefore needed:

> The PAT believes that at the root of these problems lies a structural weakness – the failure of existing structures to provide a coherent national approach to policy on young people at risk. For decades, no-one has had clear responsibility for making this happen, either in central or local government. This has allowed the increased focus on agencies' individual objectives to lead to less focus on the problems that straddle boundaries. Unless this is addressed, delivery and design of new policies may fall short of what the Government wants to achieve; indeed, there is a risk that new initiatives could actually add so much confusion that their underlying goals are seriously jeopardised. (SEU, 2000: 59)

The Labour Party leadership agreed that steps needed to be taken to improve the integration of policymaking in this area. Thus, the CYPU was tasked with leading the development of a unified children's policy framework, in addition to managing the roll-out of the Children's Fund programme.

No concrete proposals for structural reform at the local level had yet surfaced at this point. However, it seemed highly unlikely that social services departments would emerge as the central coordinating agency for child and family welfare services. They were widely considered to be part of the problem rather than part of the solution. Several ministers involved in the development of children's policy at this time were sceptical about the willingness and capacity of social services departments to deliver change and did not trust them to invest new resources effectively. Boateng, who had chaired the PAT 12 review, commented in an interview that coincided with the publication of the PAT 12 report that:

> We have to break the silos down and until we do we're not going to be able to address the needs of children and young people. So, to get hung up on what the status quo was before this government came to office, in which social services was the lead, I just do not see social services as the lead.... They have let children down year and year upon year. Now that's beginning to change. But the notion that we can just leave it to the social services is fanciful frankly. (Boateng, 2000)

Significantly, Boateng went on to chair the development of the ECM Green Paper, which included proposals for the structural reform of local authority services involving the break-up of social services departments.

The Victoria Climbié inquiry

Background

In October 1999, Frank Dobson was replaced by Alan Milburn as Secretary of State for Health. Milburn shared the concerns of the party leadership regarding the delivery of the government's social policy objectives, agreeing that investment in public services must be accompanied by structural reform to ensure that new resources were not wasted. Moreover, Milburn agreed with Blair's view that greater choice and competition were necessary to drive improvement, arguing that public services ought to be commissioned by a greater range of providers from across the public, private and voluntary sectors (Timmins, 2017: 621). In this sense, Milburn effectively abandoned the position on structural reform set out in the *Modernising Social Services* (DH, 1998a) White Paper.

The NHS Plan (DH, 2000b: ch 7) introduced the idea that new Care Trusts should oversee the commissioning of social care services from the public, private and voluntary sectors. It was stated that 'Care Trusts will be able to commission and deliver primary and community healthcare as well as social care for older people and other client groups. Social services would be delivered under delegated authority from local councils' (DH, 2000b: para 7.10). How this might work in practice was not clearly specified. Furthermore, the plan claimed that 'The new arrangements will provide better care services, *especially for older people*' (DH, 2000b: para 7.13, emphasis added). It did not respond specifically to concerns regarding the delivery of children's services. Nonetheless, it did reflect the appetite among the Labour leadership and senior ministers for the restructuring of public services. The extended remit of the Victoria Climbié inquiry and the decision to appoint Lord Laming to chair it need to be understood in this context.

Lord Laming was appointed to chair the inquiry by Milburn in April 2001. The shocking circumstances surrounding Victoria's death, but particularly the repeated opportunities missed by various agencies to intervene, meant that a detailed investigation into the case was necessary. National and local policymakers had consistently sought to learn lessons from a succession of serious child abuse cases stretching back over several decades. However, the decision to establish a *public* inquiry was unusual. Furthermore, the Victoria Climbié inquiry was the first to be set up under three separate pieces of legislation: Section 81 of the Children Act 1989; Section 84 of the NHS Act 1977; and Section 49 of the Police Act 1996 (Lord Laming, 2003: para 2.4). However, what was perhaps more unusual was the decision to ask Lord Laming to review not only the circumstances surrounding Victoria's death, but also the nationwide multi-agency arrangements for the protection of children with a view to making recommendations for wider reform (Lord Laming, 2003: para 2.5). This meant that the inquiry needed to be led by a children's policy expert rather than an independent judge. It required the leadership of someone with extensive knowledge and experience in relation to child safeguarding. As a DH official explained:

'What ministers wanted was not just an identification of the facts, the story as it were. That's purely retrospective. What they wanted was to use the evidence as a springboard to make recommendations for organisational and systems change for the future. So, what they wanted was somebody to do the inquiry who was deeply immersed in the subject matter.' (Interview with DH official)

Lord Laming was well qualified in this regard, having had a long career in social services. Starting as a social worker, he rose to the position of Director of Social Services in Hertfordshire. Having worked in the DH as the government's Chief Inspector of Social Services between 1991 and 1998, he also had extensive experience in dealing with ministers and government policymakers.

Accountability for child safeguarding

The inquiry began in May 2001 and published its findings in January 2003. Lord Laming's report catalogued a long list of failings across four social services departments, two local authority housing departments, two Metropolitan Police child protection teams, an NSPCC-managed family centre and two National Health Service (NHS) hospitals. Individual workers who encountered Victoria were criticised for failing to investigate her case properly and for missing opportunities to intervene and better protect her. However, Lord Laming's sharpest criticism was reserved for the leaders of these agencies. The report stated that 'The greatest failure rests with the managers and senior members of the authorities whose task it was to ensure that services for children, like Victoria, were properly financed, staffed, and able to deliver good quality support to children and families' (Lord Laming, 2003: para 1.23). Although this criticism was directed at the agencies judged to have failed Victoria, it had a wider resonance. To support the inquiry's broader remit to examine nationwide safeguarding arrangements, the inquiry team invited representatives from agencies in the children's sector that had not been involved in Victoria's case to participate in a series of five seminars. Seminar participants recognised many of the failings identified in Victoria's case, including the failure of public agencies to adequately prioritise the safeguarding of children. Alongside the Victoria Climbié inquiry, inspection bodies for social services, health, the police, the Crown Prosecution Service, magistrates' courts, schools, prisons and probation services also reviewed evidence relating to activity to safeguard children. The Joint Chief Inspectors' report concluded that 'The priority given to safeguarding has not been reflected firmly, coherently or consistently enough in service planning and resource allocation nationally or locally across all agencies. Other priorities have competed for attention with action on safeguarding' (DH, 2002: 3).

Most of Lord Laming's 108 recommendations addressed apparent procedural failings identified through the investigation of the social services departments, health services and police child protection teams involved in Victoria's case. However, Lord Laming concluded that more wide-ranging reform was needed:

> I strongly believe that in future, those who occupy senior positions in the public sector must be required to account for any failure to protect vulnerable children from deliberate harm or exploitation. The single most important change in the future must be the drawing of a clear line of accountability, from top to bottom, without doubt or ambiguity about who is responsible at every level for the well-being of vulnerable children. (Lord Laming, 2003: para 1.27)

Thus, the inquiry report included 17 recommendations for structural reform to ensure greater accountability for child safeguarding. The structure chart in Figure 1 summarises the changes recommended in the inquiry report.

Lord Laming's recommendations presented a major challenge to policymakers at the national and local levels. However, it is important to note that the inquiry report did not question the suitability of the legal framework provided by the Children Act 1989. Rather, it echoed concerns raised previously regarding the implementation of Sections 17 and 47. It is important to recall that Section 47 relates to children suffering or likely to suffer 'significant harm' and the requirement to instigate child protection proceedings, whereas Section 17 refers to the broader responsibility of local authorities to 'safeguard and promote the welfare of children within their area who are in need'. However, Lord Laming concluded that the categorisation of Victoria as a 'child in need' under Section 17 meant that her circumstances were not properly monitored or investigated. As the report states:

> The downgrading of cases to the status of section 17, and afterwards to closure, was becoming an attractive option to childcare teams struggling to deal with what they perceived

Figure 1: Recommended new structure

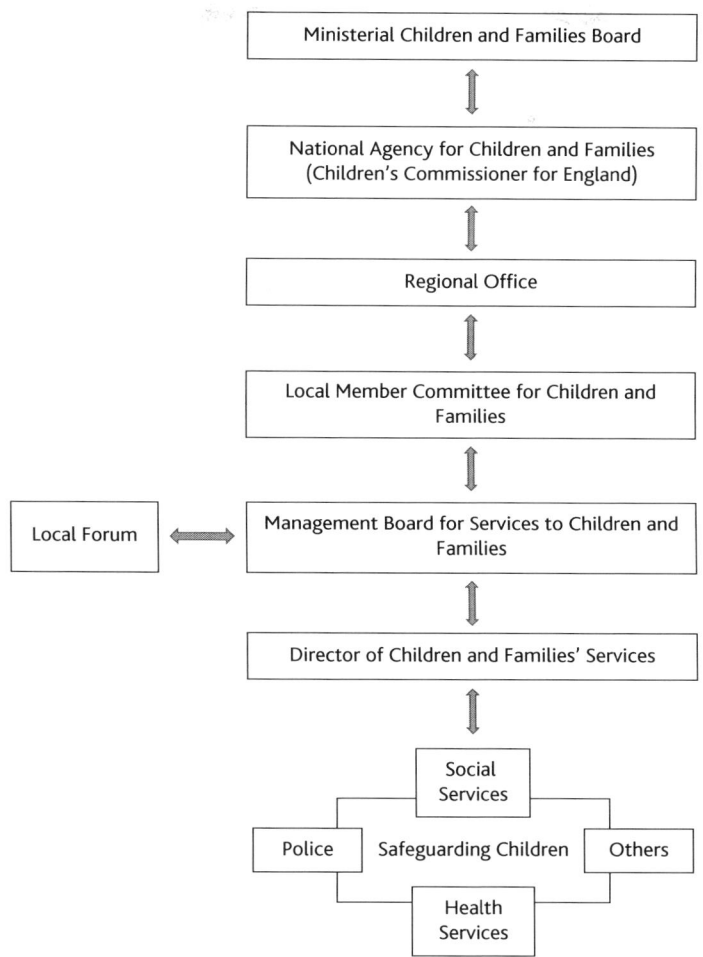

Source: Laming (2003: 370).

to be an ever-increasing number of child protection referrals, case conferences and registration. In response to social services downgrading referrals under section 17, partner agencies either tended not to make referrals or to re-frame concerns about children in a way which would attract a section 47 response. They saw the latter as the only way to access services for children they were worried about. This approach to the use of section 17 and 47 can only be

> described as dangerous. It is at odds with my understanding of the aspirations of the Children Act 1989. These factors were clearly evident in the failure to protect Victoria in the four local authorities, the two hospitals, and the one police force. (Lord Laming, 2003: paras 17.102–17.103)

Lord Laming's recommendations for structural reform aimed to improve accountability for the implementation of both Sections 17 and 47 of the Children Act 1989. It is also important to note that 'safeguarding children' is the only policy priority shown on the structure chart in Figure 1.

Furthermore, Lord Laming was clear that the line of accountability for safeguarding needed to start in central government. In his view, responsibility for child safeguarding was spread across too many separate departments, and within these departments, the issue was never deemed to be a high enough priority. To address this, he recommended the creation of a new National Agency for Children and Families, reporting directly to an inter-departmental board comprised of ministers from relevant departments and chaired by a member of the cabinet. It was also recommended that the agency incorporate the position of Children's Commissioner. The argument for creating this position was that they could report directly to Parliament on a wide range of issues affecting children. Advocates for the Children's Commissioner post argued that this would raise the political profile of children's policy generally, and thus challenge departmental policymakers to reassess their priorities. When asked at the House of Commons Health Committee which of his recommendations he thought should be implemented above all others, Lord Laming replied that 'It would be a development of a National Agency for Children and Families with the same kind of powers that the inquiry had, with powers not to do other people's job but to make sure other people did their job' (House of Commons Health Committee, 2003: para 83).

Milburn's response to the inquiry

Even before Lord Laming had published his report, it was clear that government ministers were considering proposals for structural reform. The Spending Review published in July 2002 stated that 'The Government believes there is a case for structural change to affect the better coordination of children's services, and will pilot children's trusts which will unify at the local level the various agencies involved in providing services to children' (HM Treasury, 2002: 154).

No detail was provided regarding the rationale for children's trusts, nor any indication of ministers' views on how they might operate. However, a speech made by Milburn at the National Social Services Conference in October 2002 was more revealing. By now, many of the details regarding Victoria's death had been widely reported in media coverage of the inquiry, even though Lord Laming's report had not yet been published. Milburn prefaced his announcement on children's trusts by suggesting that the failings of social services made reform necessary:

> Today I believe social services are at a crossroads. You are under scrutiny as never before. For all the millions of successes, it is the lapses in social services that still corrode public confidence. All of us know that if social services fail, the consequences fall on the most vulnerable people in our society. It would be comforting to believe the problems confronting social services stem purely from a hostile media. I do not believe they do. They stem in my view from a much deeper failure – a failure, which we all share, that has allowed the way we deliver social services to get out of step with the society we serve. (Milburn, 2002)

However, the case made for reform repeated arguments made two years earlier, in *The NHS Plan* (DH, 2000b), in favour of commissioning more services from the private and voluntary sectors. Milburn (2002) argued that 'Government, central or local, no longer needs to provide every public service. Gone are the days when Whitehall or indeed the town hall always knew best. What counts today is the quality of the services, not the origin of the provider.' Yet, it was now suggested that separate organisations were needed to oversee the commissioning of services for adults and children. As Milburn (2002) continued:

> The job of providing services to children in need is a very different job from services to the elderly person. The one size fits all approach embodied in the traditional social services department may have been OK in the 1970s, but as more councils are recognising, it does not belong today.

Thus, children's trusts were promoted as a means to 'enlist the involvement of the community, voluntary and private sectors alongside the public sector', and to 'dramatically reshape how social services [for children] are organised and delivered' (Milburn, 2002). It was announced that a pilot programme would begin in December 2002. This announcement pre-dated the publication of Lord Laming's report. Furthermore, it did not directly respond to emerging findings from the inquiry. Rather, it reflected a pre-existing commitment to extend the role played by private and voluntary services in the delivery of social services, including services to vulnerable children and families.

The final report of the Victoria Climbié inquiry (Lord Laming, 2003) was published on 28 January 2003. On the same day, Alan Milburn provided the government's response in a statement to the House of Commons (Milburn, 2003). Milburn offered the government's condolences to Victoria's family. He then provided MPs with a long list of the failings identified by Lord Laming, including the multiple missed opportunities that various agencies had had to intervene. Milburn acknowledged that Lord Laming was satisfied with the legislative framework provided by the Children Act 1989 but commented that 'Sound legislative policy and guidance is, frankly, useless unless we can be sure that it is implemented effectively and consistently' (Milburn, 2003). Immediate steps already taken, or planned, by the government to address poor implementation of the Children Act 1989 and the procedural failings highlighted in the inquiry report were announced. These included: the increased monitoring of those agencies implicated in Victoria's case; making child protection a higher priority in the national policing plan; the introduction of a new three-year social work degree; new shared national standards for health and social services for the care of children; a commitment to revise official child protection procedural guidance; the issuing of a checklist based on Lord Laming's findings to police forces, health authorities and social services departments; and a commitment to establish a new programme of joint inspections to monitor joint working across agencies.

Milburn also confirmed that the government agreed with Lord Laming's view that structural reform was necessary to ensure greater accountability for child safeguarding and to improve the effectiveness of multi-agency working. This was unsurprising given that ministers, including Milburn, were already committed to structural reform. Milburn took the opportunity to launch the children's trust pilot programme, originally scheduled to start in December 2002, and tie the government's case for reform more explicitly to the Victoria Climbié inquiry. He stated:

Victoria needed services that worked together. The report says that, instead, there was confusion and conflict. Down the years, inquiry after inquiry has called for better communication and better co-ordination, but neither exhortation nor legislation has proven adequate. The only sure-fire way to break down the barriers between those services is to remove them altogether. Fundamental reform is needed to pool knowledge, skills and resources and to provide more seamless local services for children. Therefore, I am today inviting health and social services, and other local services such as education, to become the first-generation children's trusts. (Milburn, 2003)

However, in giving evidence to the House of Commons Health Committee, Lord Laming could see no connection between children's trust and his recommendations. He stated that 'We took no evidence on children's trusts and it would be quite wrong of me to comment on them other than to say that I do not know what is in the Secretary of State's mind about children's trusts' (House of Commons Health Committee, 2003: para 48). On the other hand, it is important to acknowledge that this pilot programme did not prescribe specific arrangements for structural reform. The DH gave local authorities and their partners the freedom to design local trust arrangements, including the agencies involved and the specific functions to be jointly commissioned (University of East Anglia, 2004; Audit Commission, 2008). Furthermore, the government's substantive response to Lord Laming's proposals for structural reform was promised in a Green Paper scheduled for the following spring.

Discussion

It has been demonstrated that the case for the structural reform of local authority social services departments was under consideration long before the publication of the report of the Victoria Climbié inquiry (Lord Laming, 2003). This reflected wider debates within the government regarding the need for a more radical programme of public services reform. Moreover, at this stage, concerns regarding the effectiveness of multi-agency arrangements for child protection and safeguarding were not paramount. Boateng's argument in favour of restructuring was built on concerns regarding the effectiveness of policy delivery arrangements for key policy initiatives, such as Sure Start and the Children's Fund. Furthermore, Boateng's case for reform was consistent with the Treasury's progressive universalism perspective and the argument that the integration of policymaking and service delivery arrangements was necessary to drive a shift towards the provision of more preventative services. Although no specific proposals were revealed at this stage, it was clear the Boateng did not envisage social services departments playing a lead role.

Milburn's alternative case for reform reflected his view, shared with Blair, that the key to improving health and social care services was to commission services from a wider variety of service providers across the public, private and voluntary sectors. In this sense, he also envisaged a different role for social services departments. The circumstances surrounding the death of Victoria Climbié were alarming and some form of inquiry was warranted. However, the decision to carry out a full public inquiry was unusual, and Milburn's decision to ask Lord Laming to not only examine the circumstances surrounding Victoria's death, but also consider the effectiveness of multi-agency child protection and safeguarding arrangements nationally, was significant. The extended remit of the inquiry provided further evidence of ministers' pre-commitment to structural reform. Milburn subsequently used the inquiry report to support a narrative of failing social services departments and bolster the argument for structural reform. However, the government's substantive response to Lord Laming was made in the ECM Green Paper (HM Government, 2003), which was not published until nine months after the inquiry. The formulation of this response now needs to be carefully examined.

4

Every Child Matters and the Children Act 2004

Introduction

> Responding to the inquiry headed by Lord Laming into Victoria's death, we are proposing here a range of measures to reform and improve children's care – crucially, for the first time ever requiring local authorities to bring together in one place under one person services for children, and at the same time suggesting real changes in the way those we ask to do this work carry out tasks on our and our children's behalf. (Blair, in HM Government, 2003: foreword)

> As Lord Laming's recommendations made clear, child protection cannot be separated from policies to improve children's lives as a whole. We need to focus both on the universal services which every child uses, and on more targeted services for those with additional needs.... We need to ensure we properly protect children at risk within a framework of universal services which support every child to develop their full potential. (HM Government, 2003: 5)

When the ECM Green Paper (HM Government, 2003) was eventually published in September 2003, it was framed as a direct response to the Victoria Climbié inquiry (Lord Laming, 2003). Its publication signalled the beginning of a period of major change for all agencies working in the children's sector, however, ECM was not exclusively focused on child protection and safeguarding. The Green Paper introduced a new framework of 'five outcomes', and related performance targets, covering all aspects of children's policy. New centrally designed assessment and information-sharing processes and procedures were also introduced as part of a drive towards the earlier identification of needs and the extended provision of preventative services. However, the most controversial proposal was the merger of education and children's social care services, involving the break-up of social services departments created following the report of the Seebohm Committee (1968), to create unified children's services departments under the leadership of a single DCS in every English local authority. These structural changes were mandated under the Children Act 2004 just over a year later. This chapter considers the background to the ECM Green Paper and discusses the progression of Labour's structural reforms.

The chapter begins by examining the decision to initiate the ECM Green Paper several months before the Victoria Climbié inquiry had been published. The second section discusses the importance of the ECM five outcomes framework, which placed policy on child safeguarding alongside a range of other policies linked to the well-being of children and young people. The position of children's social care services and social work professionals under ECM is discussed in the third section. The emphasis placed on the role of universal services and the importance of prevention and early intervention are considered in the fourth section, which examines the government's ambitions for children's services departments and children's trusts. The final section of the chapter reflects on the response of NGOs to the ECM Green Paper, including the proposals on structural reform. The key theme of inquiries and scandals in children's services policymaking is addressed through an interrogation of the government's claim that Lord Laming's inquiry provided the main impetus for reform. The chapter also continues to assess the political drivers of children's services reform, including the proposition that ministers have been increasingly drawn into the micromanagement of policy implementation.

The origins of the ECM Green Paper

It was argued in Chapter 3 that by the end of Labour's first term, the party leadership had become impatient with the poor integration of policymaking in Whitehall. Furthermore, it was felt that loosely regulated service delivery partnerships at the local level, intended to bring the statutory and charitable sectors closer together, were not having the desired impact. The 2000 PAT 12 policy review expressed the view that more needed to be done to join up policymaking in Whitehall and to drive closer working between statutory and voluntary agencies responsible for policy delivery at the local level. One of the outcomes of this policy review was the establishment of the Children's Fund to provide joined-up early intervention services to 5–13 year olds judged to be at risk of social exclusion. The inter-departmental CYPU had been set up to oversee implementation.

However, the CYPU was also asked to bring together the various strands of children's policy being developed separately across Whitehall into an integrated policy framework (Eisenstadt, 2011: 80). Moreover, the integration of national policy was deemed necessary to drive the closer integration of service delivery locally. The CYPU (2001a, 2001b) developed the first iteration of an overarching framework of children's policy priorities that was further developed by officials working on the ECM Green Paper. A focus on early intervention and preventative services was an underlying theme, reflecting earlier initiatives such as Sure Start and the newly established Children's Fund. In the report *Tomorrow's Future*, it was argued that:

> Crisis situations in the lives of children and young people have been met too often and for too long with un-coordinated responses from a multiplicity of agencies. This array of people and services can add to any child's vulnerability if it is not offered in a co-ordinated and child-centred way.... Early identification of problems, and the effective marshalling of a range of support services in a co-ordinated way is critical and must feature centrally in our long-term strategy to improve the effectiveness of services to individual children and young people. (CYPU, 2001a: 28–9)

Members of the CYPU also contributed to a further review of policy under the Treasury's 2002 Spending Review (HM Treasury, 2002). This Spending Review was led by Boateng, who had been promoted to the position of Chief Secretary to the Treasury by this time. The report of the 'children at risk' review (HM Treasury, 2002: 153–55) reiterated the Treasury's commitment to addressing the well-being of children growing up in poverty, in line with the principle of progressive universalism. The review re-emphasised the greater contribution that mainstream services needed to play in this regard. Repeating the argument made two years earlier in the report of PAT 12 (SEU, 2000) and in subsequent CYPU publications (2001a, 2001b), the review stated:

> Mainstream services fail a significant minority of children and young people because they often focus on the majority and ignore specific needs. Services also focus on crisis and acute intervention rather than prevention and early identification of need. To address this, the Government

has introduced targeted programmes, such as Sure Start and the Children's Fund, with discrete delivery arrangements outside mainstream public services. However, the review recommends the adoption of a common framework for integrating the lessons learned from successful programmes so that mainstream services are better able to respond to the full range of children and young people's needs. (HM Treasury, 2002: 154)

Building on the work of the CYPU, the review identified four 'outcomes' to provide the focus for early intervention work. The four outcomes identified were: educational achievement; employment; health; and anti-social behaviour (HM Treasury, 2002). It is important to note that safeguarding was not highlighted as a specific priority at this stage.

However, the 'children at risk' review was not able to resolve the issue of structural reform. Moreover, the party leadership and ministers concluded that the CYPU was not well placed to stand up to departmental interests and take this agenda any further forward. Thus, the Labour leadership decided that a Green Paper was needed to set out proposals for potential machinery-of-government changes and structural reform at the local level. The process of developing the Green Paper was managed by the Cabinet Office and was therefore overseen by No 10. However, the appointment of Boateng to chair the process ensured that the Treasury was also closely involved. Blair and Brown agreed that policymakers in Whitehall and local children's services agencies needed to do more to address child poverty. Boateng commented:

'One of the great things that people misunderstand was that these two men [Blair and Brown] cared passionately about combating poverty, they really did. They were absolutely genuine in that, and I was very glad to be working to deliver to an agenda that they could both sign up to. But that is never the agenda of the DfE [Department for Education] or the DH.' (Interview with Paul Boateng)

The initiation of the ECM Green Paper was not a response to the Victoria Climbié inquiry, even though this was well under way at this point. Rather, it flowed from an ideological commitment to improve the well-being of children growing up in poverty and the determination of the Labour leadership, and ministers such as Boateng, to ensure the compliance of policymakers in Whitehall and local children's services agencies. Following the initiation of the ECM Green Paper (initially called the 'Children at Risk' Green Paper), departmental policymakers were instructed to cease working on any new reform proposals by Blair's Principal Private Secretary, Jeremy Heywood. A Cabinet Office official recalled:

> 'Jeremy Heywood wrote a letter saying there was a, he used the word "moratorium", on any development on children's services until the children's Green Paper was reported.... So, the decision was then taken as to who would actually hold the responsibility to respond to the Laming inquiry, and that's when in the end, while the sort of line-by-line response was done by the DH ... it was decided that the children's Green Paper would be the main response in policy terms to Laming.' (Interview with Cabinet Office official, 2018)

Milburn (2003) did use the opportunity provided by the publication of the report of the Victoria Climbié inquiry to announce the roll-out of the already-planned DH children's trust pilot programme, as the discussion in Chapter 3 revealed. However, it was clear that the development of the government's substantive response to Lord Laming's recommendations for structural reform would be led by the Cabinet Office team working on the Green Paper. DH policymakers who ordinarily led on child safeguarding policy did not lead on this aspect of the government's response.

The five outcomes framework

The focus for DH policymakers in the early Labour years had been on improving the implementation of the Children Act 1989. Furthermore, Lord Laming agreed that the Act continued to provide a sound legal framework. His recommendations for structural reform were directed towards improving multi-agency working in relation to child safeguarding. Moreover, Lord Laming's (2003) report echoed concerns expressed in the Joint Chief Inspectors' report (DH, 2002) that child safeguarding was not a high enough priority nationally or within local agencies. However, under ECM, safeguarding was not explicitly prioritised to the extent that Lord Laming and the

Joint Chief Inspectors had called for. Rather, safeguarding was positioned within a broader 'five outcomes' framework. The ECM five outcomes were:

- be healthy
- stay safe
- enjoy and achieve
- make a positive contribution
- achieve economic well-being

The four policy priorities identified in the earlier 'children at risk' review (HM Treasury, 2002) had been reframed: educational achievement became 'enjoy and achieve'; employment became 'achieve economic well-being'; health became 'be healthy'; and anti-social behaviour became 'make a positive contribution'. Policy on safeguarding was added to this framework under the 'stay safe' outcome.

The five outcomes framework did not address concern that safeguarding policy had to compete with too many other policy priorities. Furthermore, recommended structural changes at the national level were also overlooked. Lord Laming had called for a new National Agency for Children and Families to be established. Moreover, he had declared this to be the most important of all his recommendations (House of Commons Health Committee, 2003: para 83). Instead, in July 2003, and ahead of the publication of the Green Paper, the government established a new Children and Young People's Directorate (CYP Directorate) within the DfES. Policymaking resources from various Whitehall departments were moved into the new CYP Directorate, including civil servants who had led on child safeguarding policy within the DH. Margaret Hodge was appointed to oversee the work of the CYP Directorate in the new post of Children's Minister. However, the CYP Directorate's remit reflected the breadth of the five outcomes framework. Thus, policy on safeguarding competed for attention alongside a range of other policy priorities. Hodge provided an indication of the government's ambitions for the new CYP Directorate in a speech to local government leaders shortly after her appointment:

> We are constructing an entitlement for all our children and young people, a universal entitlement, into which we shall place the essential targeted support that some children will need, support because they are at risk in their home, because they have a special need or disability, because they are truanting or disengaged from education

and training or – when they are older – work, because they have developed anti-social patterns of behaviour, be it bullying or creating disruption and chaos on the estates or the communities in which they reside, or because they have offended and broken the law. Providing these targeted services within a universal context is in my view the best way of minimizing the need for targeted intervention and support. (Hodge, 2003)

Hodge's speech reflected the breadth of the five outcomes framework and the range of policy areas that the new CYP Directorate was to be responsible for. Furthermore, it restated the government's view that universal services needed to do more to help improve the well-being of children and families, a view that had provided the original impetus for the Green Paper.

Children's social care services and social work under ECM

The establishment of the CYP Directorate was designed to improve the integration of policymaking in Whitehall. The ECM Green Paper outlined plans for the integration of children's services at the local level. Previous inquiries into serious cases of child abuse consistently highlighted failings in inter-agency working. This was also one of the central messages to emerge from the Victoria Climbié inquiry (Lord Laming, 2003). Under the Children Act 1989, local authority social services departments are positioned as the central coordinating agencies for children in need, including but not limited to those judged to be at significant risk of harm. However, Lord Laming's report expressed the view that all agencies involved with children have a contribution to make and must be held accountable for any failure to adequately safeguard children. Thus, one of the key reforms introduced under ECM was the creation of multi-agency Local Safeguarding Children Boards (LSCBs). LSCBs replaced highly criticised and poorly regulated Area Child Protection Committees. This change was widely welcomed and helped to raise the profile of safeguarding work in local areas.

However, under the ECM five outcomes framework, the ambitions for multi-agency working extended much further than child safeguarding. Furthermore, the most controversial change mandated under ECM was the break-up of social services departments and the merger of children's social care services with education to create unified children's services departments. However, this was not driven explicitly by concerns relating to child safeguarding (this argument is justified later). Children's services departments were viewed as a first step towards the establishment of multi-agency children's trusts responsible for the coordination of all local children's services agencies and the delivery of all five ECM outcomes. New multi-agency working arrangements, including the Common Assessment Framework (CAF), the lead professional and the Information Sharing Index (later called Contact Point), required agencies to address the broad range of child well-being concerns linked to the five outcomes framework, not just child safeguarding. The implication was that the potential cohort of children requiring support extended far beyond the group categorised as children in need under the Children Act 1989.

The emphasis placed on the role of universal services under ECM also detracted from the crisis engulfing social services departments and the perilous state of the social work profession. Moreover, it was argued in Chapter 3 that some ministers were instinctively mistrustful of social services departments, based on their own experience of working in local government. The findings of the Victoria Climbié inquiry only served to harden attitudes and the resolve of ministers to restructure local services. Critically, the coordinating role afforded to social services departments and the social work profession under the Children Act 1989 was ignored as ministers emphasised the importance of universal services and the new children's services departments in relation to multi-agency working. Even in guidance specifically aimed at children's social care services staff published to accompany the Children Act 2004, a strong emphasis was placed on strengthening the role of universal services. This guidance made no reference to any plans to address the resourcing and management of children's social care services. Rather, the report simply stated that 'Social workers and social care workers working with other agencies will have an important role in supporting universal services in meeting a wider range of needs' (DfES, 2004a: 4).

The lack of attention directed towards the reform of children's social care services and social work reflected a view held among some ministers that they were part of the problem not the solution. A local authority director interviewed for this research commented that:

> 'When ECM came in, now I think there was an idea that we'll get all this early intervention going, Sure Start and Children's Fund, and actually we won't need all this nasty child protection stuff, and of course it didn't happen. I think there was a kind of mindset about, they didn't really like some of this social work stuff.' (Interview with local authority DCS)

Looking back, a number of interviewees acknowledged that the sharp end of safeguarding practice did not receive the attention it deserved in this period. When interviewed, Charles Clarke, the first Secretary of State with responsibility for the implementation of ECM, stated that "Where I think we failed is in terms of child safeguarding/child protection. We didn't have a targeted enough approach for that relatively small number of children for whom that was an issue, and I think that was a failure." Similarly, a senior DfES official reflected:

> 'If I have a mea culpa and critique of ECM, it is that it did not ... drive sufficiently on the nuts-and-bolts reform of children's social work.... For one reason or another, it is a very hard thing to do.... Which is a shame because it is not as if those two things – that broader systemic approach of ECM and the rigorous reform of children's social work – are necessarily in contradiction with each other. But one was given, initially at least, more attention than the other.' (Interview with DfES official)

The Victoria Climbié inquiry did lead to greater attention being paid to child safeguarding policy at the national and local levels. However, there was a failure to explicitly prioritise safeguarding ahead of other children's services policy priorities as Lord Laming had called for. Government policymakers did not allow concerns relating to safeguarding policy to detract from the broader concerns of the Labour Party leadership and ministers that had led to the initiation of the Green Paper. A close examination of proposals for the structural reform of local services provides further evidence.

Children's services and children's trusts

In the foreword to the ECM Green Paper, Blair announced the government's intention to instruct 'local authorities to bring together in one place under one person services for children' (HM Government, 2003: foreword). Each DCS would be accountable for both local authority education and children's social care services, supported by a new Lead Member for Children's Services (LMCS). The merger of education and children's social care services to create new children's services departments was presented as a first step towards the creation of children's trusts responsible for a wider range of services. Local authorities were subsequently required to implement these changes under the Children Act 2004.

As Secretary of State, Alan Milburn advocated experimentation with new ways of delivering health and social care services, including the increased commissioning of private and voluntary sector providers. He had launched the children's trust pilot programme to explore new arrangements for children's social care services following the publication of the report of the Victoria Climbié inquiry in January 2003. The guidance issued to pilot authorities did not prescribe which agencies needed to be involved and which specific aspects of children's health and social care needed to be addressed. Thus, pilots were free to trial new ways to integrate the commissioning of services to specific groups of children (University of East Anglia, 2004; Audit Commission, 2008). However, following the initiation of the ECM Green Paper, policymakers in Whitehall departments had been instructed to cease work on new policies. Thus, the influence of DH policymakers over the government's plans for structural reform was limited and the pilot programme became much less important.

The vision for children's services and children's trusts presented in September 2003 reflected the broader ambitions of the Labour leadership and those leading the formulation of the Green Paper. Under ECM, children's services and children's trusts thereafter were established as the delivery mechanisms for the ECM five outcomes. An analysis of the development of policy on children's trusts carried out by the Audit Commission commented that 'This was significantly different from the framework for the children's trust pathfinders, which had focused on projects that looked at specific groups of children; particular aspects of the local authority work; and limited geographical areas' (Audit Commission, 2008: 14). The ECM policy framework shifted the focus away from the population of children in need, defined under the Children Act 1989, and towards the general child population. Only five months into the children's trust pilot programme, and long before any findings would be available, the government announced plans for the mandatory restructuring of local government services.

The claim that the government's plans for structural reform provided a direct response to the Victoria Climbié report does not stand up to scrutiny. It is important to remember that specialist children's social care services were positioned within 'a framework of universal services which support every child to develop their full potential' (HM Government, 2003: 5). At the national level, the government also declined to set up the new National Agency for Children and Families. Labour's structural reforms did not explicitly prioritise child safeguarding to the extent that Lord Laming had called for. Rather, the inquiry was used as a device to downplay the political ambitions driving the reform of children's services. As a Treasury official confirmed:

> 'What drove us was a view that there wasn't enough of a connection between the universal services and targeted services and that what we needed to do was create the conditions where the universal services, that's both health and schools, played far more of a part in terms of the children's services agenda…. So, the narrative that this all had to do with Laming, with Victoria Climbié, is just a narrative. Government always needs a platform to be able to argue it needs change, and tragically it very often uses a platform of poor services.' (Interview with Treasury official)

To appreciate the challenge that ministers faced in pushing ahead with structural reform, it is also important to reflect on the reception that the government's plans received from NGOs.

The Children's Inter-Agency Group and the response to ECM

The Victoria Climbié inquiry highlighted the failings of multiple children's services agencies across the statutory and charitable sectors. In the run-up to its publication, representatives of the major children's charities and statutory agencies formed the Children's Inter-Agency Group (CIAG) to agree a united response. This was deemed necessary to avoid agencies blaming each other, as had occurred in the aftermath of previous child abuse inquiries. Having successfully achieved its initial objective, representatives of the CIAG became actively engaged in the development of the ECM Green Paper. Government policymakers saw the CIAG as a convenient mechanism through which to consult with the sector. That it was fronted by representatives of the charity sector was significant. It was argued in Chapter 2 that the Treasury had established a positive relationship with the major children's charities during the first term of the Labour government. They had been largely supportive of the child poverty strategy and had contributed to the development of early policy initiatives such as Sure Start and the Children's Fund. The NCB in particular had helped ministers to hone the Treasury's progressive universalism vision for children's services centred on the principles of early intervention and prevention.

Understandably, members of the Association of Directors of Social Services (ADSS) were alarmed by the prospect of structural reform.

However, they recognised that any defence of existing structures would be difficult given the deep levels of public and political hostility to social services departments and social work that the Victoria Climbié inquiry had fuelled. Moreover, ADSS members recognised the higher regard that ministers appeared to have for representatives of the major children's charities. Thus, working through CIAG was viewed as the best possible way to try to influence the government's reform proposals. As one local authority DCS explained when interviewed: "I suppose a lot of the role of the inter-agency group, and it developed this way right throughout this period, was to provide a vehicle through which more acceptable faces could engage with government than social services, who were perceived at the time to be part of the problem." Ahead of the Green Paper, CIAG members contributed to the joint position statement *Serving Children Well: A New Vision for Children's Services* (LGA et al, 2002). This document was generally supportive of the policy framework underpinning ECM, welcoming the broad range of policy priorities and the emphasis placed on multi-agency working, including the extended role for universal services. However, it proposed a new model for integrated children's services, 'Drawing on the principle of using existing structures rather than seeking structural change' (LGA et al, 2002: 15). Ultimately, this argument was lost and the Green Paper went on to propose the break-up of social services departments and the merger of education and children's social care services.

Arguably, CIAG's enthusiastic support for the broad approach of ECM added legitimacy to the reform programme and may have inadvertently contributed to the lack of focus on the sharp end of safeguarding practice. ADSS representatives interviewed for this research acknowledged that beyond the defence of existing management structures, there was no concerted effort to alert policymakers to the needs of social workers. As a local authority DCS actively involved in the work of the ADSS during this period commented:

> 'Given the critique within Laming, it was a hard time to stand up for social work, and linked to that, for a separate reason, because we wanted to stay inside the room, it was really easy to see how well received the ECM construct was … the integrated services, generic, universal approach, early intervention, how well received that was and how uncomfortable it would be constantly to say at the end of a discussion, "Oh, by the way, our social workers have got too high a caseload."' (Interview with local authority DCS)

Dame Moira Gibb was also involved in the work of the ADSS and later went on to chair the SWTF set up following the Baby P crisis in late 2008. She stated:

> 'Social workers can be difficult people. They are not easy to manage, and I think there was a desire on behalf of directors to kind of distance themselves from what social work practice was. I remember having a conversation with a colleague of mine, that we were building all of this on sand because we didn't have the competence and capability needed at the front line of practice.' (Interview with Dame Moira Gibb)

DH policymakers also had limited influence over the development of the Green Paper, thus further restricting the channels through which critics of the focus on universal services in ECM could be heard.

Discussion

The report of the Victoria Climbié inquiry (Lord Laming, 2003) did not influence Labour's structural reforms of local government to the extent claimed in official statements. Two key findings presented in this chapter indicate that party-political imperatives were a far more important driver of reform in this period. First, the ECM Green Paper was never set up as a response to the inquiry and concerns regarding child safeguarding. ECM was initiated well ahead of the publication of Lord Laming's report in response to wider concerns regarding the poor integration of children's policymaking in Whitehall and the effectiveness of local service delivery arrangements for key Labour children's policy initiatives, including Sure Start and the Children's Fund. Moreover, the wide remit of the Green Paper meant that it covered large areas of policy, including health, education, crime and anti-social behaviour, and employability. Child safeguarding was only added to this list following the publication of the inquiry report and because the Labour leadership did not want departments to develop separate reform proposals. Thus, the Cabinet Office team working on the Green Paper, overseen by Boateng in the Treasury, took over from DH policymakers in developing the government's official response to Lord Laming's recommendations for structural reform.

Second, ECM reflected predetermined party-political reform priorities far more than was officially acknowledged. The ECM five outcomes framework reflected a broad range of Labour's children's policy priorities linked to improving the general well-being of children and young people. This did not deliver the explicit prioritisation of policy on child safeguarding that Lord Laming had called for. Moreover, structural reforms at the national and local levels did not follow Lord Laming's recommendations. The establishment of the CYP Directorate was framed as the government's response to the recommendation that a National Agency for Children and Families be established. However, the CYP Directorate was established to provide the party leadership with greater control over various aspects of children's policymaking spread across Whitehall departments. This included but extended well beyond policy on child safeguarding. At the local level, the creation of children's services departments and children's trusts was designed to facilitate a shift towards prevention and early intervention in line with Labour initiatives such as Sure Start and the Children's Fund, reflecting the Treasury's progressive universalism perspective, which placed a strong emphasis on the contribution of universal services. In contrast, specialist children's social care services received less attention, even though the Victoria Climbié inquiry highlighted familiar concerns regarding the resourcing and management of the sharp end of child protection and safeguarding practice nationally.

The important role played by representatives of the children's charity sector in the early Labour period was highlighted in Chapter 3. To a certain extent, the close involvement of the CIAG in the development of the ECM Green Paper reflected a continued willingness to listen to representatives of the children's sector. However, the dismissal of opposition to proposals for structural reform, highlighted in this chapter, revealed the limitations of NGO influence over Labour's children's policy. Moreover, the government's use of the Victoria Climbié inquiry served to fuel public and political hostility towards social services and social workers, making it very difficult for NGOs to highlight the need for specific reforms in this area. Chapter 5 asks whether this pattern of policymaking changed as ministers moved on to the implementation phase of ECM, where the support of NGOs would be needed.

5

Delivering change for children

Introduction

> The services that reach every child and young person have a crucial role to play in shifting the focus from dealing with the consequences of difficulties in children's lives to preventing things from going wrong in the first place. (HM Government, 2004: foreword)

> 'Schools have always been the main obstacle to progress in this area because so long as children remain in the same department as schools, they will always lose out to schools.' (Interview with Paul Boateng)

> There are still intractable problems with the behaviour of some individuals and families, behaviour which can make life a misery for others, particularly in the most disadvantaged communities. (Blair, in Home Office, 2006: foreword)

The final two years of the Blair–Brown Labour government were fraught as Brown's long quest to replace Blair as Prime Minister approached its climax. Moreover, public service reform continued to provide one of the main battlegrounds between No 10 and the Treasury, with Blair seeking to push ahead with controversial reforms in health and education (Davis and Rentoul, 2019). Crucially, it was during this period that the challenge of implementing the ambitious ECM reforms began. The government's implementation plans were published in December 2004, in the report *Every Child Matters: Change for Children* (HM Government, 2004), shortly after the passage of the Children Act 2004. The first section of this chapter considers the early implementation of the Change for Children programme, including the role played by NGOs and the new DCSs. The continued involvement of the Treasury in children's policymaking is also highlighted. The second section considers resistance to the ECM reform agenda among educational interests within Whitehall and outside of government in the context of Blair's continued involvement in education policy. The third section reflects upon Blair's continued interest in youth crime and anti-social behaviour policy. Thus, the chapter examines the roles played by NGOs and Whitehall interests during this period in the context of unresolved tensions between the policy priorities of No 10 and the Treasury.

The Change for Children programme

In Chapter 4, it was argued that it was Blair's and Brown's interest in children's policy that led to the initiation of the ECM Green Paper. Both Labour leaders had become frustrated at the slow pace of delivery of key Labour initiatives. Moreover, structural reform at both the national and local levels was deemed necessary to address the poor integration of children's services policymaking and delivery. Blair had sanctioned the establishment of a new inter-departmental CYP Directorate in July 2003, located within the DfES, which was then under the stewardship of Charles Clarke as Secretary of State for Education. Policymaking resources from across Whitehall were moved into the new CYP Directorate, which Margaret Hodge was appointed to lead as the new Children's Minister. Following the publication of the ECM Green Paper in September 2003, Hodge oversaw the passage of the Children Act 2004 and the development the Change for Children programme.

Children's services departments and the DCS role

The Children Act 2004 required all English local authorities to create new children's services departments by merging education and children's social care services and appointing a single DCS. The Change for Children programme set out the government's expectations for children's services, including a list of performance targets and inspection criteria aligned to the ECM five outcomes framework. Children's services departments were also required to publish a plan setting out how ECM would be delivered locally. The justification provided for this level of prescription was that 'local change programmes will be stronger if set within a supportive national framework' (HM Government, 2004: 6). On the other hand, the Change for Children programme also placed a strong emphasis on the need for close working between the government and the first generation of DCSs, claiming that 'The transformation that we need can only be delivered through local leaders working together in strong partnership with local communities on a programme of change' (HM Government, 2004: 2). Ministers recognised that they needed the advice and support of those responsible for implementing ECM at the local level. Hodge seconded several representatives of the new DCS community into the CYP Directorate to support the implementation of the Change for Children programme. When Hodge was replaced in May 2005, only a few months into the programme, the new Children's Minister, Beverley Hughes, established a new regular forum for discussions between the government and DCSs. The formation of the Association of Directors of Children's Services (ADCS) in 2007 also facilitated regular dialogue between government policymakers and the leaders of local reform programmes.

However, it is important to recognise that discussions between the government and representatives of the DCS community were very much focused on the technical challenge of implementing the Change for Children programme. The breadth of the ECM outcomes framework could not be questioned. Moreover, the argument regarding the need for structural reform had been lost during the Green Paper consultation period. As Hughes recalled:

> 'I had regular meetings with them [DCSs], some individually, some together, and at some point, I started an inter-agency forum – very regular meetings with children's organisations around that table along with the ADCS. I had very close contact with the president of the ADCS.... That was not so much about new policy, but about delivery, what's working, what's not working and problems that arise along the way.' (Interview with Beverley Hughes)

An ADCS member corroborated this statement, stressing that advice was closely tied to day-to-day implementation issues, rather than the principles behind ECM: "We gave sensible advice; we didn't grandstand; we didn't put on t-shirts; we didn't lobby for money. We relentlessly tried to give sensible advice about our perspective from front-line services". A former social services director interviewed for this research was more critical of the new community of DCSs, questioning their lack of critical engagement with the DfES:

> 'What I felt at the time, and still do feel, was that children's services were a government franchise that local government was running ... there was a sort of co-option of local government leadership. So, the identity and loyalties I think of senior children' services professionals were quite

ambivalent towards local government.' (Interview with former Director of Social Services)

It is important to recognise that the new DCS community had a strong stake in the programme and a shared interest in making it work. The new DCSs had been propelled into prominent positions within local authorities through ECM. In most local authorities, the DCS commanded the largest budgets, making them de facto deputy chief executives.

Progressive universalism and the continued neglect of social work

It is important to remember that the ECM five outcomes framework brought together a range of Labour's children's policy priorities, which included but extended well beyond child safeguarding. Furthermore, it was argued in Chapter 4 that the Green Paper's focus on the role of universal services, and the importance of early intervention and prevention, reflected the progressive universalism perspective promoted by the Treasury. Although ECM had been framed as a response to the Victoria Climbié inquiry, its scope was far wider. The breadth of the government's ambition was reflected in the broad remit of the CYP Directorate, as well as the 16 ministerial signatures attached to the Change for Children programme (HM Government, 2004). The joint ministerial foreword emphasised the role of 'services that reach every child and young person' (HM Government, 2004: foreword). The continued interest and involvement of the Treasury in children's services policy ensured that ministers and officials leading on the implementation of ECM retained this focus. As Hughes commented:

> 'Well, we had this terrible phrase "progressive universalism", which largely came from the Treasury. Apart from nobody else understanding what it means, it does capture what we were about.... in the context of universal services, underneath that universal umbrella, we wanted and expected the public services, the agencies, to identify, target and deliver more to disadvantaged children because closing the gap, reducing child poverty and closing all kinds of gaps between disadvantaged children and the rest was a really top priority.' (Interview with Beverley Hughes)

The Treasury emphasised its ongoing commitment to tackling child poverty and the principle of progressive universalism in children's services in the run-up to the 2006 Budget and the 2007 Spending Review (HM Treasury and DfES, 2005, 2007). Treasury officials also maintained close informal contact with ministers and senior officials in the CYP Directorate. The Treasury's Head of Public Services, Ray Shostak, was a frequent visitor to the DfES. Shostak had advised Paul Boateng on the development of ECM, having himself led the integration of children's services in Hertfordshire well ahead of the statutory requirement to do so.

Notwithstanding the broad policy framework of ECM and the remit of the CYP Directorate, safeguarding policy did occupy a considerable portion of ministers' and officials' time. However, safeguarding policy continued to be positioned within the wider progressive universalism framework of ECM. One of the key policy developments in this period was the redrafting of the multi-agency safeguarding guidance called *Working Together* (HM Government, 2006). This new guidance replaced the 1999 version, which had defined safeguarding closely in line with the Children Act 1989 (Parton, 2014: 91–5). Commenting on the 2006 version, Parton states:

> The guidance was framed in terms of supporting all children and families in terms of the five ECM outcomes of being healthy, enjoying and achieving, making a positive contribution, achieving economic well-being, and, particularly, staying safe, which were seen as 'key to children and young people's wellbeing'. The guidance was presented as part of 'an integrated approach' so that effective measures to safeguard children were seen as those which also promoted their welfare, and should not be seen in isolation from the wider range of support and services to meet the needs of all children and families. (2014: 96)

The broader conception of safeguarding under ECM differed from the narrower focus on children in need under Section 17 of the Children Act 1989. ECM also largely overlooked the central role played by local authority social services departments under the framework of the Children Act 1989. Furthermore, it was the Children Act 1989 that had informed Lord Laming's analysis and provided the focus for officials working on child safeguarding policy in the DH, before they were transferred to the CYP Directorate within the DfES. Although the new version of *Working Together* was very important to local agencies and professionals responsible for safeguarding children, particularly social workers, it was drafted with limited input from representatives of the social work profession. Hughes commented that "I remember sweating blood over *Working Together*, over the detail line by line.... I have to say that whilst it went out for consultation, that particularly was a process that largely involved civil servants drafting and ministers approving" (interview with Beverley Hughes). Furthermore, the large majority of the new DCS community had an education rather than a social work background (Frost and Parton, 2009: 163). Social work continued to be poorly represented in policymaking circles during this period, both nationally and locally.

The centrally driven approach of the Change for Children programme also meant that insufficient attention was paid to the need of the children's workforce, including social workers. As one charity leader involved in the development of children's policy throughout the Labour period reflected:

> 'I'm very clear that that was one of the biggest mistakes....
> Put crudely, you can change everything else, you can create
> a common outcomes framework, common governance,
> planning and commissioning frameworks, you can move
> towards the co-location of services, you can develop
> common targets, common funding streams, common
> accountability through inspection, all those process things
> of trying to recalibrate the service, but unless you change
> the practice of the person on the front line working with
> a child or family, then nothing much will have changed.'
> (Interview with charity leader)

Labour did establish the Children's Workforce Development Council (CWDC) in 2005 to draw together the work of various organisations representing different professional and occupational groups within the children's workforce. However, the CWDC never received the necessary financial or political backing needed to force the various organisations represented to work more closely together. As the same charity leader just quoted commented:

> 'It was almost a complete failure because however much the
> people were willing to work together within the meeting,
> they were actually being driven by their own boards that
> had their own specific objectives being handed down to
> them either by the relevant government agency or by their

own sector that didn't see the need to change and unify.' (Interview with charity leader)

A DfES official recalled a separate social care workforce reform initiative that also failed to make an impact:

'It's not as if reform was not attempted prior to the whole Peter Connelly thing, but it was reform of the kind which exemplifies the difficulties of making any progress in the blancmange that was social work leadership. There was a programme called Options for Excellence, I think it was called, which one senior voluntary sector leader called "Options for Indifference", and it produced all sorts of wishy-washy definitions of what social work was about and absolutely was not going to get at the reform of social work.' (Interview with DfES official)

The lack of attention given to social work stood in marked contrast to the investment that Labour had made in the teaching profession. The government had placed heavy demands on teachers under the drive to raise educational standards. However, a new pay and rewards structure was also introduced alongside extensive investment in training (DfEE, 1998). The social work profession did not receive any comparable investment, even after the Victoria Climbié inquiry (Lord Laming, 2003) had pointed towards the perilous state of the profession. Hughes recognised that social work reform was not properly addressed in this period. As she stated:

'In terms of where we put the money, particularly around workforce development, [that] went into teachers and not social workers and that was a big gap. We just didn't have the money to be honest. That was a gap. Although Climbié–Laming–ECM was a very good framework, we didn't put the same emphasis into improving the quality of the workforce to deliver those things as we did in education.' (Interview with Beverley Hughes)

This failure to engage in the reform of social work was later exposed as a major fault line in the ECM framework following the Baby P crisis in late 2008. The government's response to this is discussed in Chapter 6. However, even before this, ministers and officials leading on the implementation of ECM had to respond to competing priorities pursued by No 10 while Blair remained in office.

Schools reform

The role of schools under ECM

The idea that schools have a role to play in promoting the general well-being of children was not new: 'Schools have traditionally offered medical and welfare services of some sort alongside their more traditional education function' (Baginsky, 2008: 11). Furthermore, prior to ECM, Labour introduced new requirements relating to schools' broader role, including a legal obligation to safeguard and promote the well-being of children under Section 175 of the Education Act 2002. However, ECM placed new demands on schools. The emphasis on early intervention and prevention placed schools in a central role under new multi-agency working arrangements. Moreover, the successful implementation of new multi-agency working tools, including the Information Sharing Index (later called Contact Point), the CAF and the lead professional, rested in large part on the cooperation and commitment of schools. More generally, schools were expected to play an 'extended' role in supporting the welfare of children and families, and in supporting the establishment of integrated children's services and the move towards local children's trusts. In specific guidance issued to schools under the Change for Children programme, it was stated:

> Schools and their governing bodies will want to consider what changes are happening locally so that they will be in a position to collaborate with the Local Authority as it develops its children's trust arrangements. A particular area of interest will be the development of extended services in and around schools. Many schools already offer aspects of extended services such as breakfast and after-school clubs which are shown to improve children's motivation and engagement. The Government is looking to all schools, over time, to provide a core offer of extended services either on site or across a cluster of local schools and providers. (DfES, 2004b: 3)

Bureaucratic resistance

However, this vision of the extended role of schools was not universally accepted by education interests inside and outside of government.

Furthermore, it was an obstacle to reform that Boateng clearly identified:

> 'Schools have always been the main obstacle to progress in this area because so long as children remain in the same department as schools, they will always lose out to schools because that's where the political pressure is, that's where the resources are, inevitably follow, and it's also where the strongest professional vested interests are.' (Interview with Paul Boateng)

Opponents of ECM succeeded in winning an exemption for schools under Section 10 of the Children Act 2004. This required key agencies to cooperate in the establishment of new arrangements for partnership working under the ECM five outcomes framework (Frost and Parton, 2009: 163). Blair also ignored Boateng's recommendation that a new Children's Department be established to ensure that the ECM reform programme was not blocked by education interests. Instead, Blair decided to set up a new directorate within the DfES. Significantly, Boateng's concern that ECM would become a second-order priority in a department focused on schools' more traditional educative functions turned out to be well founded. Charles Clarke was Secretary of State for Education when the new directorate was created. He conceded:

> 'I think the culture in the DfES was about schools' standards almost entirely, not about the wider agenda. I don't think that was ever the agenda of the ministers.... I think we all saw the wider agenda. That may have been a dislocate, but they saw, the officials, saw the school standards agenda as absolutely pre-eminent.' (Interview with Charles Clarke)

Beverley Hughes shared these concerns when she arrived in the DfES in May 2005 following her appointment as Children's Minister. She described a divide between the Schools Division within the DfES and the CYP Directorate. The Schools Division was comprised of separate directorates primarily focused on raising school standards and controlled the predominant share of departmental resources. As Hughes recalled:

> 'When I came in in 2005, there was a real problem in getting the Schools Division in the department to see themselves

as part of this agenda, and the children and families' agenda was just seen, I think, as a problem over there, not what the department was really about.' (Interview with Beverley Hughes)

This resistance to ECM was also felt at the local level. When interviewed, a local authority DCS commented that "Head teachers and the education community generally felt very resistant because they didn't want their position diluted and they didn't want to be held accountable for the children; they just wanted to be held accountable for their education outcomes." Thus, bureaucratic resistance slowed the early implementation of the ECM reforms. However, it is important to consider this resistance within the context of Blair's continued interest and involvement in education policy during this period.

School autonomy

The drive to improve educational standards continued to be a key domestic policy priority for Blair, with progress closely monitored by the PMDU (Barber, 2007: 50). Arguably, this was not incommensurate with the broader role ascribed to schools under ECM. However, Blair's continued focus on standards strengthened the position of the Schools Division within the DfES and made it more difficult to promote the broader aims of the CYP Directorate and the ECM reform agenda. Furthermore, Blair promoted the extension of competition and choice within the education system as the way to drive up school standards, arguing that to achieve this, schools needed to be given greater autonomy from local authorities. In *Higher Standards, Better Schools for All* (HM Government, 2005a: 7), it was stated that 'This White Paper sets out our plans radically to improve the system by putting parents and the needs of their children at the heart of our school system, freeing up schools to innovate and succeed, bringing in new dynamism and new providers.' It was proposed that the freedoms previously available only to academies and foundation schools would be made available to all schools. Alongside similar reforms in health, these proposals exposed deep divisions between No 10 and the Treasury regarding Labour's strategy for public services reform (Shaw, 2007: ch 3). As Charles Clarke explained:

'Gordon basically believed in a Fabian/Webbite model based on saying that if you make the changes at the centre and you move the levers and so on, you can deliver a change in Hartlepool. Tony was much more in favour of the social entrepreneurship model, which was essentially if you were freeing up schools, freeing up GPs [general practitioners] or whatever, to move more effectively, then that was the more effective way to get change. The Brownite argument against Tony was that it was not equitable because you couldn't, if you gave schools freedom and hospitals freedoms, inequality would grow as a result of that. The argument of Tony against the central system was that it didn't work and it demotivated local leadership. What you needed was local leadership to address the issues.' (Interview with Charles Clarke)

ECM embodied the Brown perspective on public services governance. It strove for greater integration and coordination, not competition, across children's services agencies, including schools. The Change for Children programme positioned schools alongside other agencies under the new children's services arrangements and the planned move towards children's trusts. The separation of schools from local authority control under Blair's proposals pulled in the opposite direction. Thus, while Blair remained in office, plans to develop the role of children's services departments and children's trusts were heavily constrained.

'Problem' young people

ECM also emphasised the importance of making positive activities available to young people beyond formal education (HM Government, 2003: 32–3). The rationale was that positive activities would help to prevent poor outcomes such as drug taking, teenage pregnancy and involvement in crime and anti-social behaviour. However, prior to ECM, Blair had promoted a more authoritarian perspective, exemplified by the creation of the ASBO. 'ASBO politics' prioritised perceptions of safety in the community ahead of the welfare of individual young people (Squires, 2008). Just over a year into the implementation of ECM, Blair launched the *Respect Action Plan* (Home Office, 2006). The plan attempted to rebalance Labour's children's policy away from the universal focus of ECM in favour of the more targeted interventions that Blair had consistently supported. In his foreword, Blair states:

> We will continue to build strong communities by providing opportunities for all through Sure Start, by tackling child poverty, through tax credits for hard-working families as

well as through enhanced youth and sport provision for young people. But there are still intractable problems with the behaviour of some individuals and families, behaviour which can make life a misery for others, particularly in the most disadvantaged communities. (Blair, in Home Office, 2006: foreword)

The plan promised new legislation to tackle poor behaviour in schools, the extended use of parenting contracts and new schemes to address 'irresponsible parents' backed by the threat of benefits sanctions (Home Office, 2006: 17). Louise Casey was appointed to lead the newly created Respect Unit based in the Home Office. Casey had previously been appointed by Blair to lead the drive on ASBOs following the Anti-Social Behaviour Act 2003.

As Children's Minister, Hughes had overall responsibility for the implementation of the ECM reform programme. She was also responsible for the development of the government's *Youth Matters* programme (HM Government, 2005b; DfES, 2006) setting out an overarching approach to youth policy. The development of the programme required Hughes to manage the ideological tensions between ECM and the *Respect Action Plan. Youth Matters* committed £200 million for the expansion of universal youth services under the Youth Opportunity and Youth Capital Funds (DfES, 2006: 5). The commissioning and provision of these services would be designed in accordance with the progressive universalism approach and the five outcomes established under ECM (HM Government, 2005b: ch 6). However, responding to pressure from No 10 (via Casey), Youth Matters also emphasised the need to apply a more targeted approach to deal with the problem behaviours of a relatively small number of young people involved in crime and anti-social behaviour. As the Green Paper (HM Government, 2005b) stated:

A minority of young people can get involved in behaviour that is a serious problem for the wider community, including anti-social behaviour and crime. The Government is clear that when this happens we need to respond firmly. This paper is therefore not just about providing more opportunities and support to young people, it is also about challenge. We need to strike the right balance between rights and responsibilities, appreciating the enormous contribution that young people can make while expecting them in return to appreciate and respect the opportunities available to them. (HM Government, 2005b: 4)

Thus, the commitment to refocusing resources towards early intervention programmes designed to prevent young people getting involved in crime and anti-social behaviour had to be tempered. Hughes had to ensure that the new integrated multi-agency youth support services, designed to support the early intervention approach, were also adequately focused on, and resourced to, address the behaviour of the specific groups of young people that concerned No 10.

Discussion

Ministers faced with the challenge of implementing the ambitious ECM reform programme forged new relationships with leaders of local authority children's services departments, recognising that their cooperation was needed to make the new structural arrangements work. Several people were seconded from local government to work alongside officials in the CYP Directorate. New forums to discuss policy with representatives of the new DCS community were also established. However, dialogue with the sector remained on the government's terms. Those consulted were careful not to question the underlying aims of the ECM programme and were expected to offer only technical advice to support its implementation. Significantly, the focus on the role of universal services, and the corresponding neglect of social work, was not openly criticised. Moreover, the Treasury's continued involvement in the development of children's policy in this period served to reinforce this focus.

However, intra-party tensions over children's services policy, and Labour's approach to public service reform more generally, served to constrain the implementation of ECM in this period. In the context of Blair's continued involvement in education policy, education interests in the DfES and outside of government were able to water down key aspects of ECM. Thus, the role to be played by schools under multi-agency children's trust arrangements was not clearly specified. Under the Treasury framework, schools would be required to play an extended role in supporting the well-being of disadvantaged pupils, working alongside other children's agencies. No 10's narrower focus on educational attainment and commitment to greater school autonomy pulled in the opposite direction. Blair's authoritarian perspective on youth policy provided a further constraint. Whereas ECM emphasised the role of universal services and the importance of a shift towards early intervention and prevention, Blair continued to champion more punitive policies aimed at addressing the perceived problem behaviours of a much smaller cohort of young people. Chapter 6 considers the extent to which these tensions in policy were resolved after Blair left office in June 2007.

6

The Children's Plan, 'Broken Britain' and Baby P

Introduction

> With schools, children's services, the voluntary sector and government all playing their part, we can ensure that every child has the best start in life. (Ed Balls, in DCSF, 2007: 4)

> The Social Justice Policy Unit has starkly articulated the challenges facing Britain's 'broken society'. Social workers, particularly those dealing with child protection cases, are at the sharp end of these challenges, often dealing with very difficult and damaged families. (David Cameron, in Conservative Party, 2007: 3)

> Whilst the improvements for services for children and families, in general, are welcome it is clear that the need to protect children and young people from significant harm and neglect is ever more challenging. There now needs to be a step change in the arrangements to protect children from harm. (Lord Laming, 2009: 4)

After Gordon Brown became Prime Minister and leader of the Labour Party in June 2007, immediate steps were taken to support the implementation of the ECM reform agenda. This included the creation of a new Department for Children, Schools and Families (DCSF), with Brown's former Treasury special adviser Ed Balls being appointed as the Secretary of State. Later that year, Balls published *The Children's Plan* (DCSF, 2007), providing a comprehensive statement of the Brown government's ambitions in relation to children's policy that effectively marked a relaunch of ECM. However, against the backdrop of the global financial crisis, Labour ministers had to respond to new pressures in the run-up to the 2010 election. The new Conservative Party leader, David Cameron, identified social policy as a key battleground as he sought to reposition the Conservatives and highlight Labour's failure to address the problem of 'Broken Britain'. Pressure on the Brown government was at its most intense following media reporting of the death of Baby P during the final months of 2008.

The first section of the chapter examines the development of children's policy under the DCSF and the leadership of Balls, focusing on *The Children's Plan* (DCSF, 2007), and building on the discussion of bureaucratic resistance to ECM in the previous chapter. The second section considers Conservative Party efforts to articulate alternative social policy priorities to Labour, including a review of policy on social work. The third section discusses the impact of the Baby P case on Labour children's policy, thereby addressing further the key theme of the impact of inquiries and scandals. Whereas previous chapters have highlighted the importance of *intra*-party tensions under the Blair–Brown government, this chapter examines how *inter*-party competition also emerged as a key driver of children's policy.

The Children's Plan

The ECM reform programme, and the work of the CYP Directorate more generally, was not viewed by all DfES officials with the same importance as the department's drive to raise educational attainment, as the discussion in Chapter 5 revealed. This made it difficult to ensure that schools embraced the broader welfare perspective of ECM. Furthermore, Blair's push to increase school autonomy, thereby ensuring greater freedom from local authority control, contradicted efforts to improve the integration of local children's services and establish accountability to children's trusts. However, following his appointment as Secretary of State, Balls provided a strong indication that he was fully committed to the broader aims of the ECM reform programme. As Balls commented:

> 'The first thing I did on the day I was appointed was to go to a meeting of stakeholders that had been arranged for some other reason and say, "I'm very pleased to be the first Every Child Matters Secretary of State".... I think we felt that the national government had told local areas that they had to implement the ethos of Every Child Matters, but that the national government itself had never properly done it.' (Interview with Ed Balls, 2018)

A comprehensive review of children's policy was subsequently undertaken, resulting in the publication of *The Children's Plan* (DCSF,

2007) in December 2007. Hughes recalled the challenge that this presented to departmental officials:

> 'Ed was completely clear that the two agendas [ECM and schools reform] were mutually interdependent and they had to be compatible and given equal prominence in the department.... it did shake up the department and it did emphasise the government's view, expressed through him and ministers, that the school standards agenda and the wider agenda on children, young people and families were equally important, and as I say, they were mutually interdependent, they needed each other. He really emphasised that.' (Interview with Beverley Hughes)

Revisiting the role of schools

The Children's Plan reflected the progressive universalism perspective underpinning ECM. It re-emphasised the contribution that universal services were expected to make to supporting the general well-being of all children, particularly those from disadvantaged backgrounds. However, it was more explicit in terms of the government's expectations of early-years settings and schools. The focus on raising educational attainment remained paramount, but it was argued in the plan that the broader focus of ECM supported, rather than detracted from, efforts to raise attainment:

> Almost all children, young people and families come into regular contact with early-years settings and with schools and colleges.... If these services are not integrated with more specialist provision, by looking for early warnings that children might need more help and by providing facilities for specialist services to operate so they can be easily reached by children and families, we will be hamstrung in achieving our broad ambitions for children and young people. The best schools and colleges have already shown us how that can be done and that it enhances, not compromises, attainment. (DCSF, 2007: 144)

The Children's Plan identified the '21st-century school' as one that recognised the interdependency of pupil welfare and attainment. This was consistent with the concept of 'extended schools' introduced earlier (DfES, 2004b). However, the plan signalled the government's determination to push these reforms further. It was announced that new performance indicators would be introduced to measure the contribution of schools to the delivery of the five ECM outcomes, and that these would be incorporated into Ofsted's school inspection framework (DCSF, 2007: 150).

The Children's Plan also committed the DCSF to clarifying the legal status and authority of children's trusts (DCSF, 2007 146–9). New, strengthened statutory guidance on children' trusts was subsequently published (DCSF, 2008a). There was an implicit acceptance that not enough had been done since the Children Act 2004 to ensure that agencies were focused on the same priorities and fully committed to more integrated patterns of working. The plan notified all local agencies that, in the future, they would be held more directly accountable for the delivery of the five ECM outcomes (DCSF, 2007: 148). Significantly, there was a clear expectation that schools would make a full contribution to local children's trust planning and commissioning. This marked a departure from the exemption to schools granted under Section 10 of the Children Act 2004. This exemption was later formally removed under the Apprenticeships, Skills, Children and Learning Act 2009.

Youth policy

Balls' commitment to the progressive universalism approach was also evident in changes made to youth policy. Balls agreed that it may sometimes be necessary to take tough action to address the problem behaviours of young people. However, he was not supportive of the emphasis that Blair, and officials such as Louise Casey, had placed on punitive measures over a more positive and preventative approach. He argued:

> 'I didn't mind being tough on anti–social behaviour, but I didn't like the ASBOs rhetoric.... I just thought it was headbanging and counterproductive ... when you went and spoke to police locally, or children's services, they just didn't think that was the right messaging ... so I had to have quite big arguments to stop that. I didn't want our new department to be seen to swing to more of that tough rhetoric and, if anything, to shift more towards opportunity for young people.' (Interview with Ed Balls, 2018)

Thus, *The Children's Plan* placed greater emphasis on the provision of positive activities for all young people. Chapter 6 of *The Children's Plan* began with the following statement:

We want all young people to enjoy happy, healthy and safe teenage years and to be prepared for adult life. Too often we focus on the problems of a few young people rather than the successes of the many – we want a society where young people feel valued and in which their achievements are recognised and celebrated. (DCSF, 2007: 125)

As a first step towards establishing a more positive youth policy programme, the Home Office's Respect Unit was scrapped, and responsibility for all aspects of children's policy shifted into the DCSF. Anne Weinstock, the department's youth policy lead, was simultaneously appointed to head up a Youth Task Force. Working under Beverley Hughes, Weinstock had been an advocate of the more positive aspects of the Youth Matters programme. Louise Casey, the outgoing head of the Respect Unit, was moved to a new post in the Cabinet Office to lead a review of community engagement in fighting crime (Home Office, 2007).

On the other hand, it must be acknowledged that interventions targeted at specific subsections of the child population were not abandoned altogether. Following the 'Think family' review (Cabinet Office, 2007: 6), initiated under Blair, ministers accepted that a targeted approach was needed to support the estimated 140,000 families facing multiple and complex problems. These families were seen to require more specialist interventions to address problems such as worklessness, poor mental health and substance misuse. Local Family Intervention Projects (FIPs) were established to develop more specialist packages of support targeted at these families. However, this more targeted approach was only an addendum to the focus on early intervention and prevention through universal services emphasised in *The Children's Plan*. The Treasury only committed £18 million over three years in the 2007 Spending Review to support the development of FIPs (Cabinet Office, 2007: 9). This was a relatively small amount compared to the £200 million already committed to support the expansion of positive activities under the Youth Opportunity and Youth Capital Funds (DfES, 2006).

The Conservative Party and 'Broken Britain'

The intra-party tensions that had shaped Labour children's policy largely disappeared after Brown became Prime Minister. However, the Brown government faced new competition from a resurgent

Conservative Party. Cameron recognised the electoral importance of social policy and the need to articulate alternative policies to Labour. Following his election as party leader in December 2005, Cameron spoke about 'a modern and compassionate conservatism which is right for our times and our country' (Cameron, 2005). He also famously declared that 'there is such a thing as society' as he sought to distance the Conservative Party from the dominant stress on economic policy under the Thatcher and Major governments (Cameron, 2005).

Cameron subsequently asked former Conservative Party leader Iain Duncan-Smith to lead a review of Conservative social policy, supported by the Centre for Social Justice (CSJ), which Duncan-Smith had founded in 2004. The review criticised redistributive measures introduced by the Labour government to reduce child poverty. In *Breakdown Britain* (Conservative Party Social Justice Policy Group, 2006: 3), it was argued that Labour's focus on income transfers had failed to address the needs of those living in the deepest poverty. It was claimed that the poverty of these families was linked to a range of behavioural problems and that 'five pathways to poverty' had to tackled. These included: (1) family breakdown; (2) educational failure; (3) economic dependence; (4) indebtedness; and (5) addiction (Conservative Party Social Justice Policy Group, 2006: 13). In a subsequent report, measures to tackle each of these five social problems were sketched out. The underlying argument made was that 'people must take responsibility for their own choices, but that government has a responsibility to help people make the right choices' (Conservative Party Social Justice Policy Group, 2007: 7). This analysis of poverty and welfare services came to be referred to as the 'Broken Britain' perspective (Hayton, 2012).

In the subsequent report, *Early Intervention: Good Parents, Great Kids, Better Citizens* (Allen and Duncan-Smith, 2008), a new approach to children and family's policy was advocated. The report was co-authored by Duncan-Smith and the Labour MP Graham Allen. The report claimed to be non-partisan, with Allen and Duncan-Smith (2008: 4) 'calling on all parties to unite around the radical new social policy "Early Intervention"'. The central importance of early intervention and prevention within Labour's ECM framework was ignored. However, this reflected a rejection of Labour's progressive universalism approach. The report was informed by the earlier work of Duncan-Smith and the Broken Britain perspective on poverty. Thus, the behavioural deviances of a 'dysfunctional base' in society were highlighted, while the structural and economic determinants of poverty were downplayed:

One of the most notable aspects of dysfunctional families is that founding members often come from a psychosocial background that also was damaging and dysfunctional. Dysfunctional families become incubators for the generational transfer of mental and physical ill-health and chaotic lifestyles that inhibit children's ability to lead a fulfilled life. These damaging effects can be explained neurologically, biologically and behaviourally. (Allen and Duncan-Smith, 2008: 30)

This analysis supported the argument that more targeted early interventions were needed, particularly aimed at families with children aged under three years, to prevent the 'intergenerational transmission of disadvantage' (Allen and Duncan-Smith, 2008: 29–30). Labour's progressive universalism approach was implicitly rejected in favour of 'evidence-based' programmes predominantly developed in the US (Featherstone et al, 2018: ch 3).

The Conservative Party Commission on Social Workers

The Broken Britain framework provided a critique of Labour social policies and pointed towards the development of new initiatives under a future Conservative government. In this context, the Shadow Children's Minister, Tim Loughton, persuaded Cameron that it was necessary to develop a policy position on social work with children. Loughton subsequently invited representatives of the social work profession to join the Conservative Party Commission on Social Workers. Members of the commission considered evidence provided by a wide range of individuals and organisations and made recommendations for reform in the report *No More Blame Game: The Future for Children's Social Workers* (Conservative Party, 2007). Cameron tied the commission's recommendations to the challenge of dealing with Broken Britain in his foreword to the report: 'Iain Duncan Smith's comprehensive work through the Social Justice Policy Unit has starkly articulated the challenges facing Britain's "broken society". Social workers, particularly those dealing with child protection cases, are at the sharp end of these challenges, often dealing with very difficult and damaged families' (Cameron, in Conservative Party, 2007: foreword). However, it was Labour's neglect of, and sometimes hostility towards, social work that provided the main impetus for Loughton to set up the commission. Loughton had served as Shadow Children's Minister since 2001. Reflecting on his early time in this post, he commented:

'I remember the first ADSS conference that I went to, and Alan Milburn was the Health Secretary, and it was around the time of Climbié, and Alan Milburn absolutely pointed the finger of blame at the social workers. He got up on stage at that conference and basically said, "You are a shambles; you've got to get your act together." It was very much the blame game, and that went down very, very badly. I think they were passing the buck on blame rather than appreciating that the government was part of the situation as well. So, the social work profession at that stage was feeling very bruised: they were losing a lot of people; vacancy rates were high; the calibre of recruits coming out of universities was poor; it was an ageing profession; and it was getting worse. And being told by the Secretary of State that "You are all crap" and that "Victoria Climbié is your fault" didn't exactly act as a recruitment tool.' (Interview with Tim Loughton)

It has been demonstrated in previous chapters that Labour's ECM reform programme emphasised the importance of universal services, and generally overlooked the specific challenges faced by social workers engaged at the sharp end of safeguarding and child protection work. Moreover, there is a strong body of research evidence to suggest that reforms introduced after the Victoria Climbié inquiry increased the bureaucratic demands placed on social workers and limited the time available for direct contact with children and families (Parton, 2006; Broadhurst et al, 2010a, 2010b; White et al, 2008; Wastell et al, 2010). Loughton also reached this conclusion following a series of meetings with social workers in several local authorities during his time as Shadow Children's Minister.

The commission provided an opportunity for representatives of the social work profession to express their concerns and contribute to the development of reform proposals. The first recommendation made by the commission was that 'The generic nature of social work must be maintained and resources better targeted to enable social workers to work with families in a preventative role' (Conservative Party, 2007: 57). Reference to the generic nature of social work reflected long-standing concerns regarding the specialisation of roles within the profession and the separation of social work with children from social work with adults. Furthermore, effective working with families required an acknowledgement that social workers have a role to play in preventing, not just responding to, family crises, including actual and suspected cases of child abuse. This perspective is reflected in Section 17 of the Children Act 1989. However, it has been argued in previous chapters that successive governments had failed to prioritise the implementation of Section 17. Although the Labour government had invested significant new resources in welfare services for children and families, it did not explicitly address the cohort of children in need as defined under this legislation. Rather, the Children Act 2004 emphasised the role that other agencies needed to play to improve the welfare of children more generally under the ECM five outcomes framework.

The commission also made recommendations to address the training and recruitment of social workers. Although this had not been ignored entirely under Labour, investment in the profession had been limited compared to other professions such as teaching. An advertising campaign to improve public perceptions of the profession was also recommended. The commission also highlighted the lack of input that representatives of the social work profession had had over policymaking. Thus, there was a call to encourage more social workers to join a professional body that could achieve a similar status to the British Medical Association or the Royal College of Nurses. The appointment of a Chief Social Worker to act as a champion for the profession in government and in the national media was also recommended. At the time, this Conservative-led review of policy on social work received limited publicity. However, the case of Baby P provided the Conservatives with an opportunity to expose Labour's neglect of social work and promote their alternative policies under the Broken Britain framework.

Baby P and children's policy

It was argued in the introductory chapter that media reporting of serious cases of child abuse has become closely associated with policy change. However, it has been demonstrated in Chapters 3 and 4 that the close association between the death of Victoria Climbié and Labour's reforms was overstated by the government, and that party-political imperatives were a more significant driver of policy change. The case of Baby P provides a further opportunity to test the association between serious cases and children's services reform.

In his book *The Story of Baby P: Setting the Record Straight*, Ray Jones (2014) provides a detailed account of how the media, but particularly *The Sun* newspaper, reported the case. In the weeks following the conviction of Baby P's mother and her partner, the paper ran a relentless 'campaign for justice' that primarily focused on the perceived failings of Haringey Council's DCS, Sharon Shoesmith, and the individual social workers involved in the case. Under pressure from the media, and following a damming snap inspection by Ofsted, Balls instructed Haringey Council to sack Shoesmith, even though it was later judged that he did not have the legal authority to do so. Under similar pressure, Haringey Council also sacked the social workers involved. Jones (2014: ch 5) argues that these actions had a long-lasting impact on professional practice and made it harder to recruit and retain high-calibre social workers. Evidence of a sustained increase in care applications since Baby P is deemed to indicate an increased risk aversion among professionals (Jones, 2014: 287). However, it is also important to reflect upon the impact that the case had on Labour's children's policy.

Labour's policy response

Following media reporting of the Baby P case, Balls commissioned Lord Laming to 'provide an urgent report on the progress being made across the country to implement effective arrangements for *safeguarding* children' (Lord Laming, 2009: 3, emphasis added). However, *The Protection of Children in England: A Progress Report* (Lord Laming, 2009), published in March 2009, was notable for its explicit focus on *child protection*. Furthermore, although the report was not overtly critical of Labour's response to the Victoria Climbié inquiry, Lord Laming expressed his view that much more needed to be done to ensure that child protection was sufficiently prioritised:

> Whilst the improvements for services for children and families, in general, are welcome it is clear that the need to protect children and young people from significant harm and neglect is ever more challenging. There now needs to be a step change in the arrangements to protect children from harm. (Lord Laming, 2009: 4)

Pointing towards reforms needed at the national level, Lord Laming (2009: 4–5) demanded that 'The Secretaries of State for Health, Justice and Children, Schools and Families must collaborate in the setting of explicit strategic priorities for the protection of children and young people for each of the key frontline services and ensure sufficient resources are in place to deliver these priorities.' He also called for the establishment of a new National Safeguarding Delivery

Unit to 'inject greater energy and drive into the implementation of change and support local improvement' (Lord Laming, 2009: 5). This recommendation mirrored Lord Laming's (2003) call for a new National Children and Families Agency in the report of the Victoria Climbié inquiry; however, it was pointed out in Chapter 4 that this was not followed. On this occasion, the government did follow Lord Laming's advice (HM Government, 2009).

Lord Laming (2009: 5) also highlighted the government's failure to adequately address the training and supply of front-line social workers. Even before Laming had published his report, Balls had recognised the need to re-examine policy on social work. He asked Moira Gibb, then the Chief Executive of the London Borough of Camden, to chair the SWTF. Members of the SWTF were drawn from front-line social work teams, local authority leadership, academia, the media, the voluntary sector and service user organisations (SWTF, 2009: 69–70). The final report of the SWTF (2009: 14) expressed the view that social work must be viewed as a 'single profession covering work with both children and adults'. This view had been expressed in the earlier report of the Conservative Party Commission on Social Workers. Unlike the commission, which focused its recommendations on social work with children, the SWTF (2009: 9) presented a 'single national reform programme for social work'. However, the content of this programme was broadly consistent with the recommendations made by the commission. The SWTF focused on training and recruitment, and called for the establishment of a national College of Social Work. It also repeated calls for action to improve public perceptions of the profession. All recommendations were accepted by the government and Gibb was appointed to lead the Social Work Reform Board (SWRB) to oversee the implementation of the reform programme (HM Government, 2010a).

The Baby P case forced ministers to reassess the government's overall approach to children's policy, and specifically to address the neglect of social work at the sharp end of child protection practice. Labour's broader conception of safeguarding, and the contribution that needed to be made by universal services, was epitomised in the DCSF's (2008b) *Staying Safe: Action Plan*, published in February 2008 shortly after *The Children's Plan*. Balls recognised that this plan did not focus sufficiently on child protection practice and that social work professionals had not been well represented in policymaking circles. He commented:

'The non-educational children's professionals nationally and locally in children's services departments were never given the weight they should have had, pre-Baby P, including at leadership level.... So even though, pre-Baby P, as a children's department, we were talking about play and health and prevention and the vital role of parents, the policy agenda was generally around opportunity and success, and children making the most of their potential ... so, while we also focused on safeguarding, the issues around numbers of social workers, their quality of training and their powers ... none of those were being properly surfaced pre-Baby P.' (Interview with Ed Balls, 2018)

A DfES official confirmed that the Baby P case had forced a rethink: "By the time Ed had been through the ringer on Baby P, he certainly understood why social work mattered, and then the more that the government looked at social work, the more it realised how it had been left to wither on the vine". Thus, the Baby P case did lead to an important shift in children's services policy, consistent with the view that policy change in this area often follows media reporting of serious cases of child abuse. However, it is also important to examine both the role played by the Conservative Party in this period and Balls's continued defence of Labour's ECM framework.

Conservative pressure

Media reporting of the Baby P case, and the pressure this placed on the government, was at least in part driven by the Conservative Party. DCSF ministers and officials recognised the serious practice failings evident in the Baby P case, as well as its potential political significance given the involvement of Haringey Council. However, they did not anticipate the extent to which the Conservatives would be able to exploit the case. As Balls explained:

'In the months before and the weeks before, the department was really worried about what was going to happen when it became public. But I think that the extra thing was that David Cameron and *The Sun* had basically decided that you could get great traction out of a "Broken Britain" narrative, and they were always looking for any way into that broader agenda ... it became another example for them of Labour, Gordon Brown, being out of touch about the reality of "Broken Britain".' (Interview with Ed Balls, 2018)

After a difficult start to his premiership, Brown had been praised for the courage and leadership qualities that he demonstrated in responding to the global banking crisis that unfolded in September 2008 (Seldon and Lodge, 2010: ch 5). The Baby P case provided Cameron with an opportunity to discredit Brown and the Labour government, and to promote new Conservative social policies. Importantly, the work of the earlier Conservative Party Commission on Social Workers provided the Conservatives with a strong platform from which to criticise Labour. As a party advisor explained:

> 'One of the reasons the story unfolded as it did was because the Conservatives through Tim [Loughton] were very well informed about the problems and so were able to advise David Cameron on how to respond with confidence…. One of the reasons why the party was able to kick up such a fuss was because we'd done the work. We knew where the weak spots in the government's strategy were and we were able to single them out.' (Interview with Conservative Party advisor)

Following the Levison inquiry, we also know that Cameron had a close relationship with Rebekah Brookes, the editor of *The Sun* at the time (Jones, 2014). The paper's campaign was triggered by Cameron's decision to raise the Baby P case at Prime Minister's Questions on 12 November 2008. Brown did not anticipate being asked about the case and had not been briefed by ministers. Cameron saw an opportunity to highlight failings in Labour's earlier response to the death of Victoria Climbié in the same London borough. Duncan-Smith made the same connection between the two cases and spotted the opportunity to promote his own work. In an article published in *The Guardian* newspaper the following day, he wrote that 'Without a comprehensive approach including earlier intervention with dysfunctional families to change their lives, as has been shown to work in other countries, the at-risk register will grow and we will see more sad outcomes like the tragic cases of children like Baby P and Victoria Climbié' (Duncan-Smith, 2008). It is not possible to isolate the specific factors that influenced Balls's response to the Baby P case. Balls (2016: 289) has claimed that it was the failings identified by Ofsted that triggered him to intervene in Haringey. Lord Laming's (2009) report pointed towards a need to review national policies. However, we must also take account of the pressure that the Conservatives succeeded in putting the government under in the weeks following the first reporting of the case. The Conservatives had already identified Labour's neglect of child protection and social work, and viewed the Baby P case as an opportunity to score political points.

Defending progressive universalism

Although he Baby P crisis forced Labour ministers to acknowledge that action needed to be taken to improve the sharp end of child protection and safeguarding practice, Balls remained committed to the progressive universalism approach of ECM and *The Children's Plan*. Furthermore, during the Baby P crisis, he sought to deflect criticism of national policy by asking Lord Laming to focus only on policy implementation at the local level. Writing to Lord Laming, Balls stated:

> The reforms introduced by Government following the Victoria Climbié Inquiry set a very clear direction and have significantly strengthened the framework for safeguarding children. But it is vital we ensure that these reforms are being implemented systematically by all local agencies so that children in every part of the country receive the protection they need. Your work will be crucial in allowing us to assess progress being made, and to identify any barriers to effective, consistent implementation and how these might be overcome. (Balls, in Laming, 2009: 94)

It was argued in Chapter 4 that Labour's ECM reforms did not closely follow the recommendations made in the Victoria Climbié inquiry, even though the Green Paper was framed as a direct response. Lord Laming (2009) did speak positively about Labour's reforms in his second report to the government. However, he also expressed his frustration that not enough had been done to ensure that child protection was made a high enough priority at both the local *and national* levels. Notwithstanding these concerns, Balls claimed that Laming's new report confirmed the appropriateness of Labour's response to the Victoria Climbié inquiry. In the government's response to the report, he wrote:

> Lord Laming's report confirmed that robust legislative, structural and policy foundations are in place and that our Every Child Matters reforms set the right direction and

are widely supported. He underlined the progress that has been made and the positive difference that people working with children, particularly those most at risk, are making every day. But he was also clear that there needs to be a 'step change' in the arrangements to protect children from harm. (Balls, in HM Government, 2009: foreword)

Subsequent policy documents published in the run-up to the 2010 general election also sought to defend Labour's progressive universalism approach. In *Support for All: The Families and Relationships Green Paper* (DCSF, 2010), there is a shift in tone from ECM and *The Children's Plan*, where the 'child' was situated at the heart of children's services policy. This Green Paper's emphasis on the importance of 'family' in bringing up children mirrored the narrative invoked in the Conservative Party's Broken Britain discourse and the CSJ's (2010) alternative 'Green Paper on the family', also published in the run-up to the 2010 general election. However, notwithstanding this presentational shift, the progressive universalism perspective is retained. Whereas the CSJ Green Paper emphasised the behavioural traits of dysfunctional families, the DCSF's Green Paper states:

> When examined overall, inequality can be seen as an important theme running through these family trends. For example, there is a marked contrast between the new opportunities being enjoyed by many young women from families on middle and higher incomes and the very limited horizons that teenage mothers, living in deprived areas, often describe. This emphasises the importance of ensuring modern family policy is *progressively universal* making available some help for everyone, with more directed at supporting those children and families who need help the most. (DCSF, 2010: 25, emphasis added)

In the run-up to the 2010 election, both Labour and the Conservatives acknowledged that reducing the budget deficit following the global financial crisis had to be a priority in the coming years. Both parties also accepted that significant savings to public expenditure would need to be made. However, no plans were presented detailing how these savings would be achieved and which services might be protected. Debate over children's policy in the final months of the Labour government continued to reflect the different ideological perspectives of the two parties. Alongside Balls's defence of Labour's children's policy, the government passed the Child Poverty Act 2010 just before the election to try to bind the next government to Labour's child poverty targets and protect tax and benefit changes. In contrast, the Conservatives advocated more targeted policies focused on addressing the behavioural problems of a smaller cohort of families.

Discussion

The creation of the DCSF and the development of *The Children's Plan* were designed to address resistance to the ECM reform agenda in Whitehall and beyond, whilst Blair remained in office. *The Children's Plan* (DCSF, 2007) signalled that the new Brown led government expected schools to focus on both the welfare *and* achievement of pupils, as well as contribute to the establishment of new children's trust arrangements in their local areas. Balls also promoted a shift in youth policy away from the more authoritarian aspects of Labour's approach under Blair, and towards a greater emphasis on early intervention, prevention and the provision of positive activities for young people. These adjustments to Labour policy underline the argument, made in previous chapters, that intra-party tensions played a key role in shaping children's services policy under the Blair–Brown coalition.

On the other hand, analysis of the Baby P case has confirmed that inquiries and scandals can be a key driver of policy change. The case exposed a fault-line in Labour's ECM reform programme and its response to the Victoria Climbié inquiry. Thus, Balls asked Lord Laming to produce a second report to examine progress made in relation to safeguarding and child protection since the inquiry. Lord Laming (2009) remained concerned about the insufficient prioritisation of safeguarding and child protection at the national and local levels. Balls's decision to ask Gibb to set up the SWTF showed that the government now recognised that not enough had been done to address the challenges faced by social workers working at the sharp end of safeguarding and child protection practice. However, the development of children's policy under the Brown government also continued to be shaped by wider party-political pressures. The Baby P case received the volume and ferocity of coverage that it did because Cameron identified it as a political opportunity to attack Labour's record and promote alternative Conservative social policies. Moreover, in the run-up to the 2010 election, Labour ministers and Conservative spokespeople promoted different social policies informed by competing analyses of poverty. Labour ministers defended the government's progressive universalism approach to tackling economic inequalities, while the Conservatives promoted more targeted policies to address the most problematic families. In this period, *inter*-party competition replaced *intra*-party competition as one of the key drivers of children's policy.

PART II

Children's services reform under the Coalition and Conservative governments (2010–19)

7

The priorities of the Coalition and Conservative government leaders

Introduction

> We will significantly accelerate the reduction of the structural deficit over the course of a Parliament, with the main burden of deficit reduction borne by reduced spending rather than increased taxes. (HM Government, 2010b: 15)

> People in troubled families aren't worthless or pre-programmed to fail. I won't allow them to be written off. So, we must get out there, help them turn their lives around and heal the scars of a broken society. (Cameron, 2011)

> [The government] is understandably focused on Brexit and does not seem to have the necessary bandwidth to ensure that the rhetoric of healing social division is matched with the reality. (Milburn, 2017)

The formation of the Conservative–Liberal Democrat Coalition government after the 2010 election created a great deal of uncertainty regarding the future direction of children's services policy. On the one hand, it was clear that, following the global financial crisis, reducing the UK's budget deficit would have major implications for spending on public services. Yet, party leaders continued to emphasise the importance of social policy. Cameron claimed that he was still committed to improving *social justice*, and the Liberal Democrat leader, Nick Clegg, had campaigned to improve *social mobility* during the election. In 2016, after taking over from Cameron following the victory for the Leave campaign in the EU referendum, Theresa May (2016) promised to 'make Britain a country that works not for a privileged few, but for every one of us'. Thus, this chapter focuses on the interest and involvement of the Coalition and Conservative governments' leaders in the development of social policies affecting children and families, complimenting the discussion of Blair's and Brown's involvement in Chapter 2.

The first section of the chapter considers the approach taken to tackling the UK's budget deficit. The way in which spending reductions were tied to government efforts to restructure public services is discussed in the second section. The third section considers the extent to which improving social justice and/or social mobility remained a priority under the leadership of Cameron and Clegg. The influence of the Treasury over welfare reform is discussed in the fourth section. Policy developments since May succeeded Cameron as Prime Minister in 2016 are discussed in the final section. Previous chapters covering the Labour government have demonstrated the importance of understanding the development of children's services policy within the context of wider economic and social policies and the priorities of party leaders. Thus, this chapter provides the essential context for the more detailed discussions on children's policy in Chapters 8 and 9.

Deficit reduction

The Coalition: Our Programme for Government (HM Government, 2010b) confirmed that deficit reduction would be the government's most important priority and that this implied substantial cuts in public spending. The detail of specific cuts to be made started to emerge in the weeks and months immediately after the election. Signalling the urgency attached to deficit reduction, £6 billion of in-year savings were announced by Chancellor George Osborne in an emergency Budget in June 2010. However, the full extent of the government's approach only emerged following the publication of the Spending Review in October 2010. It was stated that 'The Spending Review sets out how the Coalition Government will carry out Britain's unavoidable deficit reduction plan. This is an urgent priority to secure economic stability at a time of continuing uncertainty in the global economy and put Britain's public services and welfare system on a sustainable long-term footing' (HM Treasury, 2010: 5). The review revealed the scale and pace of the government's deficit reduction plan. Osborne's ambition was to eliminate the UK's structural deficit – the gap between revenue and expenditure – by 2014/15 (Dorey and Garnett, 2016: 60). The Director of the Institute for Fiscal studies at the time, Robert Chote, described the plan as 'the longest, deepest, sustained period of cuts to public services spending at least since the Second World War' (quoted in Timmins, 2017: 662).

The savings required were not spread evenly across policy areas or government departments. Osborne demanded that the DfE make budget savings of 12 per cent by 2014/15 (HM Treasury, 2010: 41) on top of the £670 million in-year cut announced in the emergency Budget. However, a commitment to protect funding for schools meant that the burden fell heavily on other areas of children's policy (this is discussed in more detail in Chapter 8). The impact that this would have on services was compounded by the announcement that funding for local government would be reduced by 28 per cent over the same period (HM Treasury, 2010: 49). Osborne also demanded that £11 billion be cut from the welfare budget (HM Treasury, 2010: 68), though this figure continued to rise during the course of the Parliament (Timmins, 2017: 662). Furthermore, Osborne protected spending on payments to older people, even though this accounted for 46 per cent of the welfare budget (Dorey and Garnett, 2016: 137–8). Thus, Labour's policy of using the tax and benefits system to support families and reduce child poverty was abandoned. For Osborne, cuts to spending in this area were politically expedient insofar as they played into the rhetoric of 'skivers' versus 'strivers' in the popular press (D'Ancona, 2013: 94).

However, it became clear in the following years that Osborne's plan to eliminate the structural deficit ahead of an election in 2015 was not achievable. The Chancellor's forecasts had relied not only on the delivery of spending reductions, but also on what turned out to be overly optimistic forecasts for economic growth. Osborne's 'Plan B' involved extending the timetable for public sector austerity to 2018/19 (Johnson and Chandler, 2015: 172–3; Dorey and Garnett, 2016: 61–6). Significantly, this required deeper cuts to public spending. The National Audit Office (NAO, 2018a) reported that funding allocated to local government by central government fell by 49.1 per cent in real terms between 2010/11 and 2017/18. Taking account of council tax receipts, spending power fell by 28.6 per cent. However, it also important to appreciate disparities between local authorities. A report by the think tank Centre for Cities (2019) points out that it is local authorities serving the most economically disadvantaged communities, particularly in the north of England, that are most dependent upon central government funding and that saw the most severe cuts to their budgets. For example, reduced spending in Liverpool equated to £816 for every resident, while in Oxford and Luton, spending per head increased between 2009/10 and 2017/18 (Centre for Cities, 2019: 18). Furthermore, these same communities also suffered financially through the withdrawal of welfare payments. Figures obtained by the MP Frank Field show that by 2021, spending on working-age welfare benefits will have fallen by £37 billion (Butler, 2018).

Public service reform

The Coalition leaders framed the deficit reduction plan as necessary and unavoidable. However, critics of the government argued that the plan demonstrated an ideological commitment to 'shrinking the state and opening up more of the public sector to other service providers: charities, not-for-profit organisations, private companies, social entrepreneurs and voluntary bodies' (Dorey and Garnett, 2016: 83). Both the Conservatives and the Liberal Democrats had criticised Labour's centralised approach to public service delivery. Thus, Cameron and Clegg framed the deficit reduction plan as an opportunity reorganise public services and devolve control to the local level. In their joint foreword to the Coalition programme, they stated:

> We share a conviction that the days of big government are over; that centralisation and top-down control have proved a failure. We believe that the time has come to disperse power more widely in Britain today; to recognise that we will only make progress if we help people come together to make life better. In short, it is our ambition to distribute power and opportunity to people rather than hoarding authority within government. That way we can build the free, fair and responsible society we want to see. (Cameron and Clegg, in HM Government, 2010b: foreword)

In the early days of the Coalition, Cameron also talked about the 'Big Society' taking the place of big government. Sharing this ambition, if not the language, Clegg promoted 'radical decentralisation' (Clegg, in HM Government, 2010c: foreword), an idea at the heart of the Localism Act 2011. Clegg repeated the argument that Labour's command-and-control structures needed to be dismantled in order to not only save money, but also spur innovation and make public services more responsive and accountable to the public.

However, in the context of public sector austerity, Coalition and Conservative government leaders were not as closely involved in the restructuring of public services as their Labour predecessors. The rhetoric of decentralisation was used by party leaders to distance themselves from difficult decisions taken in Whitehall departments and at the local level. In contrast, Labour's centralising approach was driven by a desire to ensure that additional resources were allocated to support the government's social policy priorities. Nevertheless, it is important to note that the outsourcing of public services has been consistently promoted as a solution to the challenge of restructuring public services. In the *Open Public Services White Paper* (HM Government, 2011a), it was stated:

> In the services amenable to commissioning, the principles of open public services will switch the default from one where the state provides the service itself to one where the state commissions the service from a range of diverse providers. Commissioning public services in this way – what is known as the purchaser/provider split – brings a host of benefits. For example, it encourages new, innovative providers to compete for contracts, allows payment by results and/or incentives for supporting particular social groups to be built into contracts, and enables the disaggregation of services into specialist functions. (HM Government, 2011a: 29)

The *Open Public Services White Paper* did not set out any specific plans in relation to the commissioning of children's services. Moreover, the idea of outsourcing welfare services to the private and voluntary sectors was nothing new (Jones, 2019). This perspective on the organisation of public services is highlighted here because it informed government thinking on the delivery of welfare services, and particularly how ministers responded to 'inadequate' local services. Chapter 9 includes a more in-depth discussion of this perspective and the implications for the organisation of local children's services.

Social policy under Cameron and Clegg

After becoming party leader in December 2005, Cameron had spoken of his intention to modernise the Conservative Party and reposition it on the electoral centre ground after three successive election defeats. The development of an alternative approach to social policy was central to this endeavour. Cameron had implied that a future Conservative government would commit to the better targeting of social policy initiatives and not completely abandon policies inherited from Labour. However, the unfolding financial crisis of 2008 provided Cameron with the opportunity to attack Labour's economic record and return to more traditional Conservative policy ground. Indeed, the financial crisis 'formed the backdrop to the 2010 election and the formation of the coalition government' (Johnson and Chandler, 2015: 159). Furthermore, reducing the budget deficit became the main priority of the new government. However, even in this context, Cameron and

Clegg claimed that they remained committed to the development of policies to improve social justice and social mobility. Cameron wanted to continue to position the Conservative Party on the electoral middle ground. Moreover, this made it easier for Clegg to justify his decision to commit the Liberal Democrats to working alongside the Conservatives.

Cameron and social justice

Cameron's decision to ask Labour MP Frank Field to oversee a review of policy on tackling child poverty conveyed the impression that the Coalition was committed to the development of new non-partisan social policies. Field was a long-standing campaigner on child poverty and therefore well qualified to lead the review. On the other hand, his opposition to the Brown Treasury's tax and benefits reforms was well known (Driver and Martell, 2006: 101). His report for the Coalition published in December 2010 was titled *The Foundation Years: Preventing Poor Children Becoming Poor Adults* (Field, 2010). The report emphasised the role of public services in supporting families to address a wide range of issues that could not be addressed through benefit payments alone (Field, 2010: 12), suggesting that:

> The evidence about the importance of the pre-school years to children's life chances as adults points strongly to an alternative approach that focuses on directing government policy and spending to developing children's capabilities in the early-years.... The Review recommends that the Government gradually moves funding to the early-years, and that this funding is weighted toward the most disadvantaged children as we build the evidence base of effective programmes. (Field, 2010: 6)

Perhaps anticipating Field's recommendation, Cameron had also commissioned Labour MP Graham Allen to conduct a review of early intervention policy. Allen's report was published in January 2011, a month after Field's, and addressed the question of the evidence base for social policy interventions focused primarily on the pre-school years. The choice of Allen to lead this was also significant. Like Field, Allen was somewhat of an outsider in the Labour Party and had not been closely involved in the development of social policy under the Labour government. Furthermore, Allen had already worked with Duncan-Smith and the CSJ on a new approach to children's policy (Allen and Duncan-Smith, 2008), as the discussion in Chapter 6 highlighted.

Allen's (2011) report for the Coalition, titled *Early Intervention: The Next Steps*, built on this earlier report.

Echoing Field, Allen recommended that public spending be redirected towards 'evidence-based' early intervention programmes targeted at pre-school children and their families. According to Allen, this required a shift towards more specific and accredited early intervention programmes directed at the most vulnerable children and families. This repeated the message in Allen's earlier report co-authored with Duncan-Smith by challenging the progressive universalism approach to children's services at the heart of ECM. One of Allen's key recommendations was the establishment of an Early Intervention Foundation (EIF) to lead on the evaluation of existing programmes and to build the evidence base for early intervention (Allen, 2011: xvii). Cameron later agreed to implement this recommendation, and the establishment of the EIF was announced by Duncan-Smith to coincide with the publication of *Social Justice: Transforming Lives* (HM Government, 2012). However, Allen did not recommend the radical reorganisation of local children's services. Seeking to reassure those working in the sector, he stated:

> Much excellent work has been done, at both local and national level, but new and additional lines of attack are needed. That is the purpose of this Report and no one need fear its proposals. They will not threaten any effective policies which are now in place, nor provide any excuse or rationale for cutbacks. Instead, they offer sharper tools to measure the execution and impact of Early Intervention, to improve the execution and impact of successful policies, to make more effective use of current public expenditure and to achieve lasting cost savings in later years. (Allen, 2011: ix)

Allen envisaged a pivotal role for Labour's Sure Start children's centres. He also recognised the vital importance of close working across organisational and professional boundaries, stating that 'Local authorities with their health partners also have a key role to play in promoting and brokering integrated working at a local level' (Allen, 2011: 54). The structural reforms introduced under the Children Act 2004 had been designed to support this.

However, arguably, Cameron's flagship social policy was the Troubled Families programme. Officially launched by Cameron in December 2011, this programme was presented as the government's response to riots that spread across the country in August 2011. In contrast with the Field and Allen reviews, which had emphasised the need to support families with young children, the Troubled Families programme promised tougher action to address the problem behaviours of older children and their parents. The authoritarian rhetoric of the programme was reminiscent of Blair's 'ASBO politics' and drew heavily on the Broken Britain analysis of the behavioural determinants of poverty and social exclusion. The programme was also notable for the bold promise made to 'turn around' the lives of 120,000 families; £448 million was committed to support the development of services to work with these families and address a range of behavioural issues linked to the 'five pathways to poverty' (Crossley, 2018). However, the launch of the Troubled Families programme provided further evidence that Cameron remained interested in social policy despite the government's prioritisation of deficit reduction.

Clegg and social mobility

In the run-up to the 2010 election, Clegg also commissioned a review of his party's position on social policy. Clegg asked Martin Narey to chair the Independent Commission on Social Mobility. At the time, Narey was the Chief Executive of Barnardo's and, in this position, also chair of the End Child Poverty Coalition. The commission made a series of recommendations in six key areas of policy: child poverty, early years, education, employment, health and communities (Independent Commission on Social Mobility, 2009). Significantly, the commission's analysis emphasised the impact of child poverty and the continued importance of redistributive policies even in the context of the financial crisis. The report stated:

> As we face the challenge of the present economic downturn, there are those who argue that we cannot afford more investment to give disadvantaged children more equal life-chances. This Commission argues that we can't afford not to…. Low income affects every aspect of children's lives: health, housing, education and family life. Low income puts children's standard of living well below what most people would deem an acceptable level for a country as wealthy as the UK. (Independent Commission on Social Mobility, 2009: 4–5)

The commission also called for continued investment in early-years settings and schools to address the challenges faced by families in the most disadvantaged communities (Independent Commission on Social Mobility, 2009: 9–11). Both recommendations were consistent with Labour's child poverty strategy and the principle of progressive universalism. The subsequent election manifesto of the Liberal Democrats (2010) called for additional funding for struggling school pupils and for there to be no increase in university tuition fees.

During negotiations with the Conservatives, Clegg agreed to abandon the pledge on university tuition fees. However, he did get Cameron to agree to establish the Pupil Premium, through which an additional £2.5 billion was allocated to schools to provide additional support for the most economically disadvantaged pupils. An additional £760 million was also secured to fund free early education places for two year olds from poorer families. Clegg also later succeeded in getting Cameron to agree to the introduction of free school meals for all infant schoolchildren. The Coalition's approach to improving social mobility was rationalised in the report *Opening Doors, Breaking Barriers: A Strategy for Social Mobility* (HM Government, 2011b). The report, introduced by Clegg, tied the Liberal Democrats' perspective on social mobility to the Conservatives' perspective on social justice and the 'five pathways to poverty', while simultaneously defending an approach closer to Labour's progressive universalism. The report states:

> Our work to increase social mobility complements the Government's ambitious agenda for social justice. We have a group of people in our society who have become detached, unable to play a productive role in the workplace, in their families or in their communities. They are often trapped by addiction, debt, educational failure, family breakdown or welfare dependency. Our social mobility strategy is about enabling people to move up the ladder of life. Our strategy for social justice is about helping these people get their foot onto the first rung. The two are inseparable components in our fight against poverty and disadvantage.... *We will take a progressive approach, focusing most resources on those from disadvantaged backgrounds*, but narrowing gaps in opportunity all the way up the income scale. (HM Government, 2011b: 11, emphasis added)

Welfare reform and the Treasury

The decision to appoint Iain Duncan-Smith as Secretary of State for Work and Pensions also suggested that Cameron remained committed to the implementation of new policies on social justice. Duncan-Smith had played a central role in the review of the Conservative Party's approach to social policy and the development of the Broken Britain framework. More specifically, it signalled Cameron's commitment to Duncan-Smith's plans for a radical overhaul of the benefits system and the implementation of Universal Credit. Over the past ten years, the implementation of Universal Credit has been beset by repeated delays and increasing costs (NAO, 2018b). Toynbee and Walker (2015: 121–2) argue that the botched implementation of Universal Credit may have been part of a deliberate ploy by Conservative ministers to discourage people from claiming benefits. Moreover, some ministers, including Osborne, pandered to media depictions of benefit claimants as 'skivers' (D'Ancona, 2013: 94) and displayed little sympathy for those affected by these implementation problems.

However, Dorey and Garnett (2016: 144) point out that those involved in the development of the original proposal for Universal Credit, including Duncan-Smith, 'studiously sought to avoid accusing the "workless" of being lazy or workshy, and instead focused primarily on the perverse incentives or practical obstacles which the social security system placed in the way of claimants who genuinely sought paid employment'. In office, Duncan-Smith continued to frame welfare reform, alongside other measures to address the five pathways to poverty, as part of the new Conservative approach to delivering social justice. In his foreword to *21st Century Welfare* (DWP, 2010: foreword), he states:

> Too often governments have tried to tackle poverty but ended up managing its symptoms. The changes outlined here are based on a recognition that poverty cannot be tackled through treating the symptoms alone.... The only way to make a sustainable difference is by tackling the root causes of poverty: family breakdown; education failure; drug and alcohol addiction; severe personal indebtedness; and economic dependency. These problems are interrelated and their solutions lie in society as a whole. However, we must recognise that the benefits system has an important role to play in supporting personal responsibility and helping to mend social ills. We are going to end the culture of worklessness and dependency that has done so much harm to individuals, families and whole communities.

Furthermore, Duncan-Smith also played a lead role in the development of cross-departmental social policies. In the Coalition's *A New Approach to Child Poverty* (HM Government, 2011c: 2), Duncan-Smith repeated earlier Conservative Party criticism of Labour's tax and benefits reforms and repeated calls for a focus on 'the powerful drivers that keep the most disadvantaged families from leaving poverty behind'. The publication of this report fulfilled a legal obligation under Labour's Child Poverty Act 2010. A year later, Duncan-Smith reframed the government's overarching approach to social policy in the report *Social Justice: Transforming Lives* (HM Government, 2012). The Broken Britain perspective on poverty was again evident in Duncan-Smith's foreword, which stated:

> For too long we have measured our success in tackling poverty in terms of the simplistic concept of income transfer. This strategy sets out a much more ambitious approach, aspiring to deliver Social Justice through life change which goes much wider than increases in family income alone. Social Justice must be about changing and improving lives, and the different ways this can be achieved. (Duncan-Smith, in HM Government, 2012: foreword)

The launch of this report was timed to coincide with the announcement that the government would fund the establishment of the EIF, as recommended by Allen's (2011) review. This appeared to signal the government's ongoing commitment to the development of targeted early intervention services and the refocusing, rather than the abandonment, of children's policy initiatives set up under Labour.

However, any assessment of the Coalition and Conservative governments' approach to social policy must consider the role played by the Treasury. As Dorey and Garnett explain:

> Although welfare reform was formally the remit of the Department for Work and Pensions, headed by Iain Duncan-Smith, the more immediate pursuit of significant savings in the social security budget was largely inspired by the Conservative Chancellor, George Osborne, who clearly viewed welfare spending as a soft target and was not hampered by excessive sentimentality towards benefit recipients. (2016: 138)

Osborne was not an admirer of Duncan-Smith and was not convinced by his ideas on improving social justice, including his plans for Universal Credit (D'Ancona, 2013: ch 5; Timmins, 2017: 699–700). Osborne only signed up to funding the development of Universal Credit after Duncan-Smith committed the Department for Work and Pensions (DWP) to finding substantial savings from the budget for working-age benefits. In the 2010 Spending Review, Osborne had announced that pensions and benefits for older people would be protected, while savings of £11 billion from working-age benefits would be made. A wholly unrealistic timetable for the delivery of Universal Credit was set and Duncan-Smith was also forced to except that benefit payments would be withdrawn at that rate of 65 pence for every pound earned as individuals transitioned from benefits and into work, rather than the 55 per cent that he had wanted (Timmins, 2017: 700). Furthermore, the £11 billion savings announced by Osborne in 2010 turned out to be just the tip of the iceberg, as emphasised earlier. Osborne repeatedly raided the working-age welfare budget between 2010 and 2015 as it became clear that his original plan to reduce the deficit could not be delivered. Speaking after the 2015 election, Osborne (2015) boasted that the Coalition had delivered savings of £21 billion.

Measures introduced to deliver these savings included a 1 per cent limit on increases to benefits and the introduction of a £26,000 benefits cap. Specific steps to limit spending on housing benefits included the introduction of what came to be known as the 'bedroom tax' for benefit claimants judged to have additional bedrooms that they did not need (officially, this was referred to as the withdrawal of the spare-room subsidy). Benefit claimants judged not to be committed to seeking work faced the prospect of tougher sanctions, including being struck off Job Seekers Allowance for three years. However, it was the treatment of people previously judged unable to work that created the greatest controversy. The private company Atos, commissioned by the DWP, was widely criticised for its insensitive management of crude work-capability tests that led to many individuals with serious illnesses or disabilities being instructed to find work or face the withdrawal of their benefit payments (Dorey and Garnett, 2016: ch 5; Timmins, 2017: 701–2).

Osborne's drive to slash the working-age welfare budget created considerable tension between the Treasury and the DWP, but also with the Liberal Democrats. Liberal Democrat Children's Minister Sarah Teather openly campaigned against the government's 2012 Welfare Reform Bill, forcing Clegg to sack her in September 2012. The Coalition's approach to welfare reform marked a clear reversal of Labour's approach to reducing child poverty but also contradicted claims made by the Coalition leaders that the government was committed to improving social justice and social mobility. Furthermore, even after £21 billion had been saved under the Coalition government,

Osborne continued to raid the working-age welfare budget. In his July 2015 Budget, after the Conservatives had won a majority at the 2015 general election, Osborne demonstrated that his attitude towards welfare had not changed. He stated:

> We have to move Britain from a low-wage, high-tax, high-welfare society to a higher-wage, lower-tax, lower-welfare economy. For Britain is home to 1% of the world's population; generates 4% of the world's income; and yet pays out 7% of the world's welfare spending. It is not fair to the taxpayers paying for it. It needs to change. Welfare spending is not sustainable and it crowds out spending on things like education and infrastructure that are vital to securing the real welfare of the people. (Osborne, 2015)

In the same speech, he announced that 'we need to find at least a further £12 billion of welfare savings' over the course of the new Parliament. Again, these savings would be taken from the working-age welfare budget as pensions and benefits paid to older people remained protected. Steps announced to deliver these savings included; scrapping the entitlement of 18–21 year olds to housing benefit; a requirement for lone parents whose youngest child is three years old or more to find work; lowering the benefits cap to £23,000; and the removal of additional tax credits or Universal Credit for families with more than two children. Significant savings would also be made by freezing the amount payable to individuals and families through all working-age benefits and by lowering the income threshold for those eligible for working tax credits or Universal Credit (Osborne, 2015). When Osborne returned to raid the welfare budget yet again in March 2016, Duncan-Smith resigned in protest. In his resignation letter to Cameron, he stated that 'There has been too much emphasis on money saving exercises and not enough awareness from the Treasury, in particular, that the government's vision of a new welfare-to-work system could not be repeatedly salami-sliced' (Duncan-Smith, 2016). By now, Duncan-Smith appeared to accept that cuts to welfare had gone too far and that his original vision for the reform of the welfare system could not be realised. The final straw proved to be Osborne's decision to remove £1.3 billion from the personal independence payment for people with disabilities while, at the same time, announcing a tax cut for the highest earners (Timmins, 2017: 703).

However, this decision must be viewed in the context of a welfare reform programme that was not delivering on the promises made by

Conservative reformers. In June 2018, the NAO (2018b) reported that the scheduled full roll-out of Universal Credit had slipped from October 2017 to March 2023. It was also reported that one in five benefits claimants who had switched to Universal Credit reported not receiving full payments on time. The NAO report also highlighted the pressure that the programme placed on local government and community organisations forced to step in to support Universal Credit claimants experiencing difficulties, linking this to the expansion of food banks. Moreover, the cumulative impact of a decade of public sector austerity and welfare reform on children and families is stark. The Joseph Rowntree Foundation (2018) reported that 4.1 million children living in the UK now live in poverty, a rise of half a million between 2011/12 and 2016/17. Furthermore, it is reported that:

> In the last five years, poverty rates have been rising for all types of working families – whether they are lone-parent or couple families and regardless of the number of adults in work or whether they are part-time or full-time workers. This is the first period in the last two decades when this has happened. It is striking that the rise has been driven by the risk of poverty rising for children in all types of working families, not by changes to how many children live in couple or lone-parent families, or by changes in the numbers of children in families with different numbers of workers or amounts of work. (Joseph Rowntree Foundation, 2018: 3–4)

After the referendum

The 2015 Conservative Party election manifesto promised a referendum on the UK's membership of the EU. Having helped to secure a small majority for the Conservatives at the election, Cameron decided that the referendum would take place early, and a vote was scheduled for June 2016, just a year into the new Parliament. Campaigning on the referendum and the splits that this exposed within the ruling party inevitably dominated the remainder of Cameron's premiership. Nonetheless, even in the context of the forthcoming referendum, and the ongoing austerity measures described earlier, Cameron continued to proclaim his commitment to improving social justice. In a speech delivered in January 2016, Cameron (2016) defended the Coalition's record on social policy and announced that the government would publish a new Life Chances Strategy in the spring. The speech marked a return to the Broken Britain perspective and the argument that improving opportunity was about more than reducing material poverty (Mason, 2016). However, the strategy was not published on time, and following victory for the Leave campaign in the EU referendum, Cameron resigned as Prime Minister.

Following her election as Conservative Party leader in July 2016, Theresa May famously declared that 'Brexit means Brexit'. This sound bite provided no indication of what the UK's future relationship with the EU would look like; however, it was clear that May's main priority was to secure the UK's withdrawal from the EU. Yet, May also set out to try to make sure that her premiership would not be exclusively defined by Brexit (Allen, 2018: 111). As she entered Downing Street, she praised Cameron for his work on economic policy, but also for his commitment to social justice. Positioning herself alongside Cameron as a 'One Nation' Conservative, May (2016) promised that 'As we leave the European Union, we will forge a bold new positive role for ourselves in the world, and we will make Britain a country that works not for a privileged few, but for every one of us.' In September 2016, the new Prime Minister announced that she would chair a Cabinet Committee on Social Reform and work to ensure that the government supported not only the most vulnerable members of society, but also those who 'just about manage' (Prime Minister's Office, 2016).

However, when faced with the reality of trying to deliver Brexit, other 'difficult issues were pushed to the side-lines of politics' (Wincott, 2018: 15). The government's lack of attention to social policy was indicated by the announcement in December 2016 that the Life Chances Strategy promised by Cameron had been shelved (Puffett, 2016). In the same month, it was also confirmed that the cross-government Child Poverty Policy Unit had been abolished (Lepper, 2016). May's job was made even more difficult when she lost the Conservative Party's majority in Parliament after calling a snap election in 2017, forcing her to enter into a confidence-and-supply agreement with the Democratic Unionist Party. The en bloc resignation of the independent Social Mobility Commission in December 2017 further highlighted the government's lack of focus on social policy. In his resignation letter to May, the commission's chair, Alan Milburn (2017), concluded that the government is 'understandably focused on Brexit and does not seem to have the necessary bandwidth to ensure that the rhetoric of healing social division is matched with the reality'. Twelve months later in December 2018, the chairs of six cross-party select committees, two of whom were Conservatives, released a joint statement expressing concern at the government's lack of focus on policies not directly connected to Brexit. They commented that:

> Long-drawn-out arguments over Brexit and delays in reaching an agreement on our future relationship with the EU are having a serious detrimental effect on the conduct of wider domestic policy. MPs of all parties and ministers should be addressing the most urgent challenges facing our country: safeguarding our NHS, improving social care for the elderly; stepping up the fight against crime and knife crime; sorting out our benefits system; improving our public transport and safeguarding the environment for future generations. The Prime Minister should return to addressing burning social injustices which she insisted, on entering Downing Street, would be her main priority. Instead, Brexit is sucking the life out of government at a time when our towns, cities and citizens face serious spending restraints. Rather than continuing to drag out the Brexit process for months more, we must bring it to a close if we are to prevent serious damage to our country. (Quoted in Helm and Courea, 2018)

Discussion

One of the central aims of this book has been to assess the importance of the political drivers of children's services policy. It has been demonstrated in previous chapters that the development of children's services policy between 1997 and 2010 was heavily shaped by the interest and involvement of the Labour leadership. The purpose of this chapter has therefore been to examine the policy priorities of the leaders of the Coalition and Conservative governments as a first step towards assessing the development of children's services policy since the 2010 election. The Coalition leaders were much less interested and directly involved in the development of policy in this area compared to Blair and Brown. This can partly be explained by the need to address the budget deficit inherited from Labour following the global financial crisis beginning in 2008. However, the target to eliminate the deficit within five years, and the decision to prioritise cuts in public spending over increasing taxes, had major implications for the public sector, including children's services. Although Cameron and Clegg promoted this as an opportunity to decentralise control over public services and extend the involvement of private and voluntary sector organisations, this also helped to distance the government from the difficult decisions that needed to be made regarding the organisation of public services at the local level. This stood in marked contrast to the much closer involvement of the Labour leadership in shaping policy-delivery structures for children's services.

On the other hand, both Cameron and Clegg claimed that the Coalition government was also committed to improving social justice and social mobility. Policy reviews on child poverty and early intervention, as well as the appointment of Duncan-Smith as Secretary of State for Work and Pensions, suggested that Cameron remained committed to the modernisation of Conservative social policy, as he had promised in opposition. Furthermore, Cameron also agreed to the introduction of the Pupil Premium, additional funding for early-years places for disadvantaged two year olds and universal free school meals for infant schoolchildren as concessions to the Liberal Democrats. New resources were also allocated in 2011 to fund the Troubled Families programme. Taken together, these measures indicate that even in the context of austerity, the government had not abandoned social policy altogether. However, the Treasury's repeated raids on the working-age welfare budget pulled in a different direction. Moreover, the rhetoric surrounding welfare reform signalled a shift away from Conservative modernisation, and back towards the 'moral authoritarianism that characterised the traditional Thatcherite approach to society' (Hayton and McEnhill, 2015: 144). Although May sought to align herself alongside Cameron as a Conservative moderniser, she was not able to steer the development of social policy while the resources of No 10 were being channelled into the enormous task of delivering Brexit. The purpose of Chapters 8 and 9 is to examine how these tensions and contradictions in policy, and the relative lack of engagement from party leaders, affected the development of children's services policy at the departmental level.

8

Schools reform and early intervention

Introduction

> Education reform is the great progressive cause of our times. It is only through reforming education that we can allow every child the chance to take their full and equal share of citizenship, shaping their own destiny, and becoming masters of their own fate. (Gove, in DfE, 2010: foreword)

> It is our ambition that Academy status should be the norm for all state schools, with schools enjoying direct funding and full independence from central and local bureaucracy. (DfE, 2010: 52)

> This Government believes that local areas are best placed to understand the needs of their local communities, to commission early intervention services to meet those needs and to deliver interventions. (Government response to the Science and Technology Select Committee's [2018] recommendation that a national early intervention strategy be put in place. (Cited in Lepper, 2019)

Michael Gove was appointed Secretary of State after shadowing Ed Balls since 2007 but the immediate renaming of the department signalled a change in course on children's services policy. In Gove's 'Department for Education', the overriding priority was the implementation of schools reform, even though responsibility for other aspects of children's policy was retained. Moreover, schools reform continued to be prioritised by the secretaries of state who followed Gove. The first section of the chapter examines the development of Gove's schools reform programme, considering the implications for the role played by schools in supporting the welfare of children. The second section examines the development of early intervention policy, taking account of Osborne's deficit reduction programme, but also Cameron's proclaimed commitment to early intervention policy and improving social justice. Policy developments on children's centres and youth services provide a good illustration of the approach taken. The final section considers the extent to which developments in early intervention policy have affected relations between government policymakers and children's sector NGOs. Thus, this chapter, alongside Chapter 9, assesses the extent to which children's services reform continued to be driven by political imperatives following the 2010 election.

The prioritisation of schools reform

The immediate renaming of the department provided an early indication that Gove was not committed to the integrated approach to education and children's policy of his Labour predecessor, and that education policy would be his overriding priority. However, the broader welfare focus of Labour's ECM framework was never officially abandoned. Tim Loughton had served as a Shadow Children's Minister since 2001 and was appointed as a junior Children's Minister serving under Gove. In this post, Loughton led on child protection and social work policy, sitting within the CYP Directorate – the section of the department responsible for all non-education aspects of children's policy. Reflecting on the Coalition's stance on ECM, he commented:

> 'It [ECM] was one of those things you had to go along with. There was no great enthusiasm for ECM.... I always saw it as a slightly gimmicky way of trying to distil down 'We believe in children, aren't we great?'. It was motherhood and apple pie. I'm not interested in the slogans. I'm much more interested in – are the services being provided that will aid those outcomes that ECM articulates? We never got excited by ECM. But in the same way, when we came into power, we did not abolish it. We were accused of 'Oh, you abolished ECM', but we never did. There was never a piece of legislation that says ECM is now defunct, this is what we do. It just naturally evolved.' (Interview with Tim Loughton)

However, Gove's position on the ECM five outcomes was slightly different. Speaking to the Education Select Committee a couple of months into his new post, Gove explained that 'They [the five ECM outcomes] are unimpeachable – gospel, even. But the point I would make is that in a way they are what every teacher will want to do....

I don't think you need a massive bureaucratic superstructure to police it' (House of Commons Education Committee, 2010). In Gove's view, the ECM reform programme had provided a distraction from the department's traditional policy agenda. Gove prioritised raising educational standards and initially showed little interest other aspects of children's policy. In the same meeting of the Education Select Committee, he stated:

> Sometimes people say, 'You really need to emphasise well-being, because there's too much emphasis sometimes on attainment.' I know where folk are coming from when they say that, but my own view is that if you come from a working-class background, what you want is a school where you will be well taught and where you will receive the qualifications that allow you to decide whether or not you're going to get a good job, go on to college or pursue an apprenticeship. Actually, the single most important thing that a school can do is equip children with the qualifications and self-confidence to take control in the future. (Gove speaking to the House of Commons Education Committee, 28 July 2010)

A similar view was expressed by Gove in November 2010 in his foreword to the White Paper *The Importance of Teaching* (DfE, 2010). Here, he declared that 'Education reform is the great progressive cause of our times. It is only through reforming education that we can allow every child the chance to take their full and equal share of citizenship, shaping their own destiny, and becoming masters of their own fate' (Gove, in DfE, 2010: foreword). Later in the White Paper, it was stated that 'Ofsted has been required to focus too much on inspecting schools against government policies, at the expense of a proper focus on the core function of schools: teaching and learning' (DfE, 2010: 68). This underlined Gove's intention to redirect the school inspection process away from the broader focus on child well-being and the delivery of the ECM five outcomes introduced under Labour's *The Children's Plan* (DCSF, 2007).

Gove's prioritisation of education policy also meant that the burden of meeting the Treasury's departmental savings targets fell heavily on the CYP Directorate. A few months after being sacked in September 2012, Loughton (quoted in Smithers, 2015: 259) complained that 'It was difficult for the children and families agenda to get a look in, in the bulldozer that was the schools reform programme.' Edward Timpson replaced Loughton as the Children's Minister responsible for child protection and social work in September 2012, serving until June 2017 when he lost his seat at the general election. He recalled:

> Prior to my tenure it was clear that there was some heavy lifting going into schools' reform that sucked in a large slice of the DfE resourcing capability. My experience of the department was an understandable, and in many ways necessary, preoccupation with school improvement and standards that at times meant the need for me and my very able team to shout more loudly so as to explain why what we were doing was just as pressing and crucial. There was also the task of better linking child protection/safeguarding into the work on schools to demonstrate the mutual benefit for both policy areas of an equal and strategically coherent footing. (Email correspondence with Edward Timpson, 2019)

Academies, free schools and children's services

The White Paper *The Importance of Teaching* (DfE, 2010) set out a range of schools reform proposals. These included measures relating to behaviour management, the curriculum, exams and the training and career progression of teachers. However, the cornerstone of Gove's reform programme was the expansion of academy schools and the introduction of free schools. In contrast to community schools, academy schools operate independently of local government and receive their funding direct from central government. Academy status was promoted because, it was claimed, greater freedom from 'external control' (DfE, 2010: 9) was key to improving the quality of teaching and raising levels of pupil attainment. Greater autonomy, and more specifically freedom from local authority interference, had been a consistent theme of education policy since the 1980s (Muschamp et al, 1999; Naidoo and Muschamp, 2002). Academies had been introduced under Blair's leadership as the means to turn around the 'failing schools' that local authorities had not succeeded in improving. Between 2003 and 2010, 203 schools became academies under Labour (DfE, 2010: 52).

However, Gove wanted to go much further than previous governments. The establishment of free schools had been included in the Conservative Party's 2010 election manifesto and formed part of his strategy. Free schools would be new schools established and run by parents or local community groups, and would enjoy the same freedoms as academy schools. More significant, and not included in the manifesto, was Gove's plan to convert existing schools to academies (Eyles et al, 2017: 108). Under the Academies Act 2010, introduced two months before the White Paper was published, schools judged by Ofsted to be 'outstanding' could apply for academy status. In November, alongside the publication of the White Paper, it was announced that this invitation would be extended to schools judged to be 'good' (DfE, 2010: 54). Gove was openly hostile towards local authorities and wider education interests, and his ambition for most schools to become academies implied a significantly diminished role for local authorities. As the White Paper stated:

> It is our ambition that Academy status should be the norm for all state schools, with schools enjoying direct funding and full independence from central and local bureaucracy.... We expect schools to use their increased autonomy to explore new ways of working together – but collaboration in the future will be driven by school leaders and teachers – not bureaucrats. (DfE, 2010: 52)

It was noted in Chapter 6 that in the final Labour years, Balls had sought to promote a broader welfare focus in schools and improve the integration of local children's services under children's trust arrangements (DCSF, 2007, 2008a). A new duty for schools to cooperate with children's trusts was introduced under the Apprenticeships and Learning Act 2009. This ensured that legal obligations placed on other children's services agencies under the Children Act 2004 now also applied to schools. However, the emphasis placed on pupil attainment and the autonomy of schools under Gove's reform programme pulled schools in the opposite direction. Gove's desire to disentangle schools from local authority structures was evident when it was announced that the duty for schools to cooperate with children's trusts would be scrapped (DfE, 2010: 29). Ultimately, this plan was blocked in the House of Lords (Whitehead, 2011), but it was clear that Gove did not view the integration of schools alongside other children's services agencies as a priority.

Furthermore, Gove distanced the DfE from Labour policy on children's trusts more generally, suggesting that local areas needed greater freedom to experiment and innovate. In October 2010, Labour's statutory guidance on the development of children's trusts was removed, even though the legal requirement to establish them under the Children Act 2004 remained in place (Easton et al, 2012). In April 2013, the DfE issued revised statutory guidance on the role of the DCS and the LMCS. This reaffirmed the legal status of both roles as set out in the Children Act 2004. However, in addressing concerns that DCSs were increasingly being asked to take on additional responsibilities, the guidance simply stated that 'Local authorities should give due consideration to protecting the discrete roles and responsibilities of the DCS and the LMCS before allocating any additional functions other than children's services' (DfE, 2013a: 4). In March 2018, the ADCS (2018a) reported that in 46 of 152 authorities, the DCS held statutory responsibility for both children's and adults' services.

Although Gove was replaced as Secretary of State in July 2014, there was no discernible change of course following his departure from the ·DfE. In March 2016, Nicky Morgan, Gove's immediate successor, announced that all schools would become academies by 2022 (DfE, 2016a). Opposition from Conservative-led authorities, among others, meant that this target was abandoned just two months later (Weale, 2016). However, in defending this U-turn, Morgan (DfE, 2016b) indicated that the DfE remained committed to extending academy status as far as possible. She stated:

> Making every school an academy is the best way to ensure every child, regardless of birth or background, has access to a world-class education. I am today reaffirming our determination to see all schools become academies. However, having listened to the feedback from Parliamentary colleagues and the education sector we will now change the path to reaching that goal. By focusing our efforts on those schools most at risk of failing young people, and encouraging 'good' and 'outstanding' schools to seize the opportunities of conversion, we will ensure the continued growth of the academy programme, empowering frontline heads and school leads, and transforming even more children's education. (Morgan, in DfE, 2016b)

After May became Prime Minister in July 2016, Morgan was replaced as Secretary of State by Justine Greening. A year later, the DfE opened a consultation on plans to replace LSCBs with new multi-agency safeguarding arrangements. This proposal followed Wood's (2016) review of LSCBs published over a year earlier, though the statutory basis for the change was provided by the Children and Social Work Act 2017. Under LSCBs, it was a requirement for schools to be involved in overseeing local arrangements for safeguarding children. However, under the new arrangements, only local authorities, the police and the health service needed to engage (Puffett, 2017a). In response, the Local Government Association (LGA) warned that 'A failure of schools to engage in local arrangements would create a hole in the system that could fundamentally compromise its effectiveness'. The ADCS also argued against the exclusion of schools from the new multi-agency safeguarding arrangements on the basis that 'education settings typically have the greatest levels of contact with children and young people as a universal service' (quoted in Lepper, 2018a). The British Association of Social Workers (BASW) expressed concern that 'the huge austerity cuts experienced by all three partner agencies will ultimately underpin what the new safeguarding arrangements look like rather than what will work best for children' (quoted in Lepper, 2018b). Notwithstanding these concerns, the decision to replace LSCBs was announced in July 2018 (HM Government, 2018b), by which time Damian Hinds had replaced Greening. In January 2019, Hinds reconfirmed the government's commitment to extending academy status and limiting the influence of 'local bureaucracies' over schools. Responding to the announcement that 50 per cent of state-funded schools in England had now been converted to academies, Hinds stated:

> Whilst there is a huge amount of diversity in our school system – and there are great schools of all types – I want more schools to choose to become an academy and enjoy the enormous benefits it provides to schools, their staff and pupils…. In the past, schools that failed were allowed to stay under local authority control for far too long. Academies have changed all that – failing schools can now be taken away from local bureaucracies who have not been able to improve them and give them to school leaders who can. (Hinds, in DfE, 2019)

Early intervention policy

Cameron claimed to still be committed to the development of new approaches to social policy during the early years of the Coalition, even though the Treasury's deficit reduction plan required significant cuts in public spending. The commissioning of independent policy reviews on child poverty (Field, 2010) and early intervention (Allen, 2011) signalled a refocusing of key areas of children's policy. Concessions offered to the Liberal Democrats on the Pupil Premium, early education funding and free school meals also appeared to indicate that the Coalition leadership was interested in more than schools reform, and that the broader welfare focus of Labour's children's policy had not been abandoned altogether. Furthermore, in March 2012, Cameron agreed to Allen's recommendation to establish the independent EIF. Initial funding of £3.5 million was provided to establish the EIF and its work to develop the evidence base for targeted early interventions. This was announced to coincide with the launch of Duncan-Smith's cross-government strategy *Social Justice: Transforming Lives* (HM Government, 2012). In his foreword, Duncan-Smith re-emphasised the importance of early intervention and preventative services, explaining that 'This starts with support for the most important building block in a child's life – the family – but also covers reform of the school and youth justice systems, the welfare system, and beyond to look at how we can prevent damaging behaviours like substance abuse and offending' (HM Government, 2012: 1). However, the development of Duncan-Smith's strategy required the cooperation of cabinet colleagues, but particularly Gove. It is therefore necessary to consider the DfE's position on early intervention policy in more detail.

Early intervention funding

Like Osborne, Gove was also not an enthusiastic supporter of Duncan-Smith's efforts to implement a new approach to tackling social justice. Gove argued that raising levels of achievement in schools was the key to improving the life chances of poorer children, as noted earlier. On the other hand, he was not openly critical of Duncan-Smith's work on social justice and recognised its continued importance to Cameron. Thus, the position he adopted on early intervention policy matched his position on Labour's ECM framework. Gove acknowledged the importance of providing services to address a broad range of social problems faced by children and families. However, he argued that the refocusing of services that Duncan-Smith advocated was best led at the local level and did not need to be directed from the centre. Moreover, this chimed with declarations made by both Cameron and Clegg that the Coalition would dismantle Labour's bureaucratic apparatus and devolve power away from Whitehall. In December 2010, it was announced that all the separate ring-fenced grants used under Labour to direct investment in children's services would be replaced by a single Early Intervention Grant (EIG) for every English local authority. Graham Allen welcomed the announcement, which was made just a month before his policy review was published, commenting that 'The essence of the grant ties in with the thinking of my review'. Gove explained that the EIG would provide a 'new flexibility to enable local authorities to act more strategically and target investment early, where it will have the greatest impact' (BBC, 2010).

However, the devolution of decision-making for early intervention policy was not driven by a commitment to the autonomy of local authorities. After all, under the academies and free schools programmes local authorities were portrayed as inefficient bureaucracies that stifled change and innovation. Rather, it enabled Gove to distance the DfE from the impact of spending cuts and the reorganisation and closure of services such as children's centres and youth services, without explicitly contradicting the Coalition leaders' proclaimed commitment to the refocusing of early intervention services. Furthermore, this approach allowed Gove to reduce the size and capacity of the CYP Directorate in order to protect resources for schools' policymaking, whilst also meeting the Treasury's savings targets.

The introduction of the EIG in 2010 marked the beginning of year-on-year cuts to funding allocated to local government for early intervention services. Furthermore, the protective ring fence for early intervention funding was removed in 2013/14 when the EIG was rolled into the Revenue Support Grant, a single pot for all local authority services. The 'big five' children's charities have analysed changes to funding allocated by central government and actual expenditure on children's services by local authorities since 2010/11 (Action for Children et al, 2019). In this analysis, expenditure on children's services includes 'early intervention services', such as children's centres and youth services, and 'late intervention' services, such as safeguarding services and children in care. Between 2010/11 and 2017/18, funding allocated by central government for children's services fell by £3 billion, a 29 per cent reduction. However, in general, local authorities have prioritised spending on children's services and have allocated resources from elsewhere to compensate for the cut in central funding. Thus, the actual fall in local authority spending on children's services was £1.7 billion, a 16 per cent cut. However, it is important to recognise that cuts to spending on children's services have varied between local authorities, with those serving the most deprived communities experiencing the largest cuts: 'Whilst the least deprived have a 21 per cent cut to funding, their level of spending has only fallen 5 per cent. In comparison, the most deprived have seen their funding cut by 37 per cent and have reduced their spending by 24 per cent' (Action for Children et al, 2019: 10). Furthermore, a significant trend over recent years has been the shift from spending on early intervention towards greater spending on late intervention. Expenditure on late intervention increased from £5.9 billion in 2010/ 11 to £6.7 billion in 2017/18, an increase of 12 per cent. Thus, early intervention services have borne the brunt of austerity. Between 2010/11 and 2017/18, spending on early intervention services by local authorities fell from £3.7 billion to £1.9 billion, a 49 per cent cut (Action for Children et al, 2019: 3).

Children's centres

The contradiction between Coalition and Conservative government statements on early intervention and the withdrawal of local services is clearly illustrated in relation to children's centres. The initiation of Labour's Sure Start programme was described in Chapter 2. Following the establishment of 250 initial programmes in areas of high deprivation, a network of 3,632 Sure Start children's centres was established by August 2009 (Sutton Trust, 2018: 4). Under Labour's progressive universalism framework, children's centres accessible to all families were vital to the early identification of problems and a shift towards more preventative services. The Conservatives recognised the popularity of children's centres, and in the run-up to the 2010 election, they signalled that they would be retained under a future Conservative government. On the other hand, in line with the Broken Britain perspective on early intervention (Allen and Duncan-Smith, 2008), the Conservatives argued that Labour's progressive universalism approach needed to be substituted with a more targeted approach. As the 2010 Conservative Party election manifesto stated:

> The Conservative Party is committed to keeping Sure Start because the network of children's centres is of enormous value to parents across the country. But we believe Sure Start needs to work better because the people who need it most – disadvantaged and dysfunctional families – are not getting enough of the benefit. We will take Sure Start back to its original purpose of early intervention, increase its focus on the neediest families, and better involve organisations with a track record in supporting families. (Conservative Party, 2010a: 43)

However, after 2010, DfE ministers chose not to get closely involved in the development of policy on children's centres and strove to maintain a distance from the politically sensitive closures and restructuring that has taken place at the local level.

Advocates for children's centres, both in Parliament and outside, have used All Party Parliamentary Groups (APPGs) and House of Commons committees to monitor the impact of spending cuts and to put pressure on the DfE to protect children's centres. In 2012, the APPG for Sure Start called on the DfE to re-establish central oversight of local authority compliance with responsibilities set out under the Childcare Act 2006 (APPG for Sure Start, 2012). In response, the DfE (2013b) published new 'core purpose' guidance on children's centres in April 2013. However, the House of Commons Education Committee (2013: 3) considered this guidance to be 'too vague and broadly worded'. The DfE's response was dismissive, stating that 'While the government understands the Committee's concerns, the government believes that focus should now be on developing services within the broad framework the core purpose document provides' (House of Commons Education Committee, 2014: 3).

It was noted in Chapter 7 that in January 2016, Cameron had promised that the government would publish a new Life Chances Strategy. The APPG for Children's Centres (2016: 7) called on the government to 'give full consideration to augmenting children's centres into Family Hubs as part of its Life Chances Strategy'. The concept of 'family hubs' had been coined by the CSJ, the think tank set up by Duncan-Smith in 2004 that had led the Conservative's 'Broken Britain' social policy review (Conservative Party Social Justice Policy Group, 2006, 2007). Family hubs would become 'local "nerve centres" which enable parents to access all family-related support including universal services and specialist help to meet their most pressing needs' (CSJ, 2014: 48). After the Life Chances Strategy was scrapped by the May government in December 2016, the DfE announced that a consultation on the future of children's centres would begin in early 2017 (Puffett, 2017b). However, national policy on children's centres has yet to be clarified. In August 2018, the Children's Minister, Nadhim Zahawi, confirmed that the promised consultation had been shelved (Lepper, 2018c). Several months later, it was announced that the EIF would carry out a review of children's centres (Parkes, 2019).

Research published by the Sutton Trust (2018) provides an overview of the impact of funding cuts and the DfE's de-prioritisation of policy on children's centres. It estimates that 1,000 registered children's centres closed between 2009 and 2018. However, it is also reported that many of the centres still open now operate on a part-time basis and offer fewer services. Furthermore, the research found that further reductions were in the pipeline as part of local authority plans to meet saving targets in the coming years. In summary:

> The result has been to move children's centres away from the original idea of an open access neighbourhood centre. Services are now 'hollowed out' – much more thinly spread, often no longer 'in pram-pushing distance'. The focus of centres has changed to referred families with high need, and provision has diversified as national direction has weakened, with local authorities employing a variety of strategies to survive in an environment of declining resources and loss of strategic direction. (Sutton Trust, 2018: 5)

Youth services

A similar pattern of disengagement by the DfE, and the government more generally, can also be observed in relation to policy on youth services. In 2011, the House of Commons Education Committee echoed the concerns expressed by the APPG for Sure Start. The report of the committee's inquiry into youth services highlighted the impact of spending cuts on the capacity of local authorities to provide sufficient activities for young people outside of school, as required under the Education and Inspection Act 2006 (House of Commons Education Committee, 2011). Again, ministers sought to distance the government from the cuts and reorganisations required at the local level. In the report *Positive for Youth* (HM Government, 2011d: 64), it was argued that this approach gave 'local authorities the flexibility and responsibility to prioritise public funding for services for children and young people according to local need'.

In January 2013, it was reported that Gove did not visit a single youth services project during his first two-and-a-half years as Secretary of State (Puffett, 2013). A few months later, he handed over responsibility for youth services policy to the Cabinet Office. This was the first time that youth policy had been removed from the education portfolio since the Second World War (McCardle, 2014). Moreover, to the disappointment of those working in the sector, youth policy remained a low priority even after the shift to the Cabinet Office. When asked about youth services in Parliament in July 2015, the minister responsible for youth policy, Rob Wilson, replied: 'I find it disappointing that local councils are making the choice to cut youth services' (quoted in Offord, 2015). There was no recognition of the role that the government played in funding and overseeing the provision of youth services.

After May became Prime Minister in July 2016, Wilson retained responsibility for youth policy but moved into the Department for Culture, Media and Sport (DCMS). Speaking in November 2016, he now acknowledged that the government needed to play a more active role. Wilson stated that 'If we work together, if we are innovative, if we keep a relentless focus on the needs of young people, we will be successful and make good progress' (quoted in Offord, 2016). A new three-year national strategy for youth services was promised in the coming months. However, after losing his seat at the 2017 election, Wilson was replaced by Tracey Crouch. In November 2017, Crouch announced that the strategy promised by Wilson had been scrapped (Puffett, 2017c). The justification given was that youth policy would be incorporated into the government's wider *Civil Society Strategy* (HM Government, 2018c), which was eventually published in August 2018. However, the strategy did not offer any new resources or provide any clarification of how the government planned to work with local authorities to improve youth services, as Wilson had promised two years earlier. The strategy simply stated:

> While the government recognises the priority that local authorities must place on functions such as child protection, it also recognises the transformational impact that youth services and trained youth workers can have, especially for young people facing multiple barriers or disadvantage.... The government will therefore review the guidance which sets out the statutory duty placed on local authorities to provide appropriate local youth services. We expect that the review will provide greater clarity of government's expectations, including the value added by good youth work. (HM Government, 2018c: 42)

A more recent inquiry by the APPG on Youth Affairs (2018) welcomed the government's promised review. However, the inquiry report highlighted the extent to which youth services have been de-prioritised at both the national and local levels, and the impact that this had had. Drawing on a report published by the YMCA (2018), the inquiry reported that spending on youth services by local authorities fell from £1.028 billion in 2008/09 to £0.338 billion in 2016/17, a reduction of 62.25 per cent (APPG on Youth Affairs, 2018: 10). The precise impact on local services has not been closely monitored. No national audit of local services has been carried out since 2007/08 (APPG on Youth Affairs, 2018: 11). Research carried out by Unison (2016: 5), based on freedom of information requests sent to local authorities, suggests that between 2012 and 2016, 3,652 youth work jobs were lost, 603 youth centres closed and 138,898 places for young people were cut. The YMCA (2018) report concludes:

> It is difficult to imagine any other services in England and Wales that could be on the receiving end of cuts of more than three fifths of their total budget over such a short period of time, with little or no scrutiny to the long-term impact this would have on our communities and the individuals missing out. Unfortunately, it is not until news of young people being isolated or incidents like the recent knife crimes in London hit the headlines, that attention seems to go to the role of youth services. However, like all news cycles, this will pass, but as set out in this research, the cuts to youth services look likely to continue. (YMCA, 2018: 11)

NGOs and early intervention policy

The role played by NGOs in policymaking under the Labour government has been discussed in previous chapters. Although early initiatives such as Sure Start were largely driven by the Treasury and Labour ministers, representatives of the sector played a key role in helping to formulate the detail of new policy initiatives, including the design of local service delivery arrangements. Initially, it was representatives of the children's charities that enjoyed the best access to government policymakers. However, it was later recognised that closer engagement with the statutory sector, particularly local government, was necessary if Labour's ambitious ECM reform agenda was to be successfully implemented. This final section of the chapter considers how this relationship changed after the 2010 election and as DfE policymakers disengaged from early intervention policy.

Trying to stay relevant

It was widely recognised that the case for ongoing investment in early intervention services needed to be made even before the 2010 election. It was clear that cuts to public spending would be made whichever party won the election. In this context, some NGOs strived to demonstrate the cost effectiveness of their services. For example, Action for Children worked with the New Economics Foundation

(NEF) to try to demonstrate the cost-effectiveness of services run by the charity, claiming that for every £1 invested in targeted early intervention services, between £7.60 and £9.20 was saved by society as problems were prevented from reoccurring (Action for Children and NEF, 2009: 8). The findings of this research were highlighted by three charities in a pamphlet sent to MPs after the election (Family Action et al, 2010: 16). A few months after the election, the Centre for Excellence and Outcomes in Children and Young People's Services (C4EO, 2010) published a practice guide to the challenges and opportunities in supporting children, families and communities through early intervention. C4EO was a consortium of children's policy and research organisations led by the NCB that had been set up in 2008 to collect and disseminate examples of best practice and support the implementation of ECM. The report reflected on changes to children's services over the previous five years, arguing that 'we have come a long way and seen massive investments in our schools and early years settings and increased attention paid to preventative services and early intervention' (C4EO, 2010: 51). However, it was also acknowledged that there was now a greater need to provide 'information of the costs of effective interventions at project level' (C4EO, 2010: 3). Cameron's decision to commission Graham Allen MP to oversee a review of the effectiveness of early intervention programmes was warmly welcomed.

However, NGOs hoping to continue to influence government policymakers also had to adapt to ideological differences between the Labour and Coalition governments. During the Labour years, NGOs from the children's sector had campaigned in favour of income transfers to poorer families and investment in universal services. Under the Coalition government, the priority was to develop services targeted at the 'dysfunctional base' in society and to address the 'five pathways to poverty' (Conservative Party Social Justice Policy Group, 2006, 2007; Allen and Duncan-Smith, 2008). In the report 'Deprivation and risk: the case for early intervention', Action for Children (2010: 2–4) acknowledged the new political reality, arguing that:

> For too long this debate has focused on income. Of course, income is important, but for families who endure hardship over generations, who are trapped in a cycle of deprivation, increasing income alone does not provide freedom.... Tackling this level of disadvantage requires intensive, targeted and challenging interventions at a point in people's lives when they are open to change. (2010: 2–4)

To try to maintain access to government policymakers and help shape future policy developments, some NGO leaders initially resisted criticising the government. One charity leader interviewed in 2012 explained that "We are carefully not that critical of government. I think everything we write at the moment isn't a 'How dare you cut?' I think that's a stupid argument, I wouldn't do it. It's more about 'What are you going to choose to prioritise?'" (interview with charity leader, October 2012). The leader of another charity also interviewed in 2012 commented:

> 'You do have to be flexible, not in terms of changing base positions, but in understanding that priorities change, that external situations change and that if you are so rigid in the policy positions that you take that you can't change and adapt yourself, then you will quickly become unhelpful and useless. So, there is something about being intellectually flexible enough, and also politically astute enough, to be able to operate in whatever the prevailing political atmosphere is.' (Interview with charity leader, December 2012)

Shouting from the sidelines

Some NGOs repositioned themselves during the early years of the Coalition government because they hoped that Cameron's proclaimed commitment to early intervention signalled an opportunity to shape policy and attract resources, even as public spending was being cut. However, it was argued earlier that under the stewardship of Gove as Secretary of State, the DfE prioritised schools reform and largely disengaged from early intervention policy. As funding for early intervention services continued to be cut, and as DfE policymakers distanced themselves from service closures and restructuring at the local level, frustration grew within the sector. A charity leader interviewed in late 2013 concluded that:

> 'We have a Secretary of State who is education obsessed, it has been very difficult to land the broader safeguarding issues … the vision, the ECM vision, which I would have lots of criticism of, but that sense of children and the totality of children I think has largely gone.' (Interview with charity leader, October 2013)

A similar view was expressed by the leader of a different charity interviewed in early 2014. They stated:

> 'I think Michael Gove, I think he's preoccupied mainly with, well, a very particular agenda on schools and there, I think, the shame is that it is a very narrow agenda and we would be really interested in thinking about how do children's non-cognitive skills and abilities and seeing children in the round contribute not only to, you know, both their learning outcomes, but also to their wider outcomes in terms of getting them prepared to be well-rounded citizens. There is no agenda for that in the department.' (Interview with charity leader, January 2014)

Over more recent years, NGOs across the charitable and statutory sectors have sought to highlight the impact of a decade of spending cuts and make the case for reinvestment in early intervention services. The research published by the 'big five' children's charities on children's services funding discussed earlier reveals the severity of cuts to early intervention services, but also highlights the prioritisation of spending on 'late intervention' children's social care services (Action for Children et al, 2019). The work of the Sutton Trust (2018) and the YMCA (2018), also referenced earlier, describes the impact that this has had on children centres and youth services provision. The ADCS, on the other hand, has drawn attention to the demand pressures placed on children's social care services over recent years and the difficulties that local authorities have therefore faced in trying to protect early intervention services. The sixth *Safeguarding Pressures* report highlights the following changes over the past ten years: increased initial contacts (+78 per cent); more referrals (+22 per cent); more Section 47 investigations (+159 per cent); more children subject to a child protection plan (+87 per cent); and more children looked after (+24 per cent). Thus, the ADCS has joined calls to reverse the spending cuts, arguing that:

> In terms of the future, there is a sense that authorities have been constantly re-designing and re-configuring services to meet needs and manage the growth in demand. They have done so whilst maintaining, passionately, a clear focus on children and their families at the heart of services. In order to stop the cycle we are seeing, and start to reduce demand and support children and families when they need it most,

we must be resourced to allow for a focus on prevention. (ADCS, 2018b: 120)

The 'Bright futures' campaign led by the LGA (2017) also called for additional funding for children's services in the run-up to the expected 2019 comprehensive Spending Review. The LGA (2019: 2) has predicted that demand pressures on local authorities over the coming years will mean that local authorities will face a funding gap of £3.1 billion for children's services by 2024/25. Independent reports published by the APPG for Children (2018) and the NAO (2019) have also drawn attention to increased pressure on children's social care services.

It is perhaps unsurprising that NGOs have been calling for central government to provide more funding. However, there have also been consistent calls for government policymakers to play a more active role to support the integration of children's services and promote a shift towards earlier intervention at the local level. The research on children's centres (Sutton Trust, 2018) and youth services (YMCA, 2018) highlights the emergence of significant variations in service provision across different local authority areas. Similarly, evidence provided to the APPG for Children (2018) describes a 'a postcode lottery of children's social care'. The ADCS (2019) has called upon the government to re-establish a national children's workforce strategy that recognises the diversity of professions and occupations that make up the sector. While welcoming the focus that the government has placed on social work, the ADCS (2019: 2) argued that 'this has largely been at the expense of the wider workforce, which has borne the brunt of a decade of austerity'. Even the LGA, an organisation that has generally campaigned for greater local government autonomy, has acknowledged the importance of a clearer national approach to children's policy, arguing that:

> The importance of local partnership working is mirrored at the national level, as the lives of children and young people are inevitably affected by decisions over which councils and their partners have little control. It is therefore vital that Whitehall approaches improved outcomes for children with one voice.... A clearly articulated ambition for children, young people and families, shared and owned across Whitehall, is crucial to ensuring that government is truly putting children first. (LGA, 2017: 6)

A review of early intervention policy by the House of Commons Science and Technology Committee (2018) considered evidence provided by a wide range of NGOs and individual experts working in the children's sector. One of the key recommendations made was that:

> The Government should make early intervention and childhood adversity a priority, and set out a clear national strategy to empower and encourage local authorities to deliver effective, sustainable and evidence-based early intervention. The Government should also ensure that it has better oversight of the provision of early intervention around the country, so that it can identify approaches that are working well, detect local authorities in need of support and hold local authorities to account. (House of Commons Science and Technology Committee, 2018: 3)

The official response to this recommendation stated that 'This Government believes that local areas are best placed to understand the needs of their local communities, to commission early intervention services to meet those needs and to deliver interventions as part of a whole system approach to produce the best outcomes for families' (quoted in Lepper, 2019). The government's continuous refusal to engage in this area of policy has meant that NGOs no longer play any significant role in the policymaking process and have therefore been largely reduced to shouting from the sidelines.

Discussion

The influence that individual ministers can have over children's policy is exemplified by the case of Michael Gove. After being appointed as Secretary of State, Gove immediately reshaped the priorities of the renamed Department *for Education*. Under Balls's *The Children's Plan* (DCSF, 2007), ECM had been placed on an equal footing with the department's more traditional education policy agenda. Moreover, schools had been positioned at the heart of new multi-agency arrangements designed to better integrate local children's services and address a diverse range of children's and young people's needs stretching well beyond educational attainment. Under Gove's schools reform programme, a more traditional focus on school and pupil attainment was reintroduced to education policy, alongside more radical changes designed to limit the influence of local authorities over schools in their areas. Furthermore, Gove's prioritisation of education policy also limited the prospects for the refocusing of early intervention policy in line with the Conservative Party's Broken Britain framework. The Conservative secretaries of state that followed Gove stuck to this reform agenda. Thus, Labour's ECM framework was severely neglected, even though it was never officially abandoned.

On the other hand, the influence of individual ministers, including Gove, needs to be considered in the context of the wider political imperatives discussed in Chapter 7. In the context of public sector austerity, ministers were granted greater autonomy as Coalition and Conservative government leaders largely sought to distance themselves from the difficult decisions that needed to be made in Whitehall departments and at the local level. Thus, even though Cameron and Clegg emphasised their shared commitment to improving social justice and social mobility during the early years of the Coalition, they did not seek to interfere in departmental policymaking to the extent that Blair and Brown did. Moreover, as the impact of public sector spending cuts and welfare reform started to be felt, the necessity for Coalition and Conservative leaders to distance themselves from unpopular social policy reforms became even more important politically. The strategy adopted by DfE ministers to avoid blame has been to support the devolution of policymaking powers and emphasise the importance of local leadership. The faint hope that a change of Prime Minister might lead to a change of course diminished quickly. After May took over from Cameron in July 2016, Brexit dominated and policy statements on the Life Chances Strategy, children's centres and youth services were either shelved or kicked into the long grass.

The abandonment of early intervention policy by the Coalition and Conservative governments has also been reflected in changes to the relationship between government policymakers and NGOs in the children's sector. A shared commitment to addressing the challenges faced by children and families growing up in poverty formed the basis of a generally constructive relationship between Labour ministers and favoured NGOs in the children's sector. Although the input of NGOs was generally on ministers' terms, organisations representing the children's charity sector and the new children's services departments in local government enjoyed good access to ministers and officials, and were valued for their technical advice. Cameron's interest in early intervention during the early years of the Coalition government raised hopes that NGOs would continue to help shape policy even in the context of public sector cuts. However, these hopes were ultimately ill founded. As ministers have disengaged from early intervention policy,

NGOs have been forced to campaign from the outside, highlighting the impact of austerity and welfare reform on local services and the children and families that depend on them. However, campaigning on the importance of early intervention and preventative services must also be viewed in the context of Coalition and Conservative policies on child and family social work, which are the subject of Chapter 9.

9

The reform of child and family social work

Introduction

> We believe we need to move towards a child protection system with less central prescription and interference, where we place greater trust and responsibility in skilled professionals at the front line. (Loughton, in DfE, 2011: foreword)

> Too many local authorities are failing to meet acceptable standards for child safeguarding. Too many children are left for too long in homes where they are exposed to appalling neglect and criminal mistreatment. (Gove, 2012: 2)

> We want a system staffed and led by the best trained professionals; dynamic and free to innovate in the interests of children; delivered through a more diverse range of social care organisations. (Morgan and Timpson, in DfE, 2016c: foreword)

Before the Baby P crisis, social work reform had not been a high priority under the Labour government. Furthermore, the reform programme initiated by the SWTF (2009) was only just starting to be implemented at the time of the 2010 election. However, the Conservatives had identified social work reform as a priority even before the Baby P case. Furthermore, the recommendations of the SWTF were consistent with those of the earlier Commission on Social Workers for the Conservative Party (2007), and it therefore seemed likely that the new sector-led reform programme would be allowed to continue. Indeed, other than schools reform, the reform of child and family social work turned out to be the most active area of children's policy under the Coalition and Conservative governments. Thus, this chapter considers the development of policy in this area, building on the wider discussions in Chapters 7 and 8.

The first section focuses on the first two years of the Coalition government, which appeared to signal a commitment to the sector-led reform programme initiated by the SWTF. This includes a discussion of *The Munro Review of Child Protection* (Munro, 2011) and the government's response. The remainder of the chapter examines the development of policy on child and family social work since the end of 2012. The second section highlights how the familiar narrative of local authority and professional failure resurfaced. This is followed by a discussion of new reforms aimed at improving the consistency of social work training, regulation and learning in the third section. The fourth section reflects on the return to structural reform as the main solution to the challenges facing local authority children's services. The final section considers the role that representatives of the social work profession have played in the development of policy on child and family social work since 2010. The chapter provides further evidence regarding the political drivers of children's policy and the influence of NGOs.

Professional renewal

During the first two years of the Coalition government, the Children's Minister, Tim Loughton, played a pivotal role in the development of policy on child and family social work. During this period, Secretary of State Michael Gove, Loughton's boss in the DfE, was preoccupied with the roll-out of his academies and free schools programmes. Loughton was unusually well qualified to lead reform in this area, having served as a shadow minister since 2001. Moreover, Loughton had worked closely with children's sector representatives to highlight Labour's neglect of social work, and had developed recommendations for reform through the Commission on Social Workers (Conservative Party, 2007). The recommendations of the SWTF (2009) closely matched those made by the commission. Unsurprisingly, therefore, Loughton offered the Coalition government's support for the work of the SWRB, chaired by Moira Gibb, which had been set up under Labour to implement the recommendations of the SWTF. In April 2012, Gibb handed over responsibility for the implementation of the reform programme to the newly established College of Social Work. The establishment of a new professional body to raise the status of the social work profession and improve the consistency of training and social work practice had been a key recommendation of the commission in 2007. Loughton also continued to advocate for the appointment of a Chief Social Worker, another recommendation made by the commission.

Loughton also promoted the rationalisation of the bureaucratic rules and procedures that had built up around the child protection duties of social workers over several decades. One of the first actions he took after being appointed was to scrap the Contact Point database created under Labour, fulfilling a promise made in the pre-election report *Child Protection: Back to the Frontline* (Conservative Party, 2010b). However, Loughton wanted to go much further in terms of rationalising centrally prescribed policies and procedures, but he needed to ensure that any further changes were carefully thought through and designed with input from social work experts. Thus, he convinced Cameron and Gove that an independent review of the child protection system was needed.

The Munro Review

Professor Munro was a well-regarded expert in child protection practice who had been critical of procedural reforms introduced under the Labour government following the Victoria Climbié inquiry (Munro, 2008). Furthermore, speaking on the BBC Panorama programme during the Baby P crisis, she criticised Labour's broad definition of child *safeguarding*, arguing that detecting child abuse is like 'trying to spot a needle in a haystack', and that 'it gets harder if you make the haystack larger' (quoted in Jones, 2014: 145). For Loughton, Munro was a logical choice to lead a new review of child protection.

Previous reviews of policy in this area had been commissioned in the aftermath of high-profile child abuse cases. Moreover, the recommendations made in these reviews, including the 166 made by Lord Laming (2003, 2009), were seen to have fuelled central government efforts to assert closer control over local services and individual professionals, particularly social workers. That this review was commissioned outside of the shadow of an individual case was significant, as Munro explained:

> 'My review was a real exception because it was done at a calm time and I think that made a very, very big difference in that it allowed me to be looking at the system as a whole rather than, "How did this terrible death happen?" It was done also without media interest because it wasn't on the back of some horrific story.' (Interview with Professor Eileen Munro)

Munro's findings were shared in a series of three reports, with the third and final report setting out 15 key recommendations. The overarching message was that much greater attention needed to be given to developing and supporting child protection practice at the front line, as opposed to the continued development of centrally prescribed policies and procedures. In the preface to her third report, Munro stated:

> This is my third and final report in which I set out recommendations that I believe will, taken together, help to reform the child protection system from being over-bureaucratised and concerned with compliance to one that keeps a focus on children, checking whether they are being effectively helped, and adapting when problems are identified. A move from a compliance to a learning culture will require those working in child protection to be given more scope to exercise professional judgment in deciding how best to help children and their families. It will require more determined and robust management at the front line to support the development of professional confidence. (Munro, 2011: 5)

Specific recommendations aimed at reducing the bureaucratic burden included a rewrite of the statutory *Working Together* guidance (HM Government, 2010d) and the development of a new approach to inspection that paid closer attention to the quality of front-line practice rather than bureaucratic compliance. Recommendations relating to social work training and regulation were consistent with the work of the SWRB (Munro, 2011: ch 6). Munro (2011: ch 7) also gave her backing to long-standing calls for the appointment of a Chief Social Worker. At the local level, she recommended the appointment of Principal Child and Family Social Workers to help support the development of professional practice and 'communicate frontline concerns to all layers of management' (Munro, 2011: 105).

Munro's analysis provided strong evidence to support the established view, shared by many social work academics and professional representatives, that child protection practice was too restricted by bureaucratic controls. Moreover, this was a view that Loughton had long accepted, and it was therefore unsurprising that he welcomed the overarching message of *The Munro Review*. In his foreword to the DfE's official response, he stated that 'We believe we need to move towards a child protection system with less central prescription and interference, where we place greater trust and responsibility in skilled professionals at the front line' (Loughton, in DfE, 2011: 2). On the other hand, the DfE's response to Munro's specific recommendations was more cautious. Nine recommendations were accepted; however, five were only 'accepted in principle', while a recommendation relating to the methodology for carrying out SCRs was marked as 'consider further'. However, notwithstanding this caution, Loughton indicated that the DfE remained committed to working closely with representatives of the sector to develop and implement a programme of reform, stating:

> The Government is committed to continuing to work in partnership with local government and leaders of children's services, the College of Social Work, the Association of Chief Police Officers, health service organisations' leaders, the education sector and children's organisations in the voluntary and community sector, the Inspectorates and others. This response is not a one-off set of recommended solutions to be imposed from the centre. Rather it is the start of a shift in mindset and relationship between central Government, local agencies and front line professionals working in partnership. (Loughton, in DfE, 2011: 3)

Furthermore, although her review focused on the *child protection* system and the role of child and family social workers, Munro (2011: ch 5) was clear that these must not be seen in isolation, arguing that:

> The case for preventative services is clear, both in the sense of offering help to children and families before any problems are apparent and in providing help when low level problems emerge. From the perspective of a child or young person, it is clearly best if they receive help before they have any, or have only minor, adverse experiences. (Munro, 2011: 69)

The role of preventative services had been a recurring theme in debates on child welfare policy for several decades. The role of local authority social workers in this regard is set out under Section 17 of the Children Act 1989. Prevention was also a key principle under Labour's ECM framework, though this placed more emphasis on the role of universal services. In her report, Munro refers to the recently published Allen (2011) review of early intervention to bring the argument in favour of preventative services up to date. The importance of preventative services to Munro was reflected in her recommendation that 'The Government should place a duty on local authorities and statutory partners to secure the sufficient provision of local *early help* services for children, young people and families' (Munro, 2011: 12, emphasis added). Even though Loughton supported this, the new early help duty was never implemented. In the context of year-on-year cuts to early intervention funding, Gove had chosen to distance the DfE from service cuts and restructuring taking place at the local level, as Chapter 8 demonstrated. Placing a new duty on local authorities would have been inconsistent with this position. Furthermore, in September 2012, Loughton was sacked and policy on child and family social work moved in a different direction.

A change of narrative

Although Edward Timpson was appointed to replace Loughton, Gove became more personally involved in the development of policy at this point. Moreover, Gove made the case for a new approach to child protection reform in a speech delivered in November 2012. In this speech, Gove was implicitly critical of the emphasis that Munro and many others placed on the importance of preventative services, arguing that social work suffered from an 'optimism bias' that clouded judgements made in relation to the safety of children. Explaining this, Gove argued that:

> Social workers are encouraged to develop relationships with adults who are careless of their own welfare and dignity. And for perfectly understandable reasons sometimes professionals are reluctant to directly and robustly challenge the behaviour of people whose trust they are trying to win. But all the time, while adults are trusted, children continue to suffer. (Gove, 2012: 6)

Gove's views on the child protection system had been influenced by the advice of Sir Martin Narey. After a long period as a civil servant in the Home Office, Narey served as the Chief Executive of Barnardo's between 2005 and 2011. His views on the care system marked him out from other leaders in the children's sector. However, he found that Gove was very interested in understanding his perspective. Reflecting on his conversations with Gove about the care system, Narey explained:

> 'Although it could be improved, my view was that the general theology, that the fewer children in care the better, was dangerous and there might be real reasons for having the numbers in care that we had. Nobody reads the research. I would give him mounds of research to read. He

read it…. I found him very refreshing.' (Interview with Sir Martin Narey, 2019)

Narey (2011) had also published a long report in *The Times* newspaper calling for reform of the adoption system. Influenced by this report, and his own positive experience of adoption, Gove launched a new action plan in March 2012 aimed at speeding up the adoption process for children who had been taken into care (DfE, 2012).

Gove resurrected the familiar narrative of service failure that had invariably accompanied previous waves of reform to support his case for a new approach to child protection. In his speech, Gove (2012) referenced the high-profile deaths of Victoria Climbié, Peter Connelly (Baby P) and Khyra Ishaq, breaking with the less emotive tone of *The Munro Review*, which Loughton had purposefully commissioned outside the shadow of the latest child abuse scandal. Moreover, Gove's (2012) speech was provocatively titled 'The failure of child protection and the need for a fresh start'. The following excerpt captures the tone of the speech:

> Too many local authorities are failing to meet acceptable standards for child safeguarding. Too many children are left for too long in homes where they are exposed to appalling neglect and criminal mistreatment. We put the rights of biological parents ahead of vulnerable children – even when those parents are incapable of leading their own lives safely and with dignity never mind bringing up children. When we do intervene, it is often too late. (Gove, 2012: 2)

Although Gove was replaced as Secretary of State in July 2014, sharp criticism of 'failing' local authorities and social work professions continued to define Coalition and Conservative government statements on child protection. In March 2015, Prime Minister David Cameron criticised social workers and police officers for failing to use 'common sense' following the publication of reports examining the systematic sexual exploitation of children by gangs of men in Rotherham (Jay, 2014) and Oxfordshire (Oxfordshire Safeguarding Board, 2015). He also announced that the government was considering plans to introduce prison sentences for professionals, including teachers and social workers, who fail to act upon evidence of child abuse (Wintour, 2015).

However, criticism of local authorities and social workers has not been reserved for the most extreme cases. In the policy statement

Putting Children First: Our Vision for Children's Social Care (DfE, 2016c), it is suggested that 'inadequate' services and poor-quality social work practice are commonplace. The report states:

> The best children's social care services in England deliver excellent help and support to children and families. But whilst there is much impressive social work in the system, evidence from frontline delivery organisations, multiple Serious Case Reviews and from Ofsted inspections points to continued inconsistency in the quality of work with children and families. Ofsted's recent Annual Report on children's social care states that, of those local authorities inspected under the current framework, a quarter have been found to be inadequate. In addition, almost half require improvement to be good. The majority of local authorities still struggle to provide consistently effective core social work practice. Similarly, fewer than half of Local Safeguarding Children Boards, which coordinate and challenge multi-agency working locally, do so in a way which is 'good'. (DfE, 2016c: 9–10)

Inconsistent professional practice has been consistently identified in numerous reviews of child protection, including *The Munro Review* (Munro, 2011). However, the strong emphasis on the failings of individual local authorities and the social work profession in official statements on child protection deflected attention from the challenge of rising demand for social care services (ADCS, 2018b; APPG for Children, 2018; NAO, 2019) at a time of public sector austerity and cuts to welfare payments to families. The rhetoric of service and professional failure has been used to promote a new reform programme that largely replaced the profession-led reform programme initiated by the SWTF (2009) that, under Loughton, the Coalition government had initially supported.

Reshaping social work: training, regulation and learning

Improving the consistency and quality of social work training and professional development had been identified as a key priority by the SWTF (2009). The SWRB subsequently worked with universities and employers to take this forward, before handing over to the College of Social Work in April 2012. However, Gove was not satisfied with the pace or direction of reform and decided that the DfE needed to play a more active role. Narey explained how his conversations with Gove about the care system provoked a wider interest in social work reform:

> 'As we got into that and he [Gove] understood the care system more, he started to become more probing about those who work in the care system. My view of social work was very positive, and I had managed 2,000 of them at Barnardo's, and I knew how this is a generally vocational group of people. I shared with him my view that I was unimpressed with the variation in social work degrees, and the fact that I was also told by Directors of Children's Services that, informally, they are trying to recruit people from some universities and not others.... It slowly culminated into an issue that we should have a look at: the training of the whole profession.' (Interview with Sir Martin Narey, 2019)

Frontline

In February 2013, Gove provided the DfE's backing for a new training scheme for child and family social work called Frontline. The programme was to be led by Josh McAlister, a graduate of the Teach First programme. The programme is modelled on Teach First, with the Frontline website boldly describing a 'mission to transform the lives of vulnerable children by recruiting and developing outstanding individuals to be leaders in social work and broader society' (Frontline, 2019). Frontline students attend an initial five-week training programme before beginning local authority placements. After two years, successful students are awarded a master's degree (Brindle, 2013). However, the scheme has been strongly criticised by social work educators elsewhere for its narrow curriculum and short duration compared to other courses (Maxwell et al, 2016). At the time, Gove's announcement was viewed as a snub to the work of more experienced social work educators and the progress made by the SWRB. A statement by the Joint University Council Social Work Education Committee (JUCSWEC) and the Association of Professors of Social Work (APSW) protested that 'Qualifying social work, through the work of the SWRB and the whole sector, is currently being carefully revised to support continuing professional development – a holistic model is being sought; Frontline's "short-termism" will not sustain change for families or useful practitioners in years to come' (JUCSWEC and APSW, 2013: 3). Even after celebrating its fifth anniversary, Frontline continues to divide opinion (Brindle, 2018;

Gupta and SocialWhatNow, 2018; Stevenson, 2018a). In May 2018, the DfE signalled its confidence in the programme by announcing additional funding. Participating local authorities have also defended Frontline (Stevenson, 2018b). However, critics of the programme argue that its effectiveness has not been properly. evaluated. In May 2018, a letter sent on behalf of the APSW, BASW, JUCSWEC and the Social Work Action Network (SWAN) was sent to Nadhim Zahawi, Children's Minister from January 2018, calling for the re-tendering of the programme to be suspended. Concerns regarding the quality and depth of initial training, as well as the impact of higher funding levels for Frontline students compared to those on other undergraduate and postgraduate courses, all remained (APSW et al, 2018).

The Knowledge and Skills Statement and social worker accreditation

Significantly, Gove also asked Narey to carry out a review of the education of *children's* social workers in order to provide a platform for more wide-ranging reforms. This provided a further signal of Gove's lack of confidence in the progress made by the SWRB and the College of Social Work. However, it also challenged the widely held view that initial social work training should have a generic basis, a view that had been accepted by the SWTF and the Commission on Social Workers (Conservative Party, 2007). In his report, published in January 2014, Narey did acknowledge the progress made by the SWRB in producing a new Professional Capabilities Framework (PCF), and was impressed by the Chief Executive of the College of Social Work, which had taken over from the SWRB. However, Narey highlighted the fact that the body then responsible for regulating social workers, the Health and Care Professionals Council (HCPC), also produced Standards of Proficiency, and pointed out that universities also had to take account of another framework, the Benchmark Statements for Social Work, produced by the Quality Assurance Agency for Higher Education. Thus, Narey called for a single document setting out 'what a newly qualified children's social worker needs to understand' and recommended that the recently appointed Chief Social Worker for Children and Families should take the lead in drafting such a document (Narey, 2014: 13).

Two separate Knowledge and Skills Statements (KSSs) were published later in 2014, covering children's and adults' social workers separately. Jones (2019: 81) suggests that two statements emerged because the DH had to make sure that adult social workers were 'not left outside of the government's script'. More significantly, Jones also argues that the statements undermined the PCF, which had been developed with much wider input from representatives of the social work profession, pointing out that the short consultation on the children's KSS took place in the holiday month of August. Furthermore, the KSS is now being used to inform a new accreditation scheme for child and family social workers being developed by the DfE in partnership with the accountancy firm KPMG. The scheme has caused considerable concern within the children's sector, drawing criticism from a range of groups, including the BASW, Unison and the ADCS. The House of Commons Education Select Committee has echoed these concerns and warned of the potential impact of a crudely designed accreditation scheme on an already fragile workforce (Jones, 2019: 82–90).

Social work regulation

The introduction of Frontline and the new accreditation scheme is only part of recent efforts by DfE policymakers to take a firmer grip on the education and practice of child and family social workers. In Narey's (2014) analysis, a lack of clarity and consistency about what was expected of a newly qualified social worker reflected an underlying problem regarding the regulation of social work. At the time of Narey's review, the HCPC was responsible for the regulation of social work, holding the power to enforce professional standards and determine who could and could not practise as a social worker. However, as the title suggests, the HCPC held responsibility for regulating a diverse range of professions in health and social care. The HCPC had only taken on responsibility for social work after the General Social Care Council (GSCC) had been scrapped by the government in 2012. However, Narey (2014) argued that the HCPC was not up to the task and recommended that the government review its role in relation to the regulation of social work. He was far more impressed with the early work of the College of Social Work and suggested that consideration should be given to transferring the regulatory functions of the HCPC to the college. Narey (2014: 27) also endorsed the college playing a more central role in relation to the quality assurance of social work degree programmes offered by higher education institutions.

However, in June 2015, it was announced that the College of Social Work was to close after only three years. The college had run into financial difficulties, partly because it had failed to recruit a large enough paying membership. However, Jones (2019: 69) suggests that the government had not had confidence in the college to deliver reform, pointing out that the collapse of the college followed a decision to award the £2 million contract to develop the new accreditation scheme to KPMG rather than the college. Yet, the government accepted the argument that a specialist regulator for social work was needed. Thus, it was belatedly agreed that a new regulator would be established. However, as Jones (2019: 70–3) explains, while the establishment of a new stand-alone regulator separate from the HCPC was broadly welcomed, the proposed relationship between Social Work England and the government provoked further concern within the children's sector. It was initially proposed that the new regulator would operate as an executive agency tied to the DfE and DH. This would have given the Secretary of State for Education much closer control over 'who could and could not be a social worker and how they were to be educated and trained, by whom, and what was to be the content of their education' (Jones, 2019: 71). Responding to widespread opposition from social work groups, the LGA and the ADCS, ministers accepted the argument that greater independence from the government was needed. However, it must be noted that the Secretary of State will be able to determine the Chair and the Chief Executive of Social Work England (Jones, 2019: 72–3). Furthermore, concerns have been expressed regarding the representation of experienced social work practitioners on the board of Social Work England (Haynes, 2019).

A national learning infrastructure

Munro (2011: 5) spoke about moving from a compliance to a learning culture in child and family social work. Ministers have responded to this by committing to the development of a 'national learning infrastructure that brings together everything we know about the best ways of helping our most vulnerable children, and makes this available and easily accessible to the whole system' (DfE, 2016c: 27–8). An important challenge for child and family social workers, as well as professionals in partner agencies, has always been to learn lessons from serious cases of child abuse. Thus, LSCBs operating independently of local authorities and other child safeguarding agencies have been responsible for overseeing local SCRs. However, ministers took the view that SCRs overseen by some LSCBs had not been sufficiently rigorous, which was a view supported by the findings of Wood's (2016) review, discussed in Chapter 8. Edward Timpson, Children's Minister between 2012 and 2017, confirmed this while also acknowledging that political responses to serious cases have also been unhelpful, commenting that:

> Too often either SCRs haven't answered the 'why' questions sufficiently well to enable proper learning, improvement and sustained reform, or the local agencies reinvent process off the back of a local review without fundamentally tackling the aspects of their service that are the root cause of their failings. Social work is still comparatively a fledgling profession and hasn't yet developed a mature learning culture, not helped by the Shoesmith episode where finger pointing achieves nothing other than a ramping up of risk averse behaviour. (Email correspondence with Edward Timpson, 2019)

Thus, under the Children and Social Work Act 2017, a new national Child Safeguarding Practice Review Panel was created. The panel is responsible for investigating cases that it believes to be of national importance. The Association of Independent LSCB Chairs (AILC) expressed concern about the independence of the new panel from ministerial control. However, it was subsequently announced that membership of the panel would include individuals with wide experience of running child protection services across local authorities, health, schools and the courts, though it is important to note that the panel was initially chaired by Timpson, after having lost his seat at the 2017 election (Jones, 2019: 66–7).

Another key component of the new national learning infrastructure is the What Works Centre for Children's Social Care. The centre was set up with an initial £20 million provided by the DfE, with the aim for it to become a fully independent self-financing organisation by March 2020. The centre's website states:

> What Works for Children's Social Care seeks better outcomes for children, young people and families by bringing the best available evidence to practitioners and other decision makers across the children's social care sector. (What Works Centre for Children's Services, 2019)

The centre has the potential to draw together a wide range of research evidence relating to children's social care in order to inform policymaking at both the national and local levels. However, it is important to note that the establishment of the centre has also been steered by individuals closely involved in the development of DfE policy on children's social care, with Sir Alan Wood, author of the

Wood Review (Wood, 2016), being appointed as the founding chair of the centre (Donovan, 2018; Jones, 2019: 98).

'Innovation' and further structural reform

The centrally directed reforms to social work training, regulation and learning processes discussed earlier have largely superseded the profession-led reform programme initiated by the SWTF. On the other hand, DfE policymakers have acknowledged that 'There is a consensus stemming from the Munro Review that over-regulation gets in the way of good social work practice and prevents social workers and other staff from putting children first' (DfE, 2016c: 35). It is therefore important to reflect on recent reform initiatives that have promised to reduce bureaucratic requirements and create the space for child and family social workers to 'innovate'.

In March 2013, the government published a new slimmed-down version of the statutory multi-agency safeguarding guide *Working Together* (HM Government, 2013), as Munro had recommended. Speaking later that year, Gove (2013: 3) declared that 'We need to break out of bureaucratic ways of working and generate the sort of innovation that delivers dramatically better results'. The speech followed the launch of the DfE's Innovation Programme. Through the programme, £300 million has been allocated since 2014 to local authorities and other organisations to 'test new approaches to tackling the most important and difficult practice questions facing the children's social care system' (DfE, 2016c: 29–30). In the first phase of the programme, the DfE funded projects that aimed to redesign organisational systems and practice frameworks, as well as projects to rethink support for adolescents in or on the edge of care (DfE, 2016c: 30). The DfE has also established the Partners in Practice initiative, through which local authorities that are engaged in the Innovation Programme have been encouraged to share their learning. It is claimed that this approach 'puts genuine partnership between local and national government at the heart of work to improve services, with our very best practitioners and leaders in the driving seat of reform for children and young people' (DfE, 2016c: 33).

Outsourcing children's social care services

However, although local authorities have been able to bid for funding to support a range of practice-centred initiatives, ministers have also actively promoted more radical structural reform. Gove (2013: 8) asked the provocative question: 'Why must all child protection services be delivered in-house?' In the same speech, he also challenged the assumption that social workers must always be managed by senior professionals and, echoing the rhetoric of the academies and free schools programmes, suggested that greater diversity in the provision of children's social care services might be needed. A few months later, in April 2014, the DfE published a consultation document on proposals to change regulations so that any organisation could be contracted to provide statutory child and family social work and child protection services (DfE, 2014).

Although various aspects of children's social care had long been contracted out to voluntary and private sector agencies, these proposals opened up the possibility that child protection investigations, decisions about initiating care proceedings and removing children from their families, and decisions about where children in care should live could now be outsourced for the first time. The short six-week consultation period on these proposals seemed designed to discourage dialogue with the sector. Notwithstanding the short window, the consultation generated significant concern, and the government's proposals were strongly criticised in a joint letter signed by 37 senior social work academics, including Professor Munro (Butler, 2014). The ADCS's (2014) response was more conciliatory, but nonetheless expressed the clear view that the delivery of child protection services 'should not be predicated on a profit motive'. Initially, it appeared as though the DfE would take heed of these concerns after it announced that the direct contracting out to profit-making companies would not be allowed. However, it later emerged that private companies would be able to bid for contracts to deliver child protection services by setting up a separate non-profit-making subsidiary (Jones, 2019: 13–17).

In July 2014, Gove was replaced as Secretary of State. However, ministers pushed ahead and the search for 'alternative delivery models for children's social care' became the explicit focus of the second phase of the Innovation Programme (DfE, 2016c: 32). In the foreword to *Putting Children First* (DfE, 2016c), Nicky Morgan, Gove's successor as Secretary of State, and Edward Timpson, who had been in the post of Children's Minister for almost four years by then, stated:

> We want a system staffed and led by the best trained professionals; dynamic and free to innovate in the interests of children; delivered through a more diverse range of social care organisations; with less bureaucracy; smarter checks and balances designed to hold the system to account in the

right ways; and new ways to intervene where services fail.
(Morgan and Timpson, in DfE, 2016c: 4–5)

Thus, the concept of innovation became increasingly associated with the outsourcing of local authority child protection services. In the previous statement, bureaucratic constraints are implicitly linked to local authorities, as they were under the academies and free schools programmes. As with schools, ministers have presented separation from local authority control as a key way to address service 'failure', empower front-line professionals and improve services to children and families. Plans to facilitate the outsourcing of child protection services did not involve detailed discussions with NGOs in the children's sector. However, conversations between DfE policymakers and the big private sector outsourcing companies did take place (Jones, 2019: 23–9). This set ministers on a collision course with key NGOs and individual experts in the children's sector ahead of the publication of the Children and Social Work Bill in May 2016.

Article 39 and the Children and Social Work Bill

Tunstill and Willow (2017: 49) point out that 'Unusually for a Bill with such wide-ranging provisions, there had been no Green or White Papers and therefore no opportunity for children, young people and families, and those who work with them, to express their views'. Under the Bill, clauses were included that would have given the Secretary of State the power to exempt local authorities from statutory obligations. Ministers argued that these *innovation clauses* would be used to enable local authorities to experiment with new ways of delivering services. However, the charity Article 39, led by Carolyne Willow, quickly raised concerns regarding the potential impact of these *exemption clauses* on the rights of vulnerable children and young people. Over 50 NGOs in the children's sector joined Article 39 to campaign against the clauses.

After winning the support of Lord Laming, Professor Munro and former Children's Minister Tim Loughton, the clauses were abandoned by the then Secretary of State for Education, Justine Greening (Tunstill and Willow, 2017; Jones, 2019: 54–61). Seemingly unperturbed by this defeat, the recently appointed Children's Minister, Nadhim Zahawi, approved the distribution of a 'myth-busting' guide to local authorities in July 2018. The guide suggested that local authorities are entitled to withdraw support currently provided to children in long-term foster placements who go missing or have run away from home. Following a legal challenge by Article 39, the DfE was also forced to withdraw this guidance in March 2019 (Allison and Hattenstone, 2019).

After the defeat of the innovation/exemption clauses, Timpson conceded that 'We were unable to build the consensus required to take forward the power to innovate' (quoted in Jones, 2019: 60). However, the DfE still has the power to instruct 'inadequate' local authorities to develop alternative delivery arrangements for children's social care services. Moreover, ministers have instructed local authorities in Doncaster, Slough, Sandwell, Birmingham, Reading and Worcestershire to contract out their children's social care services (Jones, 2019: 33–4). The contracting out of services in these authorities has been deemed necessary to bring about changes in leadership at the local level. However, structural reform has also been presented as the solution to more widespread challenges faced across the children's social care system after a decade of welfare reform and cuts to early intervention services. In *Putting Children First* (DfE, 2016c: 42–3, emphasis added), it is argued:

> Through the Innovation Programme and through Partners in Practice, we have begun to see some real excellence emerge in the provision of children's social care services. It remains the case, however, that there are too few examples of excellence and too many examples of failure or of organisations struggling to deliver strong services. Too often vulnerable children and families have not been the singular focus for how services are managed; innovation has not been given the space to thrive; data have not been used intelligently; leadership has not been strong enough; and services have not been delivered within a coherent and consistent framework, driving practice. *Local authorities are also facing an increasingly constrained fiscal climate, seeing greater demand for services and dealing with new threats to children and young people. All of this makes a clear case to do things differently.* Structural solutions and stronger accountability have an important role to play in driving change.

For critics of recent reforms, 'innovation' has been code for privatisation and the abrogation of legal obligations to provide services to vulnerable children and their families in a context of significant cuts to universal and community-based children's services and increased demand pressure on specialist social care services (Tunstill and Willow, 2017; Jones, 2019).

A profession still struggling to be heard?

Although the Labour years saw increased investment in children's services and closer working between central government and NGOs, the social work profession remained poorly represented in policymaking circles. Under Labour's ECM framework, a strong emphasis was placed on the role of universal services, while the preventative role of local authority social workers under Section 17 of the Children Act 1989 continued to be overlooked. Moreover, following the Victoria Climbié inquiry (Lord Laming, 2003), negative attitudes towards the profession hardened. Subsequent reforms aimed at improving the effectiveness of child protection practice created more bureaucratic controls and further restricted the autonomy of social workers.

In one sense, the Baby P crisis marked a nadir for child and family social workers. The volume and tone of public and political criticism directed towards professionals surpassed that of previous child abuse scandals stretching back over several decades. However, the case also provided an opportunity for professional representatives to voice their concerns regarding Labour's reforms and neglect of social work (Garrett, 2009b). Cross-party support for the recommendations of the SWTF (2009) appeared to mark the beginning of a period of professional renewal. After the formation of the Coalition government in 2010, the new Children's Minister, Tim Loughton, gave his backing to the reform programme led by the SWRB under the leadership of Gibb, which subsequently handed over to the College of Social Work. Loughton also looked to Professor Munro to advise the government on the steps that should be taken to scale back centrally imposed controls and enhance the autonomy of front-line social workers. Furthermore, although Loughton's primary interest was in improving the effectiveness of the child protection system, he did not challenge the generic basis of initial social work training, which social work educators continued to defend. He also supported the consistent emphasis that professional representatives, including Munro, had placed on the preventative role of social workers.

However, after Loughton was replaced in September 2012, the profession-led reform programme was sidelined as a new, more centrally directed programme took shape. Speaking in December 2013, Gibb reflected: "I am disappointed that the Reform Board's work has not had the continued attention from DfE in particular that it needed. It wasn't a quick win, but a ten-year programme. New things are pursued instead". The new reform programme initiated by Gove, which has been taken forward by successive secretaries of state and children's ministers, challenged the pace and direction of the work of the SWRB and the College of Social Work. Significantly, DfE policymakers identified *child and family* social work as a distinct profession, challenging the generic basis of most social work degrees. Furthermore, the emphasis placed on the importance of swifter intervention to protect children at risk from harm also challenged the widespread emphasis placed on the importance of preventative work. In this context, Timpson acknowledged taking a cautious approach to engaging with sector representatives, commenting:

> Children's services policy is and should be open to input and influence by outside expertise, although this shouldn't be viewed as always being a relentlessly positive influence. Outside organisations do help provide some important checks and balances into policy making but I was always wary of vested interests and side agendas creeping into the equation. At their best outside organisations can help vastly improve the response to a policy dilemma but at their worst can set the profession back. (Email correspondence with Edward Timpson, 2019)

However, Jones (2019: ch 3) points out that the DfE's new reform programme has been guided by a small group of individuals with surprisingly limited collective experience of managing local authority children's social care services. The influence of Sir Martin Narey over Gove's thinking on social work education and regulation was discussed earlier. The role of Josh McAlister in relation to the Frontline programme was also discussed. Jones also highlights the influence of Sir Julian Le Grand, a social policy professor at the London School of Economics and Political Science. Le Grand had previously been an advisor to Blair on public services reform and has been a strong advocate for contracting out. The influence of Sir Alan Wood in relation to the reform of LSCBs was referred to in the discussion in this chapter and Chapter 8.

Isabelle Trowler, the Chief Social Worker for Children and Families, previously worked under Wood at the London Borough of Hackney. Unlike Narey, McAlister, LeGrand and Wood, Trowler does have experience working as a social worker and as an assistant director of children's social care services. However, although the appointment of a Chief Social Worker had been a recommendation of the SWTF and *The Munro Review*, Trowler was appointed as one of two chief social workers (children and adults) when a single representative had been called for. Furthermore, according to Jones (2019: 94), Trowler has 'frequently been the public spokesperson promoting government policies for social work rather than ministers'. Her enthusiasm for the DfE's reform programme was evident in a letter to social workers published alongside the policy statement *Putting Children First* (DfE, 2016c). Here, Trowler comments:

> The fantastic and inspiring Innovation Programme, our radical Partners in Practice Programme, the new power to innovate, new opportunities for post qualification CPD [continuing professional development] and specialist accreditation under a dedicated new body for social work as one profession, a new What Work's Centre to get research into the heart of practice, are just some of the motivating changes in which government will invest. Some of you might have to suspend disbelief to become part of this progressive movement of change, and I urge you to do so. Don't let others interpret this opportunity for you and don't let it pass you by. (DfE, 2016c: 7)

Loughton, who had supported Trowler's appointment, has also criticised her 'below the radar' approach as a 'quiet adviser behind the scenes'. In his view, the Chief Social Worker should have a much higher public profile and act as a 'conduit between policymakers and professionals on the ground' (quoted in Hayes, 2016). Moreover, the absence of a critical voice within the DfE, which is a problem that the appointment of a Chief Social Worker was designed to address, has also been reflected in the marginalisation of established NGOs, such as the BASW, ADCS, LGA, APSW and JUCSWEC (Jones, 2019: 104). The absence of constructive dialogue with these groups has fermented widespread criticism and opposition to the numerous reform initiatives discussed in this chapter.

Discussion

This chapter has provided further evidence of the influence that individual ministers can have over policymaking. During the first two years of the Coalition government, the Children's Minister, Tim Loughton, played a central role in driving social work reform. Importantly, Loughton gave his backing to the work of the SWRB, set up under Labour, and worked closely with social work representatives to review bureaucratic requirements developed by successive governments to try to control professional practice. This included commissioning *The Munro Review* (Munro, 2011). Furthermore, although Loughton's main interest was in the child protection responsibilities of social workers, he accepted the generic basis of initial social work training and the argument that social workers must play a broader role in relation to the provision of preventative or 'early-help' (Munro, 2011) services. It was Gove's intervention in this area of children's policy that initiated a change of course. After Loughton was replaced, the reforms led by the College of Social Work were effectively abandoned. Moreover, new policy developments on *child and family* social work training, regulation and professional learning have ignored arguments in favour of generic training and emphasised the discrete child protection responsibilities of social workers.

Gove's intervention brought the familiar narrative of local service and professional failure back to the forefront of official policy statements. This was amplified by Cameron following the publication of inquiries into child sexual exploitation in Rotherham and Oxfordshire. This narrative has provided the justification for changes to social work training, regulation and learning processes directed by the government. However, it has also deflected attention from concerns about the deep cuts to funding for early intervention services and the impact of welfare reforms, with the freedom to innovate having been presented as the panacea to the challenge of rising demand for specialist social care services. As with the Coalition and Conservative governments' reforms to the schools system, mistrust of local government and a preference for the outsourcing of child protection services to private and voluntary sector providers have also been evident. Whereas *The Munro Review* advocated greater professional freedom from bureaucratic controls imposed by *central* government, ministers have criticised 'inadequate' *local* bureaucracies for not making best use of the increasingly stretched resources available to them. Thus, it is again important to recognise the significance of the wider political context.

The centralisation of policymaking has been reflected in changes to the relationship between the DfE and NGOs representing child and family social workers. The Baby P case had forced Labour ministers to engage with the profession after generally ignoring or even vilifying it over the previous decade. As a shadow minister, Loughton had already committed to working with social work representatives to promote the renewal of the profession. As a minister in the Coalition government, he supported the work of the SWRB and the College of Social Work, and committed the government to the rationalisation of bureaucratic controls in order to enhance the autonomy of social workers. However, this period of closer working between DfE policymakers and the profession was only brief. Some aspects of the DfE's new reform programme initiated in the latter years of the Coalition government have divided opinion among social work employers and educators. The Frontline training scheme provides the best example of this. However, the lack of dialogue with representatives of the profession has more frequently resulted in the criticism of new initiatives. Perhaps the clearest example of this has been the opposition to DfE plans to make it easier to outsource child protection services. On the one hand, the success of Article 39 in blocking clauses included in the Children's Social Work Bill suggests that NGOs can still influence policy and that campaigning remains important. On the other hand, this public battle also revealed the extent to which ministers have been determined to take on, rather than work with, NGOs in the children's sector. This campaign also needs to be understood in the context of the government's more widespread disengagement from NGOs in the children's sector and an ongoing programme of public sector austerity and welfare reform, as discussed in Chapter 8.

Conclusion: the politics of children's services reform

Introduction

Changes to child welfare policy over the last decade have strengthened the case for categorising the English system as a *child protection* rather than a *family service* system (Parton, 2014: ch 1). By examining the key drivers of policy change, this research has helped to explain this shift, while also accounting for unresolved tensions and contradictions in policy. Public and political debate about the English child welfare system has tended to take place in the shadow of high-profile child abuse inquiries and media-generated scandals. Moreover, successive waves of national reform have been framed by ministers as responses to inquiry findings and the perceived failures of local agencies and professionals, invariably social workers. This book has challenged this perception by turning the spotlight on policymaking at the national level, drawing on theories of the policymaking process and interviews with prominent policymakers under the Labour and Conservative-led governments. The purpose of this concluding chapter is to reflect on these findings by summarising the key features of children's services policymaking over the last two decades.

The national politics of local service failure

The narrative connecting children's services reform and high-profile child abuse inquiries has been reinforced by ministers. However, previous research suggests that it is media pressure that drives ministerial responses, more so than the findings of the inquiries themselves (Parton, 1985, 2014; Butler and Drakeford, 2005, 2012; Stafford et al, 2012; Warner, 2015). The Maria Colwell inquiry (Secretary of State for Social Services, 1974) has been identified as a landmark case in this regard. Following the scandal surrounding the circumstances of Maria's death, and the agencies and professionals implicated, ministers searched for ways to assert tighter bureaucratic control over social services and social workers. Moreover, following subsequent inquiries over the next two decades, the responsibilities of specialist *child and family* social workers became increasingly prescribed (Parton, 2014: ch 2). In the period covered by this research, two cases stand out for the volume and ferocity of media coverage, and the changes to child welfare policy that they came to be associated with. Labour's ECM reform programme (HM Government, 2003) was presented as a response to the Victoria Climbié inquiry (Lord Laming, 2003) and required significant changes to the way in which local children's agencies were organised. Following media coverage of the Baby P case just five years later, Labour ministers were forced to address the government's neglect of social workers, and the sharp end of safeguarding and child protection practice, under the ECM framework.

Although Parton (2014) highlights the continued importance of child abuse scandals to the development of children's services policy, he also acknowledges that it is important to assess the extent to which specific cases 'have acted as the main drivers of policy change and influenced the direction that such change has taken, or whether they act primarily as helpful vehicles for bringing about changes that were already planned' (Parton, 2014: 176). The evidence presented in this book in relation to the Victoria Climbié case points clearly towards the latter. First, the case for the structural reform of social services was being made by Labour ministers long before the publication of Lord Laming's (2003) report. Moreover, the extended remit of the inquiry established it as a springboard for structural reform even before the circumstances of Victoria's death had been properly investigated. Second, it was also argued in Chapter 4 that reform proposals included in the ECM Green Paper, including for the structural reform of local government, reflected the Treasury's progressive universalism perspective on children's services and the emphasis that this placed on the extension of early intervention and preventative services to support a wide range of child well-being concerns. ECM did not deliver the explicit prioritisation of safeguarding policy that Lord Laming had called for, and his recommendation to establish a new National Agency for Children and Families was rejected. Thus, although the Victoria Climbié inquiry did mark an important point in the development of children's services policy, it did not drive policy change to the extent that it was officially claimed. Rather, the inquiry was used to deflect widespread opposition to ministers' pre-existing plans for the structural reform of local government.

On the other hand, the Baby P case does stand out as a clearer example of policy change driven by inquiry and scandal. Labour ministers interviewed for this research, including the then Secretary of State, Ed Balls, acknowledged that the circumstances of Baby P's death forced the government to accept that not enough attention had been given to the sharp end of safeguarding and child protection practice, including the social work profession. Independent reviews of child protection (Lord Laming, 2009) and social work (SWTF, 2009) followed and the Labour government accepted the recommendations of both reviews unequivocally (HM Government, 2009: 2010). However, it is also important to recognise the role played by the Conservative opposition in provoking media and public reactions to the case, as well as the pressure that this placed on ministers. Cameron's decision to use the Baby P case to attack the Labour government was a key factor driving sustained media coverage of the case, particularly in *The Sun* newspaper (Warner, 2013; Jones, 2014). Furthermore, the Conservative Party's response to the case should also be viewed in the context of wider debates regarding the future direction of social policy. The Baby P case provided an opportunity for Cameron to critique Labour's progressive universalism policies and promote his party's alternative policies under the Broken Britain framework in the run-up to the 2010 election.

However, perhaps the most striking and consistent feature of ministerial responses to serious cases has been the use of inquiries to deflect attention from national policy and keep the spotlight on supposed policy implementation failures at the local level. The way in which the Victoria Climbié inquiry was used to help bring about pre-planned changes has already been highlighted. However, even during the Baby P crisis, Ed Balls sought to deflect criticism of Labour's response to the Victoria Climbié inquiry by instructing Lord Laming (2009) to only report on the local *implementation* of safeguarding policies misleadingly tied to the Victoria Climbié inquiry (Lord Laming, 2003). Although Balls claimed that his demand for Haringey Council to sack their DCS, Sharon Shoesmith, was made in response to a damming Ofsted inspection report, this also served to keep the spotlight on local failings. Furthermore, under the Coalition and Conservative governments' social work reform programme, the local failure narrative continues to play a critical role. Ministers have criticised local authorities and social workers for having an 'optimism bias' (Gove, 2012), and failing to take more decisive action to protect children, drawing on recent serious cases, including Baby P. Moreover, in the context of declining local authority budgets and rising demand for social care services, ministers have claimed that 'too many examples of failure or of organisations struggling to deliver services' (DfE, 2016c: 162) justify structural reforms, including the outsourcing of child protection services. As a Labour Treasury official explained: "Government always needs a platform to be able to argue it needs change, and tragically it very often uses a platform of poor services".

The priorities of party leaders and ministers

The second narrative reviewed in Chapter 1 emphasised the dominance of neoliberal ideology over the past 40 years. Social work researchers and commentators have argued that following the collapse of the post-war social-democratic consensus, consecutive governments, both Labour and Conservative led, have prioritised the deregulation of the private sector and have sought to limit spending on welfare services and curtail the power of public sector professionals. Moreover, the influence of neoliberal ideology is detected in policies on child protection and social work, including responses to high-profile child abuse inquiries (Ferguson and Woodward, 2009; Garrett, 2009a, 2016; Rogowski, 2011, 2016; Featherstone et al, 2014, 2018; Lee, 2014; Parton, 2014; Jones, 2019). First, the dominance of managerial and market controls, and the corresponding de-professionalisation of social work practice, is highlighted. In this context, social workers are expected to focus primarily on compliance with bureaucratic processes, leaving less space to exercise professional judgement and build relationships with children and families. Second, the emphasis on universal/collective welfare services and the role of social workers in working *with* families to address needs is deemed to have been undermined by policies that downplay socio-economic inequalities and promote a more authoritarian approach to identifying and responding to the perceived behavioural deviancies of parents and carers. Evidence collected for this research lends support to this perspective. With the exception of a brief period following the Baby P case, reforms to social work have generally been driven by central government policymakers, with only limited input from representatives of the social work profession, and have primarily focused on the narrow child protection responsibilities of social workers.

However, a more complex picture emerges when we take better account of reforms not directly related to social work. Moreover, significant differences in Labour and Conservative approaches to children's services reform have been identified. Although the 'New' Labour government initially adopted a cautious approach to economic and social policy, the economic determinants of poverty and life chances were recognised by the Labour leadership. Thus, the Brown Treasury used the tax and benefits system to lift almost 1 million children and families out of poverty (Brewer, 2012). It also sanctioned significant increases in spending on health and education services following the 2000 Spending Review (HM Treasury, 2000), as well as funding new initiatives such as Sure Start and the Children's Fund. Furthermore, it has been argued in this book that Labour's ECM reform programme (HM Government, 2003) built upon these earlier *progressive universalism* initiatives to try to embed a stronger focus on early intervention and preventative services, and thereby address a wider range of welfare concerns affecting the most economically disadvantaged children and families.

The overarching approach adopted by the leaders of the Coalition and Conservative governments has been markedly different. Although Cameron and Clegg claimed to be committed to improving social justice and social mobility, Cameron's statements on social policy downplayed the relevance of economic inequalities and promoted more authoritarian approaches to dealing with 'troubled' or 'dysfunctional' families. Furthermore, under Chancellor Osborne's deficit reduction plan, welfare payments to families were significantly cut, resulting in the reversal of progress made under Labour in reducing child poverty (Joseph Rowntree Foundation, 2018). Early statements on social policy made by Theresa May after she became Prime Minister in 2016 proved to be equally hollow in the context of ongoing austerity and the challenge of delivering Brexit. The period since the EU referendum has been notable for a number of promised strategies and position papers that have been shelved or kicked into the long grass, including those on Life Chances, children's centres and youth services. Thus, even though ministers continue to acknowledge the importance of providing 'early-help' services to families (HM Government, 2018a), local authorities have been forced to significantly reduce spending on services such as children's centres and youth services so that they can respond to rising demand for specialist children's social care services (Action for Children et al, 2019; ADCS, 2018b; NAO, 2019). This book has demonstrated that differences between the priorities of the Labour and Conservative leaders have been an important factor driving the English child welfare system away from a family service orientation and back towards a narrower child protection focus.

On the other hand, it is important not to overstate the extent to which children's policy has been directly influenced by party leaders. First, in the Labour period, ministers had to make sense of tensions and contradictions between the policy priorities of Blair and Brown, which spilled over into disagreements over the government's approach to public services reform. Although Blair was supportive of steps taken by the Treasury to address child poverty, his interest in education policy challenged key aspects of the Treasury's progressive universalism approach to children's services, including the delivery of the ECM reform programme. Under Blair, Labour education policies prioritised raising levels of school and pupil achievement in exams, whereas the ECM policy framework promoted a broader focus on a range of child well-being concerns, including but not limited to educational achievement. Blair's commitment to extending choice and competition in public services also required greater autonomy to be given to schools at the same time as ECM sought to better integrate local children's services and establish accountability to children's services departments and children's trusts. Furthermore, Blair also identified the electoral importance of tough policies to tackle youth crime and anti-social behaviour. However, policy initiatives such as the ASBO served to demonise some groups of young people, whereas the progressive universalism approach of ECM emphasised the importance of providing positive activities for all young people to help identify and prevent the emergence of problem behaviours. It was only after Blair left office that ECM was placed on an equal footing with education policy and a clearer position on youth services was established.

Second, it was argued in Chapter 8 that following the 2010 election, Secretary of State Michael Gove was afforded considerable autonomy in determining the children's policy priorities of the Coalition government, priorities that have not changed substantially since he was replaced in 2014. Gove made the implementation of the academies and free school programmes the number one priority for the renamed 'Department for Education'. Given Cameron's proclaimed commitment to early intervention policies and promises made to refocus key services such as children's centres, Gove could not publicly abandon the department's wider responsibilities in relation to children's services. However, under his leadership, the broader children's policy responsibilities of the DfE were largely neglected, and DfE policymakers did not engage to any great extent in the development of policies on services such as children's centres and youth services. The preventative focus of children's services policy was further undermined after Tim Loughton was replaced as Children's Minister and Gove redirected the sector-led social work reform programme in late 2012. Whereas the sector-led programme emphasised the broad responsibilities of a *generic* social work profession, the new centrally directed programme placed a much stronger emphasis on the narrow child protection responsibilities of *child and family* social workers. These findings do not undermine the emphasis that social work researchers have placed on the socio-economic context of child welfare policy. However, this book has suggested that the development of child protection and social work policies must also take account of developments in overlapping policy areas, particularly education, and recognise that different party leaders and ministers can interpret and respond to structural constraints in different ways.

The ubiquity of structural reform

The role played by party leaders and ministers in driving children's services reform also challenges the view that policymaking is generally dominated by Whitehall interests resistant to change (Marsh et al, 2001, 2003; Richards and Smith, 2002, 2004; Marsh, 2008, 2011; Richards, 2008; Marsh and Hall, 2016). The determination of Blair to assert closer control over different aspects of children's policy in Whitehall was reflected in the creation of new policy units, including the SEU, the Standards and Effectiveness Unit (for education policy) and the Anti-Social Behaviour Unit. Similarly, the Sure Start Unit and the CYPU were set up to lead the Treasury-backed Sure Start and Children's Fund programmes. The Brown Treasury held the additional advantage of being able to use the Spending Review process to influence departmental policymaking. The culmination of these efforts to 'join up' children's policy was the establishment of the CYP Directorate in the DfES, bringing together policymaking resources from across Whitehall. Although education policymakers in the DfES were initially resistant to the ECM agenda, this must be viewed in the context of Blair's education reform priorities, rather than as evidence of the capacity for Whitehall interests to resist policy change. Moreover, both Balls and Gove were able to impose their own priorities on the department. After becoming Secretary of State for the 'Department for Children, Schools and Families', Balls effectively relaunched the ECM reform programme, which had been held back while Blair remained in office. After the 2010 election, Gove moved quickly to make his academies and free schools programmes the number one priority in the 'Department for Education'. These changes are consistent with the view that British policymaking has become an increasingly politicised process over recent years (Moran, 2007; King and Crewe, 2014; Richards and Smith, 2016; Richardson, 2018; Diamond, 2019). More specifically, the findings of this research support the claim that it is generally ministers and their political advisers who direct policy, leaving civil servants to concentrate on the technical challenge of implementing politically determined reform priorities (Richards and Smith, 2016; Richardson, 2018: 225).

Moran (2007: 131) identifies 'hyper-innovation' as a hallmark of contemporary British policymaking, one of the indicators of which is the 'ubiquity of institutional reorganisation'. The changes in Whitehall described earlier fit this description. However, it is the perpetual reform of *local* structures that has arguably been the defining feature of children's services policymaking over the last two decades. Under the Labour government, the structural reform of local children's services emerged as a central theme of national policy towards the end of the first term. Initially, ministers identified closer partnership working between the public and charitable sectors as central to the effective delivery of new social policy initiatives such as Sure Start. DH (1998a: 49) policymakers warned against the restructuring of local authority social services on the basis that 'This would create new boundaries and lead to instability and diversion of management effort.' However, as the Labour leadership grew impatient with the perceived slow pace of policy delivery, this position was dropped. Alan Milburn, the new Secretary of State for Health and ally of Blair, initiated a children's trust pilot programme to encourage local authorities to experiment with new ways to commission and deliver health and social care services for vulnerable children. However, this was quickly superseded by the initiation of the ECM Green Paper (HM Government, 2003) led by the Cabinet Office and overseen by the Chief Secretary to the Treasury, Paul Boateng. Under the subsequent Children Act 2004, proposals for structural reform were passed into law and *all* English local authorities were required to break up social services and set up new children's services departments under a single DCS. The Change for Children programme (HM Government, 2004) set out clear expectations regarding the timetable for the establishment of these new arrangements, alongside a common framework of policy priorities, performance targets and planning requirements, as well as new child and family assessment processes and data-collection requirements. More detailed prescription regarding the form and function of multi-agency children's trusts was published later (DCSF, 2008a).

The detailed prescription of service delivery structures is consistent with the view that ministers under pressure to demonstrate impact are drawn into the micromanagement of policy implementation (Moran, 2007; King and Crewe, 2014; Diamond, 2019). However, the drivers of structural reform under the Coalition and Conservative governments have been more complex. On the one hand, reforms have continued to be driven by the ambitions of ministers. First, structural reform has been presented as the panacea for school improvement under the academies and free schools programmes initiated by Gove. Almost a decade into the programme, and after half of all state-funded schools have been converted to academy status, ministers have continued to push more schools to convert (DfE, 2019). Moreover, under the programmes, the authority and capacity of local children's services departments to continue to meet their responsibilities in relation to the welfare of children and young people have been challenged (Baginsky et al, 2015). This has been compounded by the scrapping of LSCBs and the exemption of schools from new multi-agency safeguarding arrangements. Second, since 2014, ministers have promoted outsourcing as the solution to 'failing' local authority children's social care services, arguing that 'Structural solutions and stronger accountability have an important role to play in driving change' (DfE, 2016c: 43).

Paradoxically, however, the restructuring of local services in recent years has also been driven by the *disengagement* of Coalition and Conservative ministers from the broad child welfare agenda. After a decade of public sector austerity, and as the impact of welfare reforms affecting children and families have been felt, local authorities have been forced to continually restructure local services in an ongoing search for financial savings and to respond to rising demand for children's social care services (ADCS, 2018b; APPG for Children, 2018; NAO, 2019). Consequently, local authority spending on early intervention services, including children's centres and youth services, was cut by 49 per cent between 2010/11 and 2017/18 (Action for Children et al, 2019: 3). Although the picture varies between local authority areas, research examining the overall impact of these cuts points towards the significant hollowing out of universal and preventative services nationally, with further restructuring planned to meet future savings targets (Sutton Trust, 2018; YMCA, 2018). Moreover, the LGA (2019: 2) has predicted a £3.1 billion shortfall in funding for children's services by 2024/25. In this context, ministers have promoted the devolution of policy decisions to avoid close association with the implications of austerity and welfare reform, enabling them to blame local leaders for unpopular decisions regarding the restructuring or closure of services. This has also helped ministers to frame subsequent service failings identified by Ofsted inspectors, or in SCRs, as a failure of local leadership and policy implementation, while avoiding the scrutiny of national policies.

The role of NGOs

This research has also examined the influence of NGOs over children's services policy. Rhodes (1997, 2007, 2017) has argued that the capacity of central government to direct policymaking has been significantly 'hollowed out' over recent decades and that policymaking has consequently become increasingly dominated by 'self-steering inter-organisational networks' (Rhodes, 1997: 5). However, this research has provided strong evidence to support the contrary view that British policymaking has become increasingly politicised over recent decades. From this perspective, the terms of NGO engagement in policymaking are largely determined by ministers. Thus, consultation tends to take places within 'restricted parameters' with reforms 'enforced against the resistance of at least some organised groups' (Richardson, 2018: 216).

In the early Labour years, representatives of the children's charity sector enjoyed unprecedented access to government policymakers. Advice and guidance provided to ministers and civil servants were critical to the development of new social policy initiatives, as the example of Sure Start has illustrated (see Chapter 2). Moreover, the input of key individuals representing the charity sector remained an important aspect of policymaking for children's services throughout the Labour period. This even involved the appointment of charity leaders to lead policy reviews, to act as special advisers to ministers and to lead the implementation of new policies in civil service posts. However, this was not an example of NGOs determining policy. First, representatives from the charity sector were valued as an alternative source of advice to counter perceived vested interests in Whitehall and local government, which were expected to be resistant to reform. The charities helped ministers to turn political priorities into more detailed policies that "would feel right to the sector" (interview with Treasury official) and to draw up plans for the implementation of new initiatives. Second, while charities were critical of some aspects of Labour's social policy, they generally shared the Treasury's commitment to tackling the economic determinants of child poverty. Moreover, many charity leaders were Labour supporters, and some had even been active in party campaigns to promote alternative economic and social policy priorities to those established under the Conservatives. Thus, the children's charities could be relied upon to support the Treasury's promotion of progressive universalism policies within the Labour government.

Labour ministers later recognised that the cooperation of representatives of the statutory sector was also essential to the successful implementation of the ECM reforms. The new DCS community was well represented through secondments to the government's new CYP Directorate and new forums where ministers could hear about progress being made with the implementation of structural reform at the local level. However, alongside their counterparts in the charity sector, the DCS community was only expected to offer technical advice. It should be recalled that the CIAG, set up ahead of the publication of the Victoria Climbié inquiry, had failed to persuade ministers that structural reform was not needed (see Chapter 4). Following the passage of the Children Act 2004, NGOs accepted that the argument on structural reform had been lost and that they needed to work constructively with ministers and officials to try to influence implementation plans. This was particularly important to members of the new DCS community because many owed their elevated status in local government to the ECM programme, and therefore held a significant stake in making sure that the new arrangements could be made to stick.

Developments since the 2010 election underline the extent to which the involvement of NGOs in the policymaking process was tied to the interest of Labour ministers. Initially, some NGOs sought to adapt to the change of government by tailoring their policy positions to take account of the Conservative Party's Broken Britain framework and by seeking to demonstrate the economic effectiveness of their services (Action for Children and NEF, 2009; Action for Children, 2010; C4EO, 2010; Family Action et al, 2010). However, in the context of public sector austerity and the prioritisation of education reform, NGOs have failed to convince ministers of the need for continued investment in early intervention and preventative services. Thus, over recent years, NGOs representing both the charitable and statutory sectors have been forced to campaign outside of government, and through various APPGs and House of Commons committees, to put pressure on the government to address shortfalls in children's services funding and a loss of strategic direction in relation to child welfare policy (LGA, 2017, 2019; ADCS, 2018b, 2019; APPG for Children, 2018; Sutton Trust, 2018; YMCA, 2018; Action for Children et al, 2019). However, in the context of Brexit and continuing austerity, campaigns on children's services have faced significant competition for attention, and have thus far been largely unsuccessful.

The case of social work reform also illustrates the extent to which NGO involvement and influence over policy has been tied to the attitudes of ministers to specific groups. Throughout most of the Labour period, social work was poorly represented in policymaking circles. Both the Seebohm Report (Seebohm Committee, 1968) and Section 17 of the Children Act 1989 emphasised the role of social services and social workers in working with families and other agencies to help prevent family break-up. Although Labour ministers supported this broader welfare focus, they generally viewed social services and social workers as part of the problem rather than the solution. Boateng (2000) took the view that social services had 'let children down year and year upon year'. Attitudes towards the social work profession only hardened after the publication of the Victoria Climbié inquiry. In this context, the leaders of local authority social services departments were unable to voice concerns relating to the impact of reform on social work practice. Furthermore, the input of civil servants who had led on safeguarding and social services policy in the DH was also limited.

For a brief period after the Baby P crisis, representatives of the social work profession were more closely involved in the development of policy. Balls asked Moira Gibb, the Chief Executive of Camden Council and a former social services director, to review policy on social work. The recommendations of the SWTF (2009) were accepted by Balls, and he subsequently agreed to set up the SWRB to lead the implementation of a sector-led reform programme. The work of the SWRB, and then the College of Social Work, also received the backing of the Conservative Children's Minister, Tim Loughton. Furthermore, Loughton commissioned Professor Eileen Munro (2011) to carry out a comprehensive review of child protection policy with a view to reducing the bureaucratic requirements placed on social workers. However, after Loughton was sacked in September 2012, a new centrally directed reform programme was developed with the support of a small clique of advisers, most of whom had limited or no experience of managing social workers (Jones, 2019: ch 3). On the one hand, the example of Article 39's successful campaign to remove the 'exemption' clauses from the Children and Social Work Bill suggests that NGOs can still influence policy in this area. However, it also illustrates the extent to which social work NGOs have been closed out of the policymaking process and the lengths to which ministers have been prepared to go to try to push their reforms. Even after the appointment of a Chief Social Worker for Children and Families, those working alongside ministers have been expected to be 'the "carriers" of ministerial ideas, willing to try to implement policies even when lacking broad policy community support' (Richardson, 2018: 225).

Concluding remarks

Children's services reform is a more politicised process than commonly recognised. Over the last two decades, the children's services workforce has had to respond to a relentless stream of reform initiatives promising to resolve local service 'failings', driven by ministers determined to demonstrate impact. Moreover, centrally developed reform programmes have invariably presented oversimplified solutions to the complex challenge of supporting families while also protecting children from harm. As bold promises fail to be delivered, new reform initiatives are developed, new promises are made and local services are forced to adapt. This approach displays what King and Crewe (2014: ch 27) describe as a 'deficit of deliberation' in their comprehensive study of policy blunders by UK governments.

The development of the Children Act 1989 serves as an example of what can be achieved when ministers and civil servants take time to develop legislation and listen carefully to those with extensive knowledge and experience of working with children and families. The Act continues to provide the main legal framework for safeguarding and child protection after 30 years of subsequent policy and legislative change. No 'magic bullet' has yet been found that can direct local agencies and professionals about how best to strike a balance between working *with* families and the need to protect children from harm (King's College London, 2016: 5), so maybe it is time to stop looking for one. Furthermore, it has been demonstrated that shifts in child welfare policy need to be considered within the context of competing party-political perspectives on social policy and the role of the state. Changes over the last ten years have largely been driven by severe cuts to public spending and a strong emphasis on the purported behavioural deviancies of parents and carers, while the wider economic determinants of poverty and life chances have been significantly downplayed. As such, it is vital that NGOs in the children's sector continue to push the economic and moral case for renewed investment in child welfare services.

APPENDIX

Chronology of key reports

Labour government (1997–2010)

Commission on Social Justice (1994) *Social Justice: Strategies for National Renewal.*

Labour Party (1997) *New Labour: Because Britain Deserves Better.*

Department for Education and Employment (1997) *Excellence in Schools.*

HM Treasury (1998) *Comprehensive Spending Review: Aims and Objectives.*

Home Office (1998) *Supporting Families.*

Department of Health (1998) *Modernising Social Services.*

Social Exclusion Unit (2000) *Report of Policy Action Team 12: Young People.*

Department of Health (2000) *The NHS Plan.*

HM Treasury (2000) *New Public Spending Plans for 2001–2004: Prudent for a Purpose: Building Opportunity and Security for All.*

Children and Young People's Unit (2001) *Tomorrow's Future: Building a Strategy for Children and Young People.*

HM Treasury (2001) *Tackling Child Poverty: Giving Every Child the Best Possible Start in Life.*

HM Treasury (2002) *Spending Review: New Public Spending Plans 2003–2006: Opportunity and Security for All – Investing in an Enterprising, Fairer Britain.*

Local Government Association, NHS (National Health Service) Confederation and Association of Directors of Social Services (2002) *Serving Children Well: A New Vision for Children's Services.*

Department of Health (2002) *Safeguarding Children: A Joint Chief Inspectors' Report on Arrangements to Safeguard Children.*

Lord Laming (2003) *The Victoria Climbié Inquiry.*

HM Government (2003) *Every Child Matters.*

HM Treasury (2004) *Spending Review: Stability, Security and Opportunity for All: Investing in Britain's Long-Term Future.*

HM Government (2004) *Every Child Matters: Change for Children.*

HM Government (2005) *Youth Matters.*

HM Government (2005) *Higher Standards, Better Schools for All: More Choice for Parents and Pupils.*

HM Treasury and Department for Education and Skills (2005) *Support for Parents: The Best Start for Children.*

Home Office (2006) *Respect Action Plan.*

Department for Children, Schools and Families (2007) *The Children's Plan.*

HM Treasury and Department for Education and Skills (2007) *Aiming High for Children: Supporting Families.*

Department for Children, Schools and Families (2008) *Staying Safe: Action Plan.*

Lord Laming (2009) *The Protection of Children in England: A Progress Report.*

HM Government (2009) *The Protection of Children in England: Action Plan.*

Social Work Task Force (2009) *Building a Safe, Confident Future: The Final Report of the Social Work Task Force.*

HM Government (2010) *Building a Safe and Confident Future: Implementing the Recommendations of the Social Work Task Force.*

Department for Children, Schools and Families (2010) *Support for All: The Families and Relationships Green Paper.*

Coalition and Conservative governments (2010–19)

Conservative Party Social Justice Policy Group (2006) *Breakdown Britain.*

Conservative Party Social Justice Policy Group (2007) *Breakthrough Britain.*

Conservative Party (2007) *No More Blame Game: The Future for Children's Social Workers.*

Allen, G. and Duncan-Smith, I. (2008) *Early Intervention: Good Parents, Great Kids, Better Citizens.*

Conservative Party (2010) *Child Protection: Back to the Frontline.*

Conservative Party (2010) *Invitation to Join the Government of Britain.*

HM Government (2010) *The Coalition: Our Programme for Government.*

Department for Work and Pensions (2010) *21st Century Welfare.*

HM Treasury (2010) *Spending Review.*

Department for Education (2010) *The Importance of Teaching: The Schools White Paper.*

Field, F. (2010) *The Foundation Years: Preventing Poor Children Becoming Poor Adults.*

Allen, G. (2011) *Early Intervention: The Next Steps.*

HM Government (2011) *A New Approach to Child Poverty: Tackling the Causes of Disadvantage and Transforming Families' Lives.*

HM Government (2011) *Opening Doors, Breaking Barriers: A Strategy for Social Mobility.*

Munro, E. (2011) *The Munro Review of Child Protection: Final Report.*

HM Government (2011) *Open Public Services White Paper.*

Department for Education (2011) *A Child-Centred System: The Government's Response to the Munro Review of Child Protection.*

Department for Education (2012) *An Action Plan for Adoption: Tackling Delay.*

HM Government (2012) *Social Justice: Transforming Lives.*

Department for Education (2014) *Powers to Delegate Children's Social Care Functions.*

Narey, M. (2014) *Making the Education of Social Workers Consistently Effective.*

Jay, A. (2014) *Independent Inquiry into Child Sexual Exploitation in Rotherham (1997–2013).*

Oxfordshire Safeguarding Board (2015) *Serious Case Review into Child Sexual Exploitation in Oxfordshire: From the Experiences of Children A, B, C, D, E, and F.*

Department for Education (2016) *Putting Children First: Our Vision for Children's Social Care.*

References

Aberbach, J.D. and Rockman, B.A. (2002) 'Conducting and coding elite interviews', *Political Science & Politics*, 35(4): 673–6.

Action for Children (2010) *Deprivation and Risk: The Case for Early Intervention*, www.actionforchildren.org.uk/media/3265/deprivation_and_risk_the_case_for_early_intervention.pdf

Action for Children and NEF (New Economics Foundation) (2009) *Backing the Future: Why Investing in Children is Good for Us All*, www.actionforchildren.org.uk/resources-and-publications/research/backing-the-future-why-investing-in-children-is-good-for-us-all/

Action for Children, National Children's Bureau, NSPCC (National Society for the Prevention of Cruelty to Children), The Children's Society and Barnardo's (2019) *Children and Young People's Services: Funding and Spending 2010/ 11 to 2017/ 18*, www.childrenssociety.org.uk/what-we-do/resources-and-publications/children-and-young-people%E2%80%99s-services-funding-and-spending

ADCS (Association of Directors of Children's Services) (2014) *Response to the Consultation on the Powers to Delegate Children's Social Care Functions*, https://adcs.org.uk/care/article/consultation-response-on-powers-to-delegate-childrens-social-care-functions

ADCS (2018a) 'ADCS DCS update – as of 31 March 2018', https://adcs.org.uk/assets/documentation/ADCS_DCS_data_update_2017-18_FINAL.pdf

ADCS (2018b) *Safeguarding Pressures Phase 6*, https://adcs.org.uk/safeguarding/article/safeguarding-pressures-phase-6

ADCS (2019) *ADCS Position Paper: Building a Workforce That Works for All Children*, https://adcs.org.uk/assets/documentation/ADCS_Building_a_workforce_that_works_for_all_children_FINAL_11_March_2019.pdf

Allen, G. (2011) *Early Intervention: The Next Steps*, London: Cabinet Office, https://assets.publishing.service.gov.uk/government/uploads/system/uploads/attachment_data/file/284086/early-intervention-next-steps2.pdf

Allen, G. and Duncan-Smith, I. (2008) *Early Intervention: Good Parents, Great Kids, Better Citizens*, London: Centre for Social Justice and the Smith Institute, www.centreforsocialjustice.org.uk/library/early-intervention-good-parents-great-kids-better-citizens

Allen, N. (2018) '"Brexit means Brexit": Theresa May and post-referendum British politics', *British Politics*, 13(1): 105–20.

Allison, E. and Hattenstone, S. (2019) 'Government backs down over "myth-busting" guide on child protection', *The Guardian*, 24 March, www.theguardian.com/society/2019/mar/24/government-backs-down-over-myth-busting-guide-on-child-protection

Annesley, C. and Gamble, A. (2003) 'Economic and welfare policy', in S. Ludlam and M. Smith (eds) *Governing as New Labour*, Basingstoke: Palgrave Macmillan.

APPG (All Party Parliamentary Group) for Children (2018) *Storing up Trouble: A Postcode Lottery of Children's Social Care*, www.ncb.org.uk/storinguptrouble

APPG for Sure Start (2011) *Sure Start Delivery in 2011/12: An Inquiry, Interim Report*, London: All Party Parliamentary Group for Sure Start.

APPG on Children's Centres (2016) *Family Hubs: The Future of Children's Centres*, https://democracy.leeds.gov.uk/documents/s150825/app%208%20appg%20on%20childrens%20centres%20-%20family%20hubs%20report%20final.pdf

APPG on Youth Affairs (2018) *Youth Work Inquiry*, https://nya.org.uk/wp-content/uploads/2018/10/APPG-Summary-and-Recommendations-FINAL.pdf

APSW (Association of Professors of Social Work), British Association of Social Workers, Joint University Social Work Education Council Social Work Education Committee and Social Work Action Network (2018) 'Proposed expansion of the fast-track social work programme', www.basw.co.uk/media/news/2018/may/open-letter-urges-government-suspend-proposed-tender-expand-fast-track-children

Audit Commission (2008) *Are We There Yet? Improving Governance and Resource Management in Children's Trusts*, London: Audit Commission, https://lx.iriss.org.uk/sites/default/files/resources/AreWeThereYet29Oct08REP.pdf

Bache, I. (2003) 'Governing through governance: education policy control under New Labour', *Political Studies*, 51(2): 300–14.

Baginsky, M. (2008) *Safeguarding Children and Schools*, London: Jessica Kingsley Publishers.

Baginsky, M., Driscoll, J. and Manthorpe, J. (2015) 'Thinking aloud: decentralisation and safeguarding in English schools', *Journal of Integrated Care*, 23(6): 352–63.

Balls, E. (2016) *Speaking Out: Lessons in Life and Politics*, London: Hutchinson.

Barber, M. (2007) *Instruction to Deliver: Tony Blair, Public Services and the Challenge of Achieving Targets*, London: Politico's.

BBC (British Broadcasting Corporation) (2010) 'Early Intervention Grant is cut by 11%', www.bbc.co.uk/news/education-11990256

Beech, M. (2008) 'New Labour and the politics of dominance', in M. Beech and S. Lee (eds) *Ten Years of New Labour*, Basingstoke: Palgrave Macmillan.

Biehal, N. (2019) 'Balancing prevention and protection: child protection in England', in L. Merkel-Holguin, J.D. Fluke and R.D. Krugman (eds) *National Systems of Child Protection: Understanding the International Variability and Context for Developing Policy and Practice*, Cham: Springer International Publishing.

Blair, T. (1996) 'Labour Party conference speech', 1 October, www.britishpoliticalspeech.org/speech-archive.htm?speech=202

Blair, T. (1998) 'New politics for the new century', *Independent*, 21 September, www.independent.co.uk/arts-entertainment/new-politics-for-the-new-century-1199625.html

Blair, T. (1999a) 'Beveridge lecture', 18 March, www.bris.ac.uk/poverty/downloads/background/Tony%20Blair%20Child%20Poverty%20Speech.doc

Blair, T. (1999b) 'Speech to venture capitalists', 6 July.

Blair, T. (2002) *The Courage of Our Convictions: Why Reform of the Public Services is the Route to Social Justice*, London: Fabian Society.

Blair, T. (2010) *A Journey*, London: Arrow Books.

Boateng, P. (2000) 'Interview with *Community Care*', *Community Care*, 19 October.

Brewer, M. (2012) 'Labour's effort to cut child poverty was exceptional', *The Guardian*, 12 June, www.theguardian.com/society/2012/jun/12/labours-effort-cut-child-poverty-exceptional

Brindle, D. (2013) 'Frontline founder: "Social work needs life-changing professionals"', *The Guardian*, 11 September, www.theguardian.com/society/2013/sep/11/josh-macalister-social-work-frontline

Brindle, D. (2018) 'It's time to end the feud over fast-track training for children's social workers', *The Guardian*, 5 September, www.theguardian.com/society/2018/sep/05/time-end-feud-fast-track-training-childrens-social-workers

Broadhurst, K., Wastell, D., White, S., Hall, C., Peckover, S., Thompson, K., Pithouse, A. and Davey, D. (2010a) 'Performing "initial assessment": identifying the latent conditions for error at the front-door of local authority children's services', *The British Journal of Social Work*, 40(2): 352–70.

Broadhurst, K., Hall, C., Wastell, D., White, S. and Pithouse, A. (2010b) 'Risk, instrumentalism and the humane project in social work: identifying the informal logics of risk management in children's statutory services', *The British Journal of Social Work*, 40(4): 1046–64.

Brown, G. (2017) *My Life, Our Times*, London: The Bodley Head.

Buckler, S. and Dolowitz, D.P. (2004) 'Can fair be efficient? New Labour, social liberalism and British economic policy', *New Political Economy*, 9(1): 23–38.

Butler, I. and Drakeford, M. (2005) *Scandal, Social Policy and Social Welfare*, Bristol: Policy Press.

Butler, I. and Drakeford, M. (2012) *Social Work on Trial: The Colwell Inquiry and the State of Welfare*, Bristol: Policy Press.

Butler, P. (2014) 'Privatise child protection services, Department for Education proposes', *The Guardian*, 16 May, www.theguardian. com/society/2014/may/16/privatise-child-protection-services-department-for-education-proposes

Butler, P. (2018) 'Welfare spending for UK's poorest shrinks by £37bn', *The Guardian*, www.theguardian.com/politics/2018/sep/23/welfare-spending-uk-poorest-austerity-frank-field

Cabinet Office (2007) *Reaching Out: Think Family – Analysis and Themes from the Families at Risk Review*, http://webarchive.nationalarchives. gov.uk/20080804201836/http://www.cabinetoffice.gov.uk/~/media/assets/www.cabinetoffice.gov.uk/social_exclusion_task_force/think_families/think_families%20pdf.ashx

Cairney, P. (2012) *Understanding Public Policy: Theories and Issues*, Basingstoke: Palgrave Macmillan.

Cameron, D. (2005) 'Conservative Party leadership victory speech', 6 December, http://news.bbc.co.uk/1/hi/uk_politics/4504722.stm

Cameron, D. (2011) 'Speech on troubled families', www.gov.uk/government/speeches/troubled-families-speech

Cameron, D. (2016) 'Life Chances speech', January, www.gov.uk/government/speeches/prime-ministers-speech-on-life-chances

Centre for Cities (2019) *Cities Outlook 2019*, www.centreforcities.org/publication/cities-outlook-2019/

C4EO (Centre for Excellence and Outcomes in Children and Young People's Services) (2010) *Grasping the Nettle: Early Intervention for Children, Families and Communities*, www.bl.uk/collection-items/grasping-the-nettle-early-intervention-for-children-families-and-communities

Charman, S. and Savage, S. (2008) 'Controlling crime and disorder: the Labour legacy', in M. Powell (ed) *Modernising the Welfare State: The Blair Legacy*, Bristol: Policy Press.

Clarke, J. and Newman, J. (1997) *The Managerial State*, London: Sage.

Clarke, J., Gewirtz, S. and McLaughlin, E. (2000) *New Managerialism, New Welfare?*, London: Sage.

Commission on Social Justice (1994) *Social Justice: Strategies for National Renewal*, London: Vintage.

Conservative Party (2007) *No More Blame Game: The Future for Children's Social Workers*, www.conservatives.com/~/media/Files/Downloadable%20Files/No%20More%20Blame%20Game.ashx?dl=true%20-%202008-09-12

Conservative Party (2010a) *Invitation to Join the Government of Britain*, http://conservativehome.blogs.com/files/conservative-manifesto-2010.pdf

Conservative Party (2010b) *Child Protection: Back to the Frontline*, London: Conservative Party.

Conservative Party Social Justice Policy Group (2006) *Breakdown Britain*, www.centreforsocialjustice.org.uk/core/wp-content/uploads/2016/08/Breakdown-Britain.pdf

Conservative Party Social Justice Policy Group (2007) *Breakthrough Britain*, www.centreforsocialjustice.org.uk/core/wp-content/uploads/2016/08/BBChairmansOverview.pdf

Crossley, S. (2018) *Troublemakers: The Construction of 'Troubled Families' as a Social Problem*, Bristol: Policy Press.

CSJ (Centre for Social Justice) (2010) *Green Paper on the Family*, www.centreforsocialjustice.org.uk/library/green-paper-family

CSJ (2014) *Fully Committed? How a Government Could Reverse Family Breakdown*, www.centreforsocialjustice.org.uk/core/wp-content/uploads/2016/08/CSJJ2072_Family_Breakdown.pdf

Cutler, T. and Waine, B. (2000) 'Managerialism reformed? New Labour and public sector management', *Social Policy & Administration*, 34(3): 318–32.

CYPU (Children and Young People's Unit) (2001a) *Tomorrow's Future: Building a Strategy for Children and Young People*, https://dera.ioe.ac.uk//19113/

CYPU (2001b) *Building a Strategy for Children and Young People*, London: Children and Young People's Unit.

D'Ancona, M. (2013) *In it Together: The Inside Story of the Coalition Government*, London: Penguin.

Davies, J.S. (2002) 'The governance of urban regeneration: a critique of the "governing without government" thesis', *Public Administration*, 80(2): 301–22.

Davies, P.H.J. (2001) 'Spies as informants: triangulation and the interpretation of elite interview data in the study of the intelligence and security services', *Politics*, 21(1): 73–80.

Davis, J. and Rentoul, J. (2019) *Heroes or Villains? The Blair Government Reconsidered*, Oxford: Oxford University Press.

DCSF (Department for Children, Schools and Families) (2007) *The Children's Plan*, http://webarchive.nationalarchives.gov.uk/20130401151715/https://www.education.gov.uk/publications/eOrderingDownload/Childrens_Plan_Summary.pdf

DCSF (2008a) *Children's Trusts: Statutory Guidance on Inter-Agency Cooperation to Improve Well-Being of Children, Young People and their Families*, https://dera.ioe.ac.uk/6336/1/ACF9F23.pdf

DCSF (2008b) *Staying Safe: Action Plan*, https://webarchive.nationalarchives.gov.uk/20100202135027/http://www.dcsf.gov.uk/everychildmatters/resources-and-practice/IG00312/

DCSF (2010) *Support for All: The Families and Relationships Green Paper*, http://webarchive.nationalarchives.gov.uk/20130401151715/http://www.education.gov.uk/publications/eOrderingDownload/00148-2010BKT-EN.pdf

DfE (Department for Education) (2010) *The Importance of Teaching: The Schools White Paper*, https://assets.publishing.service.gov.uk/government/uploads/system/uploads/attachment_data/file/175429/CM-7980.pdf

DfE (2011) *A Child-Centred System: The Government's Response to the Munro Review of Child Protection*, www.gov.uk/government/publications/a-child-centred-system-the-governments-response-to-the-munro-review-of-child-protection

DfE (2012) *An Action Plan for Adoption: Tackling Delay*, www.gov.uk/government/publications/an-action-plan-for-adoption-tackling-delay

DfE (2013a) *Statutory Guidance on the Roles and Responsibilities of the Director of Children's Services and the Lead Member for Children's Services*, www.gov.uk/government/publications/directors-of-childrens-services-roles-and-responsibilities

DfE (2013b) *Sure Start Children's Centres Statutory Guidance*, https://assets.publishing.service.gov.uk/government/uploads/system/uploads/attachment_data/file/678913/childrens_centre_stat_guidance_april-2013.pdf

DfE (2014) *Powers to Delegate Children's Social Care Functions*, https://assets.publishing.service.gov.uk/government/uploads/system/uploads/attachment_data/file/304660/Powers_to_Delegate_Con_Doc.pdf

DfE (2016a) *Educational Excellence Everywhere*, www.gov.uk/government/publications/educational-excellence-everywhere

DfE (2016b) 'Next steps to spread educational excellence everywhere announced', 6 May, www.gov.uk/government/news/next-steps-to-spread-educational-excellence-everywhere-announced

DfE (2016c) *Putting Children First: Our Vision for Children's Social Care*, www.gov.uk/government/publications/putting-children-first-our-vision-for-childrens-social-care

DfE (2019) 'Education Secretary calls on more schools to become an academy', 23 January, www.gov.uk/government/news/education-secretary-calls-on-more-schools-to-become-an-academy

DfEE (Department for Education and Employment) (1997) *Excellence in Schools*, www.educationengland.org.uk/documents/wp1997/excellence-in-schools.html

DfEE (1998) *Teachers: Meeting the Challenge*, www.educationengland.org.uk/documents/gp1998/teachers-change.html

DfES (Department for Education and Skills) (2004a) *Every Child Matters: Change for Children in Schools*, https://dera.ioe.ac.uk/7670/7/DFES-1089-200MIG748_Redacted.pdf

DfES (2004b) *Every Child Matters: Change for Children in Social Care*, http://dera.ioe.ac.uk/7673/

DfES (2006) *Youth Matters: Next Steps*, http://webarchive.nationalarchives.gov.uk/20100408095957/http://www.dcsf.gov.uk/everychildmatters/_download/?id=3287

DH (Department of Health) (1995) *Child Protection: Messages from Research*, London: HMSO.

DH (1998a) *Modernising Social Services*, London: Department of Health.

DH (1998b) 'The Quality Protects programme: transforming children's services', http://webarchive.nationalarchives.gov.uk/20130107105354/http://www.dh.gov.uk/prod_consum_dh/groups/dh_digitalassets/@dh/@en/documents/digitalasset/dh_4012636.pdf

DH (1999) *The Government's Objectives for Children's Social Services*, London: Department of Health.

DH (2000a) *Framework for the Assessment of Children in Need and their Families*, London: Department of Health.

DH (2000b) *The NHS Plan*, http://1nj5ms2lli5hdggbe3mm7ms5.wpengine.netdna-cdn.com/files/2010/03/pnsuk1.pdf

DH (2002) *Safeguarding Children: A Joint Chief Inspectors' Report on Arrangements to Safeguard Children*, http://webarchive.nationalarchives.gov.uk/+/www.dh.gov.uk/assetRoot/04/06/08/34/04060834.pdf

Diamond, P. (2014) *Governing Britain: Power, Politics and the Prime Minister*, London: I.B. Tauris.

Diamond, P. (2019) *The End of Whitehall?*, London: Palgrave Macmillan.

Dobrowolsky, A. and Lister, R. (2008) 'Social investment: the discourse and dimensions of change', in M. Powell (ed) *Modernising the Welfare State: The Blair Legacy*, Bristol: Policy Press.

Dolowitz, D.P. (2004) 'Prosperity and fairness? Can New Labour bring fairness to the 21st century by following the dictates of endogenous growth?', *The British Journal of Politics and International Relations*, 6(2): 213–30.

Dominelli, L. (2010) *Social Work in a Globalizing World*, Cambridge: Polity Press.

Donovan, T. (2018) 'Alan Wood to chair £20m social care evidence centre', *Children and Young People Now*, 5 July, www.cypnow.co.uk/cyp/news/2005516/alan-wood-to-chair-gbp20m-social-care-evidence-centre

Dorey, P. and Garnett, M. (2016) *The British Coalition Government: A Marriage of Inconvenience*, London: Palgrave Macmillan.

Driver, S. (2008) 'New Labour and social policy', in M. Beech and S. Lee (eds) *Ten Years of New Labour*, Basingstoke: Palgrave Macmillan.

Driver, S. and Martell, L. (2006) *New Labour*, Cambridge: Polity Press.

DSS (Department for Social Security) (1999) *Opportunity for All: Tackling Poverty and Social Exclusion*, https://dera.ioe.ac.uk/15121/1/Opportunity%20for%20all%20-%20tackling%20poverty%20and%20social%20exclusion.pdf

Duncan-Smith, I. (2008) 'Mend broken homes to end tragedy', *The Guardian*, 13 November, www.theguardian.com/commentisfree/2008/nov/13/baby-p-dysfunctional-families

Duncan-Smith, I. (2016) 'Resignation letter', 18 March, www.bbc.co.uk/news/uk-politics-35848891

DWP (Department for Work and Pensions) (2010) *21st Century Welfare*, www.gov.uk/government/consultations/21st-century-welfare

Easton, C., Hetherington, M., Smith, R., Wade, P., Aston, H. and Gee, G. (2012) *Local Authorities' Approaches to Children's Trusts Arrangements*, www.nfer.ac.uk/publications/LGCH01/LGCH01.pdf

Eisenstadt, N. (2011) *Providing a Sure Start: How Government Discovered Early Childhood*, Bristol: Policy Press.

Eyles, A., Machin, S. and McNally, S. (2017) 'Unexpected school reform: academisation of primary schools in England', *Journal of Public Economics*, 155: 108–21.

Family Action, Children England and Action for Children (2010) *The Smart Money: Making Tomorrow Better for Children and Families*, www.actionforchildren.org.uk/media/3290/the_smart_money.pdf

Faucher-King, F. and Le Galès, P. (2010) *The New Labour Experiment: Changes and Reform under Blair and Brown*, Stanford, CA: Stanford University Press.

Featherstone, B., White, S. and Morris, K. (2014) *Re-imagining Child Protection: Towards Humane Social Work with Families*, Bristol: Policy Press.

Featherstone, B., Gupta, A., Morris, K. and White, S. (2018) *Protecting Children: A Social Model*, Bristol: Policy Press.

Ferguson, I. and Woodward, R. (2009) *Radical Social Work in Practice: Making a Difference*, Bristol: Policy Press.

Field, F. (2010) *The Foundation Years: Preventing Poor Children Becoming Poor Adults*, https://webarchive.nationalarchives.gov.uk/20110120090141/http://povertyreview.independent.gov.uk/media/20254/poverty-report.pdf

Frontline (2019) 'Changing lives', https://thefrontline.org.uk/the-charity/

Frost, N. and Parton, N. (2009) *Understanding Children's Social Care: Politics, Policy and Practice*, London: Sage.

Garrett, P.M. (2009a) *Transforming Children's Services? Social Work, Neoliberalism and the 'Modern' World*, Maidenhead: Open University Press.

Garrett, P.M. (2009b) 'The case of "Baby P": opening up spaces for debate on the "transformation" of children's services?', *Critical Social Policy*, 29(3): 533–47.

Garrett, P.M. (2016) 'Questioning tales of "ordinary magic": "resilience" and neo-liberal reasoning', *The British Journal of Social Work*, 46(7): 1909–25.

Giddens, A. (1998) *The Third Way: The Renewal of Social Democracy*, Cambridge: Polity.

Giddens, A. (2002) *Where Now for New Labour?*, Cambridge: Polity.

Giddens, A. (2007) *Over to You Mr Brown*, Cambridge: Polity.

Gilbert, R., Kemp, A., Thoburn, J., Sidebotham, P., Radford, L., Glaser, D. and MacMillan, H.L. (2009) 'Recognising and responding to child maltreatment', *The Lancet*, 373(9658): 167–80.

Goldstein, K. (2002) 'Getting in the door: sampling and completing elite interviews', *Political Science & Politics*, 35(4): 669–72.

Goodwin, M. and Grix, J. (2011) 'Bringing structures back in: the "governance narrative", the "decentred approach" and "asymmetrical network governance" in the education and sport policy communities', *Public Administration*, 89(2): 537–56.

Gove, M. (2012) 'The failure of child protection and the need for a fresh start', www.gov.uk/government/speeches/the-failure-of-child-protection-and-the-need-for-a-fresh-start

Gove, M. (2013) 'Getting it right for children in need', speech, 12 November, www.gov.uk/government/speeches/getting-it-right-for-children-in-need-speech-to-the-nspcc

Gregory, A. (2019) 'UK government communication: the Cameron years and their ongoing legacy', *Public Relations Review*, 45(2): 202–16.

Gupta, A. and SocialWhatNow (2018) 'Frontline training scheme poses a threat to social work education', *The Guardian*, 16 October, www.theguardian.com/society/2018/oct/16/frontline-training-scheme-threat-social-work-education

Hall, P. (1976) *Reforming the Welfare: The Politics of Change in the Personal Social Services*, London: Heinemann.

Hall, S. (2003) 'New Labour's double-shuffle', *Soundings*, 24(24): 10–24.

Hall, S. and Jacques, M. (1983) *The Politics of Thatcherism*, London: Lawrence and Wishart.

Harris, J. (1998) 'Scientific management, bureau-professionalism, new managerialism: the labour process of state social work', *The British Journal of Social Work*, 28(6): 839–62.

Hay, C. (1999) *The Political Economy of New Labour: Labouring under False Pretences?*, Manchester: Manchester University Press.

Hayes, D. (2016) 'Loughton criticises "quiet" Chief Children's Social Worker', *Children and Young People Now*, 25 May, www.cypnow.co.uk/news/article/loughton-criticises-quiet-chief-children-s-social-worker

Haynes, L. (2019) 'Lack of registered social workers on Social Work England board criticised', *Community Care*, 18 April, www.communitycare.co.uk/2019/04/18/social-work-englands-failure-appoint-registrants-board-criticised-sector/

Hayton, R. (2012) 'Fixing broken Britain', in T. Heppell and D. Seawright (eds) *Cameron and the Conservatives*, Basingstoke: Palgrave Macmillan.

Hayton, R. and McEnhill, L. (2015) 'Cameron's Conservative Party, social liberalism and social justice', *British Politics*, 10(2): 131–47.

Heffernan, R. (2000) *New Labour and Thatcherism*, Basingstoke: Palgrave Macmillan.

Helm, T. and Courea, E. (2018) 'Brexit deadlock "is blocking vital domestic policy reforms"', *The Guardian*, www.theguardian.com/politics/2018/dec/15/mps-warn-brexit-deadlock-sucking-life-out-of-government

Hill, M. (2009) *The Public Policy Process* (5th edn), Edinburgh: Pearson Education Limited.

HM Government (2003) *Every Child Matters*, https://assets.publishing.service.gov.uk/government/uploads/system/uploads/attachment_data/file/272064/5860.pdf

HM Government (2004) *Every Child Matters: Change for Children*, www.education.gov.uk/publications/standard/publicationdetail/page1/DfES/1081/2004

HM Government (2005a) *Higher Standards, Better Schools for All: More Choice for Parents and Pupils*, http://webarchive.nationalarchives.gov.uk/20130401151715/http://www.education.gov.uk/publications/eOrderingDownload/Cm%206677.pdf.pdf

HM Government (2005b) *Youth Matters*, http://webarchive.nationalarchives.gov.uk/20100408095957/http://www.dcsf.gov.uk/everychildmatters/_download/?id=3286

HM Government (2006) *Working Together to Safeguard Children: A Guide to Inter-Agency Working to Safeguard and Promote the Welfare of Children*, http://webarchive.nationalarchives.gov.uk/20130401151715/http://www.education.gov.uk/publications/eOrderingDownload/WT2006%20Working_together.pdf

HM Government (2009) *The Protection of Children in England: Action Plan*, https://assets.publishing.service.gov.uk/government/uploads/system/uploads/attachment_data/file/327238/The_protection_of_children_in_England_-_action_plan.pdf

HM Government (2010a) *Building a Safe and Confident Future: Implementing the Recommendations of the Social Work Task Force*, http://webarchive.nationalarchives.gov.uk/20130401151715/http://www.education.gov.uk/publications/eOrderingDownload/00306-2010DOM-EN.pdf

HM Government (2010b) *The Coalition: Our Programme for Government*, www.gov.uk/government/uploads/system/uploads/attachment_data/file/78977/coalition_programme_for_government.pdf

HM Government (2010c) *Decentralisation and the Localism Bill: An Essential Guide*, www.communities.gov.uk/publications/localgovernment/decentralisationguide

HM Government (2010d) *Working Together to Safeguard Children: A Guide to Inter-Agency Working to Safeguard and Promote the Welfare of Children*, www.workingtogetheronline.co.uk/documents/wt_2010.PDF

HM Government (2011a) *Open Public Services White Paper*, www.gov.uk/government/publications/open-public-services-white-paper

HM Government (2011b) *Opening Doors, Breaking Barriers: A Strategy for Social Mobility*, www.gov.uk/government/uploads/system/uploads/attachment_data/file/61964/opening-doors-breaking-barriers.pdf

HM Government (2011c) *A New Approach to Child Poverty: Tackling the Causes of Disadvantage and Transforming Families' Lives.*

HM Government (2011d) *Positive for Youth: A New Approach to Cross-Government Policy for Young People Aged 13 to 19*, www.gov.uk/government/publications/positive-for-youth-a-new-approach-to-cross-government-policy-for-young-people-aged-13-to-19

HM Government (2012) *Social Justice: Transforming Lives*, www.gov.uk/government/uploads/system/uploads/attachment_data/file/49515/social-justice-transforming-lives.pdf

HM Government (2013) *Working Together to Safeguard Children: A Guide to Inter-Agency Working to Safeguard and Promote the Welfare of Children*, https://webarchive.nationalarchives.gov.uk/20130403143649/https://www.education.gov.uk/publications/standard/publicationDetail/Page1/DFE-00030-2013

HM Government (2018a) *Working Together to Safeguard Children: A Guide to Inter-Agency Working to Safeguard and Promote the Welfare of Children*, https://assets.publishing.service.gov.uk/government/uploads/system/uploads/attachment_data/file/779401/Working_Together_to_Safeguard-Children.pdf

HM Government (2018b) *Working Together: Transitional Guidance*, https://assets.publishing.service.gov.uk/government/uploads/system/uploads/attachment_data/file/722306/Working_Together-transitional_guidance.pdf

HM Government (2018c) *Civil Society Strategy: Building a Future that Works for Everyone*, www.gov.uk/government/publications/civil-society-strategy-building-a-future-that-works-for-everyone

HM Treasury (1998) *Comprehensive Spending Review: Aims and Objectives*, http://webarchive.nationalarchives.gov.uk/20071204130111/http://hm-treasury.gov.uk/media/E/C/460.pdf

HM Treasury (2000) *New Public Spending Plans for 2001–2004: Prudent for a Purpose: Building Opportunity and Security for All*, http://webarchive.nationalarchives.gov.uk/20060213205517/http://hm-treasury.gov.uk/Spending_Review/Spending_Review_2000/Spending_Review_Report/spend_sr00_repindex.cfm

HM Treasury (2001) *Tackling Child Poverty: Giving Every Child the Best Possible Start in Life*, www.bris.ac.uk/poverty/downloads/keyofficialdocuments/TacklingChildPoverty%20pre%202002%20budget%20report.pdf

HM Treasury (2002) *Spending Review: New Public Spending Plans 2003–2006: Opportunity and Security for All – Investing in an Enterprising, Fairer Britain*, http://webarchive.nationalarchives.gov.uk/20071204130111/http://hm-treasury.gov.uk/spending_review/spend_sr02/report/spend_sr02_repindex.cfm

HM Treasury (2004) *Spending Review: Stability, Security and Opportunity for All: Investing in Britain's Long-Term Future*, http://webarchive.nationalarchives.gov.uk/20071204130111/http:/hm-treasury.gov.uk/spending_review/spend_sr04/spend_sr04_index.cfm

HM Treasury (2010) *Spending Review*, www.gov.uk/government/publications/spending-review-2010

HM Treasury and DfES (Department for Education and Skills) (2005) *Support for Parents: The Best Start for Children*, http://webarchive.nationalarchives.gov.uk/20130401151715/https://www.education.gov.uk/publications/eOrderingDownload/HMT-Support-parents.pdf

HM Treasury and DfES (2007) *Aiming High for Children: Supporting Families*, http://webarchive.nationalarchives.gov.uk/20130401151715/http://www.education.gov.uk/publications/RSG/publicationDetail/Page1/PU188

Hodge, M. (2003) 'Speech to the Local Government Association', 8 July, www.theguardian.com/society/2003/jul/08/childrensservices.comment1

Home Office (1998) *Supporting Families*, https://dera.ioe.ac.uk/4194/1/Supporting%2520families%2520summary%2520of%2520responses.pdf

Home Office (2006) *Respect Action Plan*, http://webarchive.nationalarchives.gov.uk/+/homeoffice.gov.uk/documents/respect-action-plan.html

Home Office (2007) 'Government spotlight on young people with creation of new youth taskforce', 5 October.

House of Commons Education Committee (2010) 'Minutes', 28 July.

House of Commons Education Committee (2011) *Services for Young People*, www.publications.parliament.uk/pa/cm201012/cmselect/cmeduc/744/744i.pdf

House of Commons Education Committee (2013) *Foundation Years: Sure Start Children's Centres*, https://publications.parliament.uk/pa/cm201314/cmselect/cmeduc/364/364.pdf

House of Commons Education Committee (2014) *Foundation Years: Sure Start Children's Centres: Government Response to the Committee's Fifth Report of Session 2013–14*, https://publications.parliament.uk/pa/cm201314/cmselect/cmeduc/1141/1141.pdf

House of Commons Health Committee (2003) 'Minutes', 27 March, https://publications.parliament.uk/pa/cm200203/cmselect/cmhealth/570/3032703.htm

House of Commons Science and Technology Committee (2018) *Evidence-Based Early Years Intervention*, https://publications.parliament.uk/pa/cm201719/cmselect/cmsctech/506/506.pdf

Independent Commission on Social Mobility (2009) *Report from the Independent Commission on Social Mobility*, www.dmss.co.uk/pdfs/Social-Mobility-Report-Final.pdf

Jay, A. (2014) *Independent Inquiry into Child Sexual Exploitation in Rotherham (1997–2013)*, www.rotherham.gov.uk/downloads/file/1407/independent_inquiry_cse_in_rotherham

John, P. (2012) *Analyzing Public Policy*, London: Routledge.

Johnson, P. and Chandler, D. (2015) 'The Coalition and the economy', in A. Seldon and M. Finn (eds) *The Coalition Effect: 2010–2015*, Cambridge: Cambridge University Press.

Jones, C. (2001) 'Voices from the front line: state social workers and New Labour', *The British Journal of Social Work*, 31(4): 547–62.

Jones, R. (2014) *The Story of Baby P: Setting the Record Straight*, Bristol: Policy Press.

Jones, R. (2015) 'The end game: the marketisation and privatisation of children's social work and child protection', *Critical Social Policy*, 35(4): 447–69.

Jones, R. (2019) *In Whose Interest? The Privatisation of Child Protection and Social Work*, Bristol: Policy Press.

Joseph Rowntree Foundation (2018) *UK Poverty 2018*, file:///C:/Users/k1642099/Downloads/web_jrf_-_uk_poverty_2018%20(1).pdf

JUCSWEC (Joint University Council Social Work Education Committee) and APSW (Association of Professors of Social Work) (2013) 'A joint statement on the "Frontline" proposal', www.celticknot.org.uk/dir/swecletter.pdf

King, A. and Crewe, I. (2014) *The Blunders of our Governments*, London: Oneworld.

King's College London (2016) 'The Children Act and children's needs: make it the answer not the problem', www.kcl.ac.uk/scwru/pubs/2016/reports/tunstill-etc-2016-children-act-report.pdf

Labour Party (1997) *New Labour: Because Britain Deserves Better*, www.labour-party.org.uk/manifestos/1997/1997-labour-manifesto.shtml

Laffin, M. (2013) 'A new politics of governance or an old politics of central–local relations? Labour's reform of social housing tenancies in England', *Public Administration*, 91(1): 195–210.

Lee, C. (2014) 'Conservative comforts: some philosophical crumbs for social work', *The British Journal of Social Work*, 44(8): 2135–44.

Lee, S. (2008) 'The British model of political economy', in M. Beech and S. Lee (eds) *Ten Years of New Labour*, Basingstoke: Palgrave Macmillan.

Lee, S. (2009) *Boom and Bust: The Politics and Legacy of Gordon Brown*, Oxford: Oneworld.

Lepper, J. (2016) 'Cross-government Child Poverty Unit scrapped', *Children and Young People Now*, www.cypnow.co.uk/cyp/news/2002924/cross-government-child-poverty-unit-scrapped

Lepper, J. (2018a) 'Lack of duty on schools "could compromise safeguarding shake-up"', *Children and Young People Now*, www.cypnow.co.uk/cyp/news/2004743/lack-of-duty-on-schools-could-compromise-safeguarding-shake-up

Lepper, J. (2018b) 'Social workers criticise "regressive" changes to child protection arrangements', *Children and Young People Now*, www.cypnow.co.uk/cyp/news/2004714/social-workers-criticise-regressive-changes-to-child-protection-arrangements

Lepper, J. (2018c) 'Children's centre consultation ditched, confirms DfE', *Children and Young People Now*, 10 August, www.cypnow.co.uk/cyp/news/2005645/childrens-centre-consultation-ditched-confirms-dfe

Lepper, J. (2019) 'MPs slam government over rejection of early intervention strategy', *Children and Young People Now*, www.cypnow.co.uk/cyp/news/2006361/mps-slam-government-over-rejection-of-early-intervention-strategy

Levitas, R. (2005) *The Inclusive Society? Social Exclusion and New Labour*, Basingstoke: Palgrave Macmillan.

Leys, C. (2001) *Market-Driven Politics: Neoliberal Democracy and the Public Interest*, London: Verso.

LGA (Local Government Association) (2017) *Bright Futures: Getting the Best for Children, Young People and Families*, www.local.gov.uk/sites/default/files/documents/Bright%20Futures%20-%20LGA%20children%27s%20social%20care%207%20point%20plan__15_8_2017.pdf

LGA (2019) 'Children's care cash crisis: nine in 10 councils pushed into the red', 8 January, www.local.gov.uk/about/news/childrens-care-cash-crisis-nine-10-councils-pushed-red

LGA, NHS (National Health Service) Confederation and Association of Directors of Social Services (2002) *Serving Children Well: A New Vision for Children's Services*, http://webarchive.nationalarchives.gov.uk/20130401151715/https://www.education.gov.uk/publications/eOrderingDownload/serving-children-well.pdf

Liberal Democrats (2010) *Manifesto 2010*, www.markpack.org.uk/files/2015/01/Liberal-Democrat-manifesto-2010.pdf

Liebenberg, L., Ungar, M. and Ikeda, J. (2015) 'Neo-liberalism and responsibilisation in the discourse of social service workers', *The British Journal of Social Work*, 45(3): 1006–21.

Lilleker, D.G. (2003) 'Interviewing the political elite: navigating a potential minefield', *Politics*, 23(3): 207–14.

Lister, R. (2003) 'Investing in the citizen-workers of the future: transformations in citizenship and the state under New Labour', *Social Policy & Administration*, 37(5): 427–43.

Lord Laming (2003) *The Victoria Climbié Inquiry*, www.gov. uk/government/publications/the-victoria-climbie-inquiry-report-of-an-inquiry-by-lord-laming

Lord Laming (2009) *The Protection of Children in England: A Progress Report*, www.gov.uk/government/publications/the-protection-of-children-in-england-a-progress-report

Marinetto, M. (2003) 'Governing beyond the centre: a critique of the anglo-governance school', *Political Studies*, 51(3): 592–608.

Marsh, D. (2008) 'Understanding British government: analysing competing models', *The British Journal of Politics and International Relations*, 10(2): 251–68.

Marsh, D. (2011) 'The new orthodoxy: the differentiated polity model', *Public Administration*, 89(1): 32–48.

Marsh, D. and Hall, M. (2007) 'The British political tradition: explaining the fate of New Labour's constitutional reform agenda', *British Politics*, 2(2): 215–38.

Marsh, D. and Hall, M. (2016) 'The British political tradition and the material–ideational debate', *The British Journal of Politics and International Relations*, 18(1): 125–42.

Marsh, D. and Rhodes, R. (1992) *Policy Networks in British Government*, Oxford: Clarendon Press.

Marsh, D., Richards, D. and Smith, M. (2001) *Changing Patterns of Governance in the United Kingdom*, Basingstoke: Palgrave.

Marsh, D., Richards, D. and Smith, M. (2003) 'Unequal plurality: towards an asymmetric power model of British politics', *Government and Opposition*, 38(3): 306–32.

Mason, R. (2016) 'PM says "no conflict" between fighting poverty and cutting benefits', *The Guardian*, www.theguardian.com/society/2016/jan/11/david-cameron-no-conflict-improving-lives-cutting-benefits-poverty

Maxwell, N., Scourfield, J., Le Zhang, M., De Villiers, T., Hadfield, M., Kinnersley, P., Metcalf, L., Pithouse, A. and Tayyaba, S. (2016) *Independent Evaluation of the Frontline Pilot*, www.gov.uk/government/publications/frontline-pilot-independent-evaluation

May, T. (2016) 'Downing Street speech', July, www.telegraph.co.uk/news/2016/07/13/theresa-mays-pledges-to-fight-injustice-and-make-britain-a-count/

McCardle, L. (2014) 'Youth services "decimated" despite Cabinet Office move', *Children and Young People Now*, 1 July, www.cypnow.co.uk/cyp/news/1145179/youth-services-decimated-despite-cabinet-office-move

Milburn, A. (2002) 'Speech to the National Social Services Conference', 16 October, www.communitycare.co.uk/2002/10/17/alan-milburns-speech-to-the-national-social-services-conference/

Milburn, A. (2003) 'Speech to the House of Commons', 28 January.

Milburn, A. (2017) 'Resignation letter', www.independent.co.uk/news/uk/politics/alan-miilburn-resigns-letter-read-in-full-statement-latest-theresa-may-social-mobility-tsar-a8089026.html

Moran, M. (2007) *The British Regulatory State: High Modernism and Hyper-Innovation*, Oxford: Oxford University Press.

Munro, E. (2004) 'The impact of audit on social work practice', *The British Journal of Social Work*, 34(8): 1075–95.

Munro, E. (2008) 'Lessons learnt, boxes ticked, families ignored', *The Independent*, 16 November, www.independent.co.uk/voices/commentators/eileen-munro-lessons-learnt-boxes-ticked-families-ignored-1020508.html

Munro, E. (2011) *The Munro Review of Child Protection: Final Report*, https://assets.publishing.service.gov.uk/government/uploads/system/uploads/attachment_data/file/175391/Munro-Review.pdf

Muschamp, Y., Jamieson, I. and Lauder, H. (1999) 'Education, education, education', in M. Powell (ed) *New Labour, New Welfare State?*, Bristol: Policy Press.

Naidoo, R. and Muschamp, Y. (2002) 'A decent education for all?', in M. Powell (ed) *Evaluating New Labour's Welfare Reforms*, Bristol: Policy Press.

NAO (National Audit Office) (2018a) *Financial Sustainability of Local Authorities 2018*, www.nao.org.uk/report/financial-sustainability-of-local-authorities-2018/

NAO (2018b) *Rolling Out Universal Credit*, www.nao.org.uk/report/rolling-out-universal-credit/

NAO (2019) *Pressures on Children's Social Care*, www.nao.org.uk/wp-content/uploads/2019/01/Pressures-on-Childrens-Social-Care.pdf

Narey, M. (2011) *The Narey Report: A Blueprint for the Nation's Lost Children*, www.thetimes.co.uk/article/the-narey-report-a-blueprint-for-the-nations-lost-children-7b2ktmcrf0w

Narey, M. (2014) *Making the Education of Social Workers Consistently Effective: Report of Sir Martin Narey's Independent Review of the Education of Children's Social Workers*, www.gov.uk/government/publications/making-the-education-of-social-workers-consistently-effective

Nelson, B. (1984) *Making an Issue of Child Abuse*, Chicago, IL: University of Chicago Press.

Newman, J. (2001) *Modernising Governance: New Labour, Policy and Society*, London: Sage.

Offord, A. (2015) 'Minister "very disappointed" with council youth service cuts', 6 July, www.cypnow.co.uk/cyp/news/1152352/minister-very-disappointed-with-council-youth-service-cuts

Offord, A. (2016) 'Government set to publish three-year youth strategy', *Children and Young People Now*, 8 November, www.cypnow.co.uk/cyp/news/2002734/government-set-to-publish-three-year-youth-strategy

Osborne, G. (2015) 'Budget speech', July, www.gov.uk/government/speeches/chancellor-george-osbornes-summer-budget-2015-speech

Oxfordshire Safeguarding Board (2015) *Serious Case Review into Child Sexual Exploitation in Oxfordshire: From the Experiences of Children A, B, C, D, E, and F*, www.oscb.org.uk/wp-content/uploads/Serious-Case-Review-into-Child-Sexual-Exploitation-in-Oxfordshire-FINAL-Updated-14.3.15.pdf

Parkes, K. (2019) 'DfE launches children's centres review', *Children and Young People Now*, 8 May, www.cypnow.co.uk/cyp/news/2006682/dfe-launches-childrens-centres-review

Parton, N. (1985) *The Politics of Child Abuse*, Basingstoke: Macmillan.

Parton, N. (2006) 'Changes in the form of knowledge in social work: from the "social" to the "informational"?', *The British Journal of Social Work*, 38(2): 253–69.

Parton, N. (2014) *The Politics of Child Protection*, Basingstoke: Palgrave Macmillan.

Peck, J. (1999) 'New labourers? Making a new deal for the "workless class"', *Environment and Planning C: Government and Policy*, 17(3): 345–72.

Peston, R. (2005) *Brown's Britain*, London: Short Books.

Prabhakar, R. (2003) 'New Labour and the reform of public services', in S. Ludlam and M. Smith (eds) *Governing as New Labour*, Basingstoke: Palgrave Macmillan.

Prime Minister's Office (2016) 'PM reaffirms commitment to bold programme of social reform', www.gov.uk/government/news/pm-reaffirms-commitment-to-bold-programme-of-social-reform

Puffett, N. (2013) 'Gove "fails to visit any youth project" during time at DfE', *Children and Young People Now*, 21 January, www.cypnow.co.uk/news/article/gove-fails-to-visit-any-youth-project-during-time-at-dfe

Puffett, N. (2016) 'Government confirms Life Chances Strategy has been dropped', *Children and Young People Now*, www.cypnow.co.uk/cyp/news/2002923/government-confirms-life-chances-strategy-has-been-dropped

Puffett, N. (2017a) 'DfE plans 15-month transition period to replace LSCBs', *Children and Young People Now*, www.cypnow.co.uk/cyp/news/2004392/dfe-plans-15-month-transition-period-to-replace-lscbs

Puffett, N. (2017b) 'DfE commits to children's centres consultation', *Children and Young People Now*, www.cypnow.co.uk/cyp/news/2002933/dfe-commits-to-childrens-centres-consultation

Puffett, N. (2017c) 'Government ditches youth policy statement', 17 November, www.cypnow.co.uk/cyp/news/2004514/government-ditches-youth-policy-statement

Rhodes, R. (1997) *Understanding Governance: Policy Networks, Governance, Reflexivity and Accountability*, Buckingham: Open University Press.

Rhodes, R. (2007) 'Understanding governance: ten years on', *Organization Studies*, 28(8): 1243–64.

Rhodes, R. (2017) *Network Governance and the Differentiated Policy: Selected Essays Volume 1*, Oxford: Oxford University Press.

Richards, D. (1996) 'Elite interviewing: approaches and pitfalls', *Politics*, 16(3): 199–204.

Richards, D. (2008) *New Labour and the Civil Service*, Basingstoke: Palgrave Macmillan.

Richards, D. and Smith, M. (2002) *Governance and Public Policy in the UK*, Oxford: Oxford University Press.

Richards, D. and Smith, M.J. (2004) 'Interpreting the world of political elites', *Public Administration*, 82(4): 777–800.

Richards, D. and Smith, M.J. (2016) 'The Westminster model and the "indivisibility of the political and administrative elite": a convenient myth whose time is up?', *Governance*, 29(4): 499–516.

Richardson, J. (2018) 'The changing British policy style: from governance to government?', *British Politics*, 13(2): 215–33.

Richardson, J. and Jordan, A. (1979) *Governing under Pressure: The Policy Process in a Post-Parliamentary Democracy*, Oxford: Martin Robertson and Company Limited.

Rogowski, S. (2011) 'Social work with children and families: challenges and possibilities in the neo-liberal world', *The British Journal of Social Work*, 42(5): 921–40.

Rogowski, S. (2016) *Social Work with Children and Families: Reflections of a Critical Practitioner*, London: Routledge.

Rose, R. (1976) *The Problem of Party Government*, Harmondsworth: Penguin.

Sabatier, P.A. (1991) 'Toward better theories of the policy process', *Political Science & Politics*, 24(2): 147–56.

Secretary of State for Social Services (1974) *Report of the Inquiry into the Care and Supervision Provided in Relation to Maria Colwell*, London: HMSO.

Secretary of State for Social Services (1988) *Report of the Inquiry into Child Abuse in Cleveland*, London: HMSO.

Seebohm Committee (1968) *Report of the Committee on Local Authority and Allied Personal Social Services*, London: HMSO.

Seldon, A. and Lodge, G. (2010) *Brown at 10*, London: Biteback Publishing.

SEU (Social Exclusion Unit) (1999) *Bridging the Gap: New Opportunities for 16–18 Year Olds Not in Education, Employment or Training*, https://dera.ioe.ac.uk/15119/

SEU (2000) *Report of Policy Action Team 12: Young People*, London: Cabinet Office.

Shaw, E. (2007) *Losing Labour's Soul? New Labour and the Blair Government 1997–2007*, Oxon: Routledge.

Shoesmith, S. (2016) *Learning from Baby P: The Politics of Blame, Fear and Denial*, London: Jessica Kingsley Publishers.

Simon, C. and Ward, S. (2010) *Does Every Child Matter? Understanding New Labour's Social Reforms*, Abingdon: Routledge.

Smith, M. (2003) 'Conclusion: defining New Labour', in S. Ludlam and M. Smith (eds) *Governing as New Labour*, Basingstoke: Palgrave Macmillan.

Smith, M. (2014) 'Globalisation and the resilience of social democracy: reassessing New Labour's political economy', *The British Journal of Politics and International Relations*, 16(4): 597–623.

Smithers, A. (2015) 'The Coalition and society II: education', in A. Seldon and M. Finn (eds) *The Coalition Effect 2010–2015*, Cambridge: Cambridge University Press.

Squires, P. (2008) 'The politics of anti-social behaviour', *British Politics*, 3(3): 300–23.

Stafford, A., Parton, N. and Vincent, S. (2010) *Child Protection Reform Across the UK*, Edinburgh: Dunedin Academic Press.

Stafford, A., Parton, N., Smith, C. and Vincent, S. (2012) *Child Protection Systems in the United Kingdom: A Comparative Analysis*, London: Jessica Kingsley.

Stanley, N. and Manthorpe, J. (2004) *The Age of Inquiry: Learning and Blaming in Health and Social Care*, London: Routledge.

Stevenson, L. (2018a) 'Five years of Frontline: the impact, the debate and the future of fast-track social work training', *Community Care*, 3 October, www.communitycare.co.uk/2018/10/03/five-years-frontline-impact-debate-future-fast-track-social-work-training/

Stevenson, L. (2018b) 'Frontline social work training costs "excellent value for money", minister told', *Community Care*, 17 May, www.communitycare.co.uk/2018/05/17/frontline-social-work-training-costs-excellent-value-money-minister-told/

Sutton Trust (2018) *Survival, Decline or Closure? Children's Centres in England, 2018*, www.suttontrust.com/wp-content/uploads/2018/04/StopStart-FINAL.pdf

SWTF (Social Work Task Force) (2009) *Building a Safe, Confident Future: The Final Report of the Social Work Task Force*, http://webarchive.nationalarchives.gov.uk/20130401151715/http://www.education.gov.uk/publications/eOrderingDownload/01114-2009DOM-EN.pdf

Timmins, N. (2017) *The Five Giants: A Biography of the Welfare State*, London: William Collins.

Toynbee, P. and Walker, D. (2015) *Cameron's Coup: How the Tories Took Britain to the Brink*, London: Guardian Books.

Tunstill, J. and Willow, C. (2017) 'Professional social work and the defence of children's and their families' rights in a period of austerity: a case study', *Social Work & Social Sciences Review*, 19(1): 40–65.

Unison (2016) *A Future at Risk: Cuts in Youth Services*, www.unison.org.uk/content/uploads/2016/08/23996.pdf

University of East Anglia (2004) *Children's Trusts: Developing Integrated Services for Children in England*, http://webarchive.nationalarchives.gov.uk/20130401151715/http://www.education.gov.uk/publications/eOrderingDownload/RR617%5B1%5D.pdf

Warner, J. (2013) ' "Heads must roll"? Emotional politics, the press and the death of Baby P', *The British Journal of Social Work*, 44(6): 1637–53.

Warner, J. (2015) *The Emotional Politics of Social Work and Child Protection*, Bristol: Policy Press.

Wastell, D., White, S., Broadhurst, K., Peckover, S. and Pithouse, A. (2010) 'Children's services in the iron cage of performance management: street-level bureaucracy and the spectre of Švejkism', *International Journal of Social Welfare*, 19(3): 310–20.

Watson, M. and Hay, C. (2003) 'The discourse of globalisation and the logic of no alternative: rendering the contingent necessary in the political economy of New Labour', *Policy & Politics*, 31(3): 289–305.

Weale, S. (2016) 'Nicky Morgan accused of creating chaotic mess despite academies U-turn', *The Guardian*, www.theguardian.com/education/2016/may/09/nicky-morgan-chaotic-mess-academies-u-turn

What Works Centre for Children's Social Care (2019) 'About', https://whatworks-csc.org.uk/about/

White, S., Hall, C. and Peckover, S. (2008) 'The descriptive tyranny of the common assessment framework: technologies of categorization and professional practice in child welfare', *The British Journal of Social Work*, 39(7): 1197–217.

Whitehead, F. (2011) 'Lords amend Education Bill to retain schools "duty to co-operate" with children's services', *The Guardian*, www.theguardian.com/education/2011/oct/07/education-bill-duty-to-cooperate

Wilson, D. (2003) 'Unravelling control freakery: redefining central–local government relations', *The British Journal of Politics and International Relations*, 5(3): 317–46.

Wincott, D. (2018) 'Brexit and the state of the United Kingdom', in P. Diamond, P. Nedergaard and B. Rosamond (eds) *The Routledge Handbook of the Politics of Brexit*, London: Routledge.

Wintour, P. (2015) 'Jail those who turn a blind eye to child abuse, says Cameron', *The Guardian*, www.theguardian.com/society/2015/mar/03/david-cameron-child-abuse-ignore-jail

Wood, A. (2016) 'Wood Review of Local Safeguarding Children Boards', www.gov.uk/government/publications/wood-review-of-local-safeguarding-children-boards

YMCA (Young Men's Christian Association) (2018) *Youth & Consequences: A Report Examining Local Authority Expenditure on Youth Services in England & Wales*, www.ymca.org.uk/wp-content/uploads/2018/04/Youth-Consequences-v0.2.pdf

Index